The Walton Street Tycoons

Jim Lesczynski

East River Press

This is a work of fiction. Any resemblance to any events, locales or persons, living or dead, is purely coincidental.

Copyright © 2007 by Jim Lesczynski

All rights reserved. No part of this book may be reproduced or transmitted in any form or by any means, electronic or mechanical, including photocopying, recording, or by any information storage and retrieval system, without permission in writing from the publisher.

Published by East River Press, New York, New York.
www.eastriverpress.com

Library of Congress Control Number: 2006937668

ISBN 13: 978-0-9791283-0-1
ISBN 10: 0-9791283-0-7

First Edition

For Dawn

with all my love

Contents

Chapter One: Something Fishy	7
Chapter Two: School Daze	16
Chapter Three: An Elephant Never Forgets	25
Chapter Four: Hook, Line and Stinker	37
Chapter Five: Dopey Dads	51
Chapter Six: Making Some Dough	65
Chapter Seven: Out of the Baking Pan, Into the Fire	77
Chapter Eight: Desserts Express	93
Chapter Nine: Brownies for Bullies	101
Chapter Ten: Halloween	118
Chapter Eleven: Sharing and Caring	127
Chapter Twelve: Christmas	142
Chapter Thirteen: New Money	150
Chapter Fourteen: Break-In at Daybreak	160
Chapter Fifteen: The Hostile Takeover	171
Chapter Sixteen: Valentine's Day	183
Chapter Seventeen: The Sentence	191
Chapter Eighteen: The Secret Customer	203
Chapter Nineteen: Flying Pies	211
Chapter Twenty: Let's Make a Deal	219
Chapter Twenty-One: Growing Pains	232
Chapter Twenty-Two: Easter	243
Chapter Twenty-Three: Missing Pieces	254
Chapter Twenty-Four: Family Reunion	261
Chapter Twenty-Five: Mark's Birthday	266

Chapter One

Something Fishy

"NPR sucks," I muttered.

Whap! "Ow! Knock it off, Frank!" I yelled.

Frank tried to smack me again, but this time I was able to duck. The only reason he caught me off-guard the first time was because I was looking at the cereal I was pouring instead of at him. I scooped up the cereal flakes that scattered across the table when he hit me and dumped them in my bowl. Reaching for the milk carton, I kept an eye on Frank, but he was already engrossed in the radio broadcast.

I suppose I should have seen it coming. Frank loved National Public Radio, especially "Morning Edition," although I couldn't imagine anything duller. Okay, "All Things Considered" is worse, I suppose, but "Morning Edition" is right up there. Maybe when I was forty-eight like Frank instead of twelve like I was, I would appreciate it. But it was the same thing every day—the announcer talked about unemployment, inflation, the GDP (whatever that was), and the war. All of them were getting worse, and had been for as long as I could remember. "Morning Edition" was a current events program on NPR that would try to "humanize" the story by showing how unemployment or the economy or the war affected actual people. More human, maybe, but still just as dull, as far as I was concerned. I guess I care about people—people who aren't creeps, anyway—but NPR made me wonder if there was something wrong with me.

"...Mr. Stepowicz of Twinsburg, Ohio, doesn't know what he will do when his family receives their final welfare payment this week. All this thirty-one-year-old father of three knows is that the steel mill that laid him off six years ago won't be re-opening anytime soon. All he can do is wait—and hope."

Frank shook his head solemnly. I snickered, which caused my little brother Sam to shoot milk out his nose.

"What's so funny?" Frank snarled.

"That guy is gonna have a long wait if he thinks that steel mill is gonna re-open," I replied. "What was he thinking getting a job in a dying industry and having three kids? I mean, I could see feeling bad for him if he was sixty, but jeez, thirty-one?"

"You think you're pretty smart," Frank scoffed. "I'd like to see you earn a living and support a family, you little brat."

"I'd be a cowboy," Sam offered through his mouth full of cereal.

I smiled. "You'd probably have a better chance of earning a living as cowboy than that dope does as a steelworker today."

Frank probably would have tried to smack me again, but my mom had just walked into the kitchen.

"Look at all the handsome men," she cooed. It was a little white lie. Sam and I were years away from being men, and I doubt that Frank had ever been handsome. Our mom leaned over and kissed me on my forehead. She walked around the table and did the same to Sam. When she got to Frank she wrapped her arms around his neck and gave him a long, gross kiss that almost caused Sam and me to lose our breakfast. As it was, we made our standard barfing noises. My mom arched an eyebrow as she glanced away from Frank toward us.

I never understood what my mom saw in Frank. She was kind of pretty for a mom, I thought. Sure she was old (forty last May), but she had shoulder-length red hair, which she usually wore in a bun, smooth pink skin with only a few tiny wrinkles around her green eyes (laugh lines, as she called them), and she was always smiling. And she wasn't fat, like most of the mothers in the neighborhood, even though she ran her own dessert shop.

Frank, on the other hand—blecch. Like I said, he was forty-eight, but he looked about ten years older, except that he still had zits. He was almost completely bald on top, but he combed his hair over to try to hide it. I think he had been skinny when he was younger, but he was growing a big belly that stretched the pants of the cheap suits he always wore.

About the only thing Frank had going for him, as far as I could tell, was job security, which was becoming more of a plus every day. He was the superintendent of our school system in Walton, New York, a little suburb about an hour north of New York City. Our mom admitted as much, more or less, when she sat Sam and me down to discuss Frank moving in with us, shortly after her last birthday. Business was slow at her dessert shop. She had used up her savings just keeping up the mortgage payments since our dad went away, and if we didn't want to move, our household would need more income. Moving would have been fine with Sam and me, but our mom said she didn't know if she could find another job somewhere else, and besides, she added, Frank was a good man.

"The entertainment started early this morning," Frank said sarcastically. "Mark is particularly precocious today. It must be the excitement over the first day of the new school year."

My mom took the pot from the coffeemaker and poured herself a cup. "Speaking of which, you boys better finish your breakfast and get moving," she reminded us. "You don't want to be late on the first day."

"Who has an appetite with Frank kissing you and smacking me?" I asked.

"Frank would never hit you, Mark," our mom said as she grabbed Sam's and my lunch bags from the refrigerator.

"Whatever." I flipped Frank the finger while my mom wasn't looking. "Are you ready to go, Sam?"

"Aw, gee," Sam whined. My sentiments exactly.

Unfortunately, it was indeed the first day of school. I was entering the seventh grade, while Sam was starting third grade. If we wanted to catch the school bus, we really would have to hurry. Taking one last gulp of cereal and milk, I pushed myself from the table and dragged myself toward my mom. Sam, who at this stage of his life copied me so much that I wondered how he functioned when I wasn't around, followed behind me.

"Don't forget your knapsacks," our mom said as she handed us our lunches and gave us each a kiss goodbye.

I rolled my eyes. Only our mother would call them knapsacks instead of backpacks. "Yeah, yeah. Bye, Mom," I said.

"Bye, Mom," Sam echoed.

Our mom glanced from Sam and me to Frank, as if to suggest that we should kiss him goodbye too. Yeah, right. I pretended not to see her as I walked over to the base of the stairs, picked up my backpack and slung it over my shoulder, slowly opened the door, and skulked off to the bus stop with my brother tailing behind.

The bus stop was only about fifty yards up from our house on Walton Street, which was the "main street" of our small community, but the hard part was crossing the busy roadway. Or at least it used to be. Most of our neighbors at one time commuted to New York City, which made for a lot of traffic at that time of morning. But with all the recent layoffs, there was hardly any traffic today, even less than when school let out last June. Sam, who our mom had brainwashed to live in mortal fear of crossing the street without holding onto someone, looked both ways and bravely pulled his hand from mine before sprinting across the blacktop to the other side. We walked atop the half-buried, corroded drainpipe that ran parallel to the road until we reached the bus stop.

About six kids were already there. My friends Neil Jones and Vic Sanjay were playing soccer with a crushed beer can.

"Hey," I said as I tried to block the can from getting to Vic with my foot. I missed.

"Hey," Vic said.

"Hey," Neil said. "You guys ready for Saturday?"

"Sure," Vic said.

"What's Saturday?" I asked as I made another attempt at the beer can, this time successfully deflecting it with my foot and launching it into the road.

"Don't give me that," Neil replied as he hustled after the can and kicked it backward with his heel to Vic. "You know what Saturday is."

I looked to my brother for a clue, but Sam was busy rolling in the grass with a couple of the other third graders he knew. "No, I don't. Honest."

Vic rolled his eyes and threw his hands in the air dramatically. "It's Labor Day weekend," he exclaimed. "Our big fluke fishing trip."

Oh yeah. Every year for as long as I could remember, the three of us and our fathers, plus Sam last year, had driven out to Long Island on the Saturday of Labor Day weekend and chartered a boat for a day of fluke fishing. I hadn't even thought about it this year, since so much had changed.

"Come on, guys," I said. "You know I can't do that this year. Not with my dad gone." Neil and Vic glanced quietly at me and then at each other. They obviously had forgotten that my dad was in prison and were embarrassed.

"Oh, well, what about Frank?" Neil asked.

"Do you want to spend your day on a boat with Frank?" I asked.

"No, I guess not," Neil replied.

"Me neither," said Vic.

"Me neither," I added. "So much for that. The bad part is he's the one guy who could actually afford the trip this year. Have either of you even asked your dads if they're still planning to go?"

Neil's parents had both been laid off from their jobs for several months, and Vic's father was recently downsized as well. At least that's what they called it. Laid off and downsized just sounded like a wimpy way of saying "fired," if you ask me. Just a few years ago, Neil's dad could have at least made a little income on the side as a part-time gunsmith until a full-time job came along, but between the bad economy and all the new gun laws, there weren't a lot of people shooting or hunting in our town anymore.

Vic shook his head. "That's a good point, I guess," he said.

"Shoot!" Neil exclaimed. "You mean none of us are going fishing this year? We have to go back to school, and we don't even get to go fishing? Jeez."

All three of us heard the diesel engine sputter and turned to see the school bus approaching. As its squeaky air brakes brought the bus to a grinding halt just past where we were standing, a black, stinky cloud of smoke spurted out its exhaust pipe into our faces. The cloud matched my dark, foul mood.

No more summer vacation.

No fishing.

This stank, all right.

We climbed aboard the bus and found some seats together. Neil squeezed into a seat next to Vic, which made sense. Neil was what our moms called "husky." Another wimpy word that adults liked to use, I thought. Neil was fat. Why couldn't anybody just say that? Of course, he also had muscles underneath that fat, since he was one of the strongest kids I knew. With his crew cut and reddish complexion, not to mention his short temper, he reminded me of a marine drill sergeant. Vic was the opposite—short, skinny and brown-skinned Indonesian-American. He had stringy, dark brown hair that always looked uncombed and in need of cutting. My dad always called the two of them Mutt and Jeff, which I think was the name of some old cartoon.

I sat in the seat behind Vic and Neil by myself, and I hoped that no one else would sit next to me. I was the tallest of the three of us—in fact I was the tallest kid in my class—and I was already having difficulty fitting my legs comfortably under the seat in front of me. How miserable would this ride be in two years if I kept growing, I wondered. If my brother Sam wanted to sit next to me, I wouldn't have minded, because he takes up hardly any legroom, but he was sitting up front with his little friends. With my backpack occupying the space on the seat next to me, I stretched my legs across so that my feet dangled in the aisle.

Vic turned around toward me and said, "That's too bad we're not going fishing. I've been finding a whole bunch of night crawlers under the pines in my backyard that would make great bait."

Neil snorted. "You can't use night crawlers for fluke fishing, dummy. Those are only good for catching freshwater fish."

"Shut up, Neil," Vic replied. "If you're so smart, how come I caught more fluke than you did last year?"

"Did not!"

"Did too."

I reached over the seat to grab each of them by the hair and knock their heads together, Three Stooges style, but I couldn't keep my grip on Neil's short hair and Vic squirmed loose quickly. "All right, knuckleheads, knock it off," I said.

"Oh, wise guy, huh?" Neil replied in a falsetto voice, pushing the palm of his hand toward my face. That summer had been our inauguration into the world of the Three Stooges. Vic's dad turned us on to the Stooges when a local TV station started airing them during rained-out Yankees games. Personally, I preferred "The Animaniacs" and "South Park," but we all had to admit that there was something about those old Stooges shows that kind of grew on us.

"What we *could* do," I said, "since we're stuck here in Walton anyway, and Vic has this big supply of night crawlers, is go bass fishing instead."

Before its development as a remote suburb of New York City, Walton had been highly regarded by anglers for its many ponds teeming with smallmouth bass. A few of the ponds still held a decent fish population, but they were mostly on private property. When I was much younger, we used to be able to fish the ponds in the state park, but our township banned fishing on them after some dumb old fart fell into the water wearing hip waders and drowned. One jerk was too stupid to take care of himself, so the rest of us had to suffer.

"That would be cool," Vic said. "But where? None of us has a pond."

Good point. I tried to think of someone we knew who would let us fish on their pond, but I was drawing a blank. Neil and Vic didn't look like they were coming up with anything either. We sat there in silence, considering our options, as the bus continued the drive to our prison, I mean school.

As we pulled into the school parking lot, I noticed that Vic was trying to get my attention by raising his eyebrows and glancing behind me.

"What?" I asked. Vic continued to raise his eyebrows and look over my shoulder. I slowly turned around to see who or what he was looking at. All I saw were two girls from our class, Karen Thomas and Wendy Siegel.

Then it hit me. Karen lived on a large, wooded property with a decent-sized pond right behind her house. There had to be some smallmouth in there, I thought. Neil caught on about the same time I did and nodded his head as he smiled.

"You think?" I asked my friends.

"Sure, why not?" Vic replied. "What have we got to lose?"

I shrugged. "Okay, ask her," I whispered.

Vic shook his head. "You ask her."

"It was your idea, you ask her," I protested.

"No way, you're sitting closer," Vic said. He was generally shy, and he especially didn't like talking to girls.

"Besides," Neil said with a mischievous smile, "she likes you, Mark."

"Yeah, right," I mumbled. Truthfully, however, Neil was right. Karen always did seem to like me, ever since we were in kindergarten. She usually didn't bother with boys any more than I ever had anything to do with girls, but she always smiled at me and said hi whenever I saw her. When we were in first grade, some big kids had taken away her Powerpuff Girls lunchbox and were holding it above her head, taunting Karen while she cried. I worked up the courage to sneak up from behind and snatch the lunchbox out of their hands and return it to her. Even though it cost me a massive wedgie, it was worth it to see Karen Thomas smile at me. She was very pretty, I had to admit, with curly blond hair down to her shoulders, peaches-and-cream skin, and a tiny turned-up nose. When she stopped crying and smiled at me with tears still streaked across her cheeks as she clutched her lunchbox, it was a great feeling. I guess that sealed it as far as her liking me, although I didn't think about it too much, because, come on, she was a girl.

But desperate times called for desperate measures, or so I heard.

Chapter Two

School Daze

As the bus came to a halt in the parking lot of John Dewey Elementary and Middle Schools and all of the kids shoved into the aisle, I made sure to squeeze in just in front of Karen and Wendy. I don't know why, but I was sort of nervous about asking her what I had to ask. Maybe it was because I felt like I was sort of using her. If we didn't have such a bug to go fishing, I probably wouldn't have said more than hello.

"Hey, Karen," I said with a smile.

She smiled back at me. "Hi, Mark. How was your summer?"

I shrugged. "It was okay, I guess. How about you?"

"Wonderful. I went away for four weeks to horse riding camp. My daddy bought me my own horse for my birthday!"

"You're kidding!" I exclaimed, genuinely surprised. Her own horse? Four weeks of camp? I had no idea what her parents did for a living, but whatever it was, they obviously weren't hurting as bad as most folks in Walton.

"No, really! I named her Starlight, and I learned to do all kinds of tricks—"

"That's terrific," I said, cutting her off. Her summer camp story wasn't that interesting, and I had important business to discuss. We filed out of the bus and were making our way toward the entrance of the middle school building. I only had a few minutes before the bell would ring. "Speaking of camp, did you do any fishing while you were there?"

Karen giggled. "No, silly. It was an equestrian camp. We just learned how to ride and take care of our horses."

"Oh, I'm sorry. That's too bad," I said. Of course, I already knew perfectly well that she didn't do any fishing there.

"Besides," Karen said, "I don't know how to fish." Bingo.

"You're kidding!" I said. This was going perfectly. "I love fishing. Maybe I could teach you how to fish sometime."

Karen slowed the pace of her stride and glanced at me. Oh-oh. Did she suspect something? "Sure, Mark. That would be nice, I guess."

"Great," I said with a big smile. "Say, I just thought of something. I'll bet that pond behind your house has lots of fish in it. I could come over this weekend and give you your first fishing lesson."

"This weekend? I don't know, Mark…"

"Sure, it would be fun. I'll bet there's lots of smallmouth bass in there."

The bell rang. We both looked at each other and then glanced up and down the hall. Vic and Neil were gone. So was Karen's friend Wendy, and almost all of the other kids. Karen started running down the hall.

"Hey!" I yelled as I ran next to her.

"I can't believe I'm going to be late for the first day of seventh grade!" Karen yelled in panic.

I tried not to laugh. For me, being late to class was a way of life, but Karen was one of those typical girls who lived in fear of getting in trouble. Not that I hadn't seen her participate in her share of mischief over the years, slipping notes to her friends in class, chewing gum in class, even running in the halls like she was doing right now. Only she made a point of never, ever getting caught. Karen took the teachers very seriously when they warned us about incidents going in our permanent records, which would follow us for the rest of our lives.

Me, I stopped believing in permanent records about the same time I stopped believing in the Easter Bunny. I tried to keep a sense of perspective. This was middle school, after all. A complete waste of time in my book. I knew how to read and write before I ever set foot in John Dewey Elementary, I've always had an exceptional vocabulary—my mom calls me the walking dictionary—and I usually picked up new math concepts five minutes after the teacher introduced them to us. History, science and the other subjects could have been interesting, I suppose, but it was the same stuff every year. First grade we learned that Columbus discovered America. Second grade we learned it again, just in case we weren't paying attention in first grade. Third grade we learned that Columbus discovered America for the king and queen of Spain. Fourth grade we learned that again and that Columbus discovered America in 1492. Fifth grade we learned all of that, plus some trivia about his ships named the *Nina*, the *Pinta* and the *Santa Maria*. Sixth grade, another refresher on Columbus, and we learned that he landed on the island of Hispaniola, which now consisted of the countries of Haiti and the Dominican Republic. What would they add this year, what Columbus had for lunch when he arrived?

The worst part was that the teachers were wrong about Columbus! The Vikings discovered America hundreds of years before him. When we had a test last year that asked who discovered North America, I wrote Eric the Red, and my creepy teacher marked it wrong. Vic wrote, "the Indians who crossed the Bering Strait," and our teacher marked his answer wrong too, even though it was the most correct of all. Neil laughed at both of us when we got our tests back. The fink wrote "Christopher Columbus," even though it was Neil who gave me the book about Vikings and Eric the Red where I learned that stuff in the first place. Just goes to show you that it's smarter to give the answer the teacher wants to hear than the right answer, but that's one lesson I stubbornly refused to learn.

So unlike Karen, I wasn't too worried about being late for the first day of the seventh grade. The teachers didn't scare me, and I didn't expect to learn anything new until maybe March at the earliest.

"Who's your teacher this year?" I asked.

"Miss Farkas," Karen said, reading the room numbers as she ran.

"Hey, me too. Here's her classroom," I said as we stopped in front of Room 116. Karen had a pained look on her face as she reached for the door handle. She really dreaded the idea of getting in trouble. "Wait!"

I didn't mean to upset her more, but she just about jumped out of her skin. "What?" she gasped.

"What about fishing Saturday?"

"Mark!" she said with a tone of exasperation that would have been more suited to someone twice her age. "I don't know. How can you think about fishing at a time like this?"

"Come on," I said, trying not to sound like I was begging. "It'll give you something to look forward to and take your mind off your *permanent record.*"

"That's not funny. Fine, come over Saturday, as long as my parents don't find out I was late for the first day of school and kill me."

"Oh and—." I wanted to ask her if it was okay if Vic and Neil came too, but Karen wasn't listening to me any longer. She worked up the courage to turn the knob and open the door.

As Karen and I walked into the classroom, Miss Farkas was writing something on the blackboard. She stopped, turned and pointed at us with the chalk in her hand.

"And who are you?" she asked icily. It was hard to say how old Miss Farkas was. She didn't have any wrinkles or gray hair, but she dressed like an old lady. She was a tall, heavyset ("husky" kids grow up to be "heavyset" adults) black woman with a short haircut, no make-up and a long gray dress that mercifully hid most of her body. Her hooves, I mean feet, were covered by those ugly old lady shoes with the big foam-rubber bottoms.

"My name is Karen Thomas. That's Mark Hoffman."

"Mr. Hoffman can speak for himself, Miss Thomas," replied Miss Farkas.

"I'm Al Coholic," I answered. The class burst into laughter as Miss Farkas glared at me. It's always great to warm up the audience with some proven material.

"I see," said Miss Farkas. "Well, Mr. Hoffman, you and the other children who laughed obviously are too immature to know that there is nothing funny about alcoholism." She was wrong. I knew lots of drunks, including an uncle who died of liver failure, and they were *always* hilarious. The Three Stooges have nothing on a guy who could wrap a car around a telephone pole and walk away from it whistling. "Why are you children late?"

I started to open my mouth, but Karen cut me off, clearly not wanting any further guilt by association this morning. "We were both mailed the wrong room assignment. The schedule said Room 106, not Room 116." She started to open her backpack. "I have it right here."

"That's fine; don't bother," replied Miss Farkas. Very smooth, Karen, I thought. Miss Farkas eyed the seating chart on her desk. "Miss Thomas, your desk is that fourth one in the last row by the window." Karen quickly separated herself from me and made her way to her desk.

"Mr. Hoffman," Miss Farkas continued, pausing to look again at the chart and then at the only open seat in the room. It was in the last row, next to Neil. Cool. But then she walked over to one of the kids sitting in the front row, right in front of her desk. This wasn't good. "Miss Kendall," she said to the girl sitting in front of her, "why don't you move to that empty desk in the back and give this seat to Mr. Hoffman, where I can keep an eye on him."

Dang. I went too far, too early, apparently. Susie Kendall gathered her stuff from under her desk, while I smiled meekly and shrugged. As I waited for my desk to become available, Miss Farkas returned to the blackboard.

She was writing a list of the six courses we would be "studying" over the next nine months, along with the corresponding textbooks. The subjects were English, arithmetic, spelling, art (three days a week), gym (on the other two days), world history (oh boy, Columbus again) and civics. Civics? What kind of nonsense was that?

"Now then," said Miss Farkas as she turned to face the class. "As you can see, there are stacks of textbooks and workbooks along the windowsill. I want you to proceed one row at a time, beginning with the row closest to the windows, and take one of each book. Due to severe budget cuts, we were not able to order any new textbooks this year, and many of these old books are in poor condition. Some of the covers are beginning to fray and fall off. You are each responsible for taking care of these books and seeing that their condition does not worsen."

We made our way over to the stacks of books, and I saw that Miss Kendall was right. The textbooks were dog-eared and stained, and some had ripped covers. Most of the workbooks already had the answers filled in. I just hoped that my workbooks had belonged to smart students who had filled in the *right* answers.

The morning dragged on at a painfully slow place. There was no honeymoon period, no thrill of something new to make the whole thing more bearable. English was a waste of time; we reviewed a bunch of parts of speech that I knew intuitively, if not by their actual names, since kindergarten. In arithmetic, we went over cardinal numbers (one, two, three, four...) and ordinal numbers (first, second, third, fourth...). Even the dumbest kids in the class could all count by the age of twelve, although that didn't stop some brown-noses from asking lots of pointless questions repeating what we all already knew. The first unit of the spelling book was a list of words obviously compiled by retards.

It took all of my willpower just to sit still in my seat. I couldn't be this bored only two hours into the school year, I kept telling myself. I had to pull myself together. At this rate, I would have a breakdown by October. I'd seen it happen before. Some poor kid bursting with youthful energy and curiosity, forced to stifle both traits in a smothering classroom for seven hours a day until he snaps. And then, it's off to the school psychiatrist's office for a mandatory Ritalin prescription to correct his attention deficit disorder.

We got a bit of relief in art class. At least we didn't have to listen to Miss Farkas drone on. She handed out drawing paper, colored pencils and rulers to each of us, and she gave us instructions to draw something using pictures from a collection of old magazines as models. Before heading out to the teacher's lounge for the rest of the period, Miss Farkas appointed one of the students, Susie Kendall, to be her fink and write down the names of anyone who talked during her absence.

There wasn't much to choose from in the pile of magazines on the teacher's desk. *National Geographic*, *Time*, *Newsweek* and about a hundred women's and teen magazines. No hunting or fishing magazines, not even a *Sports Illustrated*. I glumly flipped through a *National Geographic*, hoping to spot a photograph of a native fishing. I had fishing on the brain today. Neil had already found what he was looking for—a close-up shot of an AK-47 military rifle from *Newsweek*. This art project wouldn't be much of a challenge for him; Neil could draw an AK-47 or pretty much any other gun with his eyes closed. About the only thing that Neil liked more than guns was spaceships.

"So what'd she say?" Neil whispered to me.

I put down the *National Geographic* and picked up another one. "What did who say?" I asked.

"Karen! Can we go fishing in her backyard on Saturday?"

Someone's throat cleared behind us. Neil and I turned around to see Susie Kendall shaking her head disapprovingly as she wrote something on her paper. Neil was busted.

Not wanting to get myself in further trouble this morning—I had to pace myself—I returned to the magazine I was holding. Neil nudged me with his elbow. As I glanced at him, he raised his eyes and held out his hands, palms up, in a gesture that repeated his question. I nodded, and Neil smiled and gave me a thumbs-up.

Wait a minute. Karen didn't exactly say that *we* could go fishing, I remembered. I had only asked if *I* could come over to show her how to fish. After Karen said yes, my next question was going to be to ask if Neil and Vic could come too, but Karen was already rushing into the classroom. Now I shook my head, which caused a look of concern on Neil's face. I pointed to my chest to indicate that only I was invited so far, then pointed in succession to Neil, Karen and the clock on the wall to show that I would ask Karen about him later.

Neil scrunched up his face in a confused expression. Even though his mouth was closed, I could almost hear him asking what the heck I was talking about.

"She only invited me!" I finally answered in a loud, exasperated whisper. "But I'll ask about you and Vic later."

More clucking noises from the back of the classroom. We didn't have to turn around that time. Susie Kendall was adding my name to her list of scofflaw talkers, and probably putting a check next to Neil's name for his second offense. Oh well. So much for staying out of further trouble this morning.

As I returned once more to the *National Geographic* and turned the page, I came across a photograph of a large African elephant, its rear toward the camera, pooping on a dusty trail.

"Look," I said, holding up the page so that Neil and anyone paying attention (including Susie Kendall) could see it. "This is a live shot of the teachers' lounge. Miss Farkas is taking a dump!"

The classroom burst into laughter, but some of the laughs were laced with nervousness. Man, these kids have to lighten up, I thought. Even Neil looked uncomfortable.

"I don't think that's funny." Only it wasn't Neil who said that.

It was Miss Farkas, standing behind me.

Chapter Three

An Elephant Never Forgets

Lunch couldn't arrive fast enough for me. It was always my favorite part of the school day, except maybe for the final bell. But today I really needed lunch period more than usual. I had to get out of that classroom and get my bearings.

Neil and I found Vic in the cafeteria, and the three of us sat at the same table together, as we had been doing for years. I removed my lunch bag from my backpack and absent-mindedly emptied its contents on the table in front of me. My thoughts were so stuck on my lousy morning that I hardly noticed Vic and Neil ogling each item of food as I set it down. They had been doing it for so many years that I barely paid attention.

I didn't have a lot of advantages in life, especially lately, but I did have one bit of good fortune that my friends never let me forget. My mother owned her own dessert shop and bakery. As a result, my brother Sam and I always enjoyed brownbag lunches that were the envy of the school.

"Look at that apple strudel," Neil sighed as he leaned across the table for a closer look.

"Cut it out, Neil," I said as I pulled the dessert closer to me. "You'll get drool all over it."

I unwrapped my smoked ham (real ham, not processed lunchmeat) and cheddar sandwich on fresh-baked sourdough bread, but I didn't bite into it right away. My mind was still wandering. Neil and Vic glanced at the soggy Wonder Bread sandwiches in their own hands, then at my sandwich, then back at their own desserts (broken Oreos for Neil, a bruised banana for Vic), and then back at my homemade apple strudel.

"Trade you my banana for half the strudel?" Vic offered.

"Can I have half your sandwich, Mark?" Neil asked.

"You can have a knuckle sandwich," I replied.

"Come on," Neil whined. "You're not even eating it. You're just staring at it."

Exhaling deeply, I said, "Yeah, I was just thinking about that big elephant, Miss Farkas."

Neil guffawed. "I can't believe the first day of school isn't half over, and you already have two detentions."

"Really?" Vic asked as he raised his eyebrows. "You keep going like that, and they'll have you on Ritalin by the end of the week."

I shook my head and sighed. "I know. I was thinking about that myself."

Neil, giving up his attempt to con me into a bad trade, bit into his soggy tuna sandwich as he looked around the cafeteria. Gesturing with his head toward some tables in the rear of the room, he said through a mouthful of food, "My mom heard from Kevin Dougherty's mom that they've boosted Kevin up to 500 milligrams a day."

Vic and I spotted Kevin in the direction Neil was gesturing, quietly eating his lunch at a table by himself. We all nodded solemnly. None of us had the slightest idea how much 500 milligrams was, but it sounded like a lot. Up until about a year-and-a-half ago, Kevin was one of us. He used to be one of the funniest kids I knew, always laughing and horsing around. Neil used to get so flustered at Kevin's practical jokes that his face would turn purple, which would make the rest of us laugh even more. But even when he bore the brunt of Kevin's jokes, Neil was probably his biggest fan. Everybody liked Kevin Dougherty.

Well, almost everybody. One day in the middle of fifth grade, on the bus ride to school, Kevin slipped a dead mouse into the backpack of a particularly uptight girl. (At least the mouse was dead when she opened the bag. I never did ask Kevin if the mouse went into the bag alive.) When the girl got to school and found the mouse, she screamed like a banshee, whatever that is. Despite her hysteria, she managed to guess that Kevin was the culprit, especially with him doubled over in laughter at his own prank, and the girl regained her composure long enough to slap Kevin across the face. Now Kevin was not the type of guy to take that, even from a girl, and he promptly punched her in the nose, sending a stream of blood down her face and blouse.

That was the last straw for our teacher and principal, who were already tired of Kevin's disruptions. After a few quick sessions with the school psychiatrist, Kevin was diagnosed with attention deficit disorder and a tendency toward violent behavior. The psychiatrist gave him a prescription for Ritalin, which was administered twice a day by the school nurse. His parents tried to protest, but they were told the prescription was non-negotiable, and if they pressed the matter, the county social workers would get involved and who knew where that would lead. We had seen kids taken from their parents for lesser infractions.

Kevin was never the same after that. No more pranks, no more laughter, just a zombie who sat quietly in his seat for seven hours a day. A model student.

It was a lesson we should have all taken to heart, especially me. I felt like a normal, healthy kid, and I loved to learn stuff. Just not the stuff they taught in school. Well, that wasn't true, either. Some of the stuff they taught in school looked like it could have been interesting—should have been interesting—but it was always either the same old stuff we'd been reviewing for years with a few new wrinkles, or the teacher just made it as boring as possible. Sometimes, I would go to the library during the summer and find myself reading about the same stuff I ignored during the school year. Who knows, maybe I should have been medicated, but I was determined to avoid it.

"So what did she say?" Vic asked.

"Huh?" My mind had wandered again.

"What did Karen say about fishing on Saturday?" Vic asked again.

Neil answered for me. "Lamebrain got himself invited for fishing, but he left us out in the cold."

"I just didn't get around to it yet!" I protested.

"Well, get around to it," Vic said.

"Yeah, unless—" Neil paused for dramatic effect "—you and Karen want to be alone."

"Aww," Vic cooed.

They both made loud kissing and sucking noises directed at me.

"You guys keep that up, and maybe I will go fishing without you," I said.

That quieted them, but only for a moment, before Vic replied, "Oh yeah? Well, you'll be going without my night crawlers."

"And without my dad's homemade jigs and spoons."

"All right, calm down," I said. In addition to enjoying their company, I really did want Vic's night crawlers and Neil's dad's homemade tackle. I didn't have money to buy those things, I didn't particularly enjoy sneaking out after dark with my flashlight to hunt for night crawlers, and I certainly didn't have the skill to make my own lures. "Everybody has something to contribute. Vic will provide the bait, Neil will provide the tackle, and I'll provide the pond."

"You mean Karen will provide the pond," Vic countered.

"Suit yourself," I said, folding my arms. "There she is two tables behind you. Go get your own invitation."

Vic smiled weakly, glanced over his shoulder towards Karen and Wendy, and then stared down at his food. He wasn't going anywhere without me.

The girls must have noticed us glancing over at them, because they were giggling and looking back at us as they whispered in each other's ears. To my surprise, Karen stood up and walked toward our table, while Wendy watched from her seat.

"Hi, Mark," Karen greeted me with her pretty, dimpled smile. "Hi, Vic. Hi, Neil."

"Hey," my friends replied in disinterested unison. Way to sell yourselves, guys, I thought. Make me do all the work.

"Hey, Karen," I said. "We were just talking about you. I told Neil and Vic that I was teaching you how to fish on Saturday, and they offered to help. Right, guys?" I looked to my friends, who nodded in agreement.

"Oh, really?" Karen asked as she raised an eyebrow suspiciously.

"Sure. In fact, we need them. They're both experienced fishermen, plus Vic can bring some great night crawlers—"

Karen winced. "We have to use worms? Gross!"

"Yeah. Well, be don't have to, but—uh—plus Neil can bring some great fishing tackle, and some of his lures don't even need a live worm at all."

Neil finally spoke up. "Yeah. A good night crawler is the best thing for smallmouth, but I have some surface lures that'll work great."

Karen twirled a strand of her curly blond hair around a finger as she looked us over. She looked over at Wendy, who giggled again.

"So now you *and* your two friends get to come over my house fishing Saturday? And what do I get out of it again?"

I was taken aback. It didn't seem like Karen to be so cynical. Maybe her suspicion was part of the same cautiousness that allowed her to avoid trouble so much better than I did.

"Why, you get to learn how to fish—bait and tackle included," I replied innocently.

She shook her head. "I was already getting that when it was just you. What else do you have?" I looked up at her in disbelief, and Karen looked back with a sly grin. Some days, nothing comes easy.

What did I have? I thought about it for a moment, and then I noticed that Karen was not quite looking me in the eye. Her gaze seemed to be fixed on the table surface in front of me.

Suddenly, I had a hunch where this was heading, and I didn't like it.

Now silent Vic decided to pipe up, and I sort of wished he had continued to keep his mouth shut. "How about the apple strudel?" he volunteered.

"Yeah," Neil agreed. "You know how good Mrs. Hoffman's desserts are, Karen. That's a great trade."

Great for you guys, I thought. There would be time to deal with them later. I wasn't about to blow the deal now, when we were so close.

"Well?" I asked Karen.

She looked down at the strudel and nodded. "You give me that piece of strudel, and you can bring anyone you'd like."

"Deal," said Neil.

Now all eyes were on me. I shrugged. Why not? Today was already a loss, and eating dessert sure wasn't going to salvage it for me. Might as well trade it for a great day on Saturday, I figured. I took one last look at the flaky, golden crust and the moist filling that was pressed up against the plastic wrap that still covered the pastry. Not wanting to look like the loser in this negotiation, I picked it up and handed the strudel to Karen with a smile, as if she had played right into my hands.

"You got it," I said. "We'll see you on Saturday."

"See ya's" were exchanged all around, and Karen returned to her table with a satisfied smirk on her face. I couldn't help watching as she and her friend Wendy happily shared my strudel.

"I thought you were going to blow it there for a minute," Neil remarked.

"Just shut up and give me one of those Oreos."

After lunch, we went outside for recess. Just getting out of that miserable school improved my mood greatly. We played an intense game of Kill the Carrier, also known as Smear the Queer, which is sort of like rugby but with no scoring. The rules are simple—tackle the guy with the ball, beat the snot out of him until he lets go of the ball, grab the ball and run with it until you are tackled, beaten, let go, and so on. About twenty of us seventh-graders played, and it felt great to unleash some of the morning's frustration. I was so fired up that I ended up with the ball about every third round, and even when it was my turn for a beating, I didn't mind it at all. It was still far better than being back in the classroom.

The bell rang, bringing recess to a halt. Sweaty, breathless and refreshed, we trudged back to the school building to endure a few more hours of tedium.

"Feeling any better?" Neil asked me as we made our way back to our classroom.

"Now that we're fishing on Saturday, sure."

"Yeah," Neil huffed between short gasping breaths as we climbed the stairs, "this really worked out great. I haven't been bass fishing in years."

"You guys are going bass fishing? Where?" asked a new voice. Neil and I glanced over our shoulders to see Drew Baxter, one of the kids from our class. Drew was a decent-enough guy, I suppose, but maybe somewhat of a geek. As far as I knew, his interests were limited to computers and math. I was surprised to hear him ask about anything that takes place outdoors.

"Yeah, that's right," I answered. "Nowhere special. We're just going to fish in that pond in Karen Thomas's backyard."

"Oh," Drew said. After a short pause, he added, "Do you suppose I could go fishing with you?"

Now that was really a surprise. Like I said, Drew was a nice-enough kid, but he had never really hung out with Neil, Vic or me. He mostly associated with the other computer geeks.

I should mention here that all of us were sort of computer geeks, in that every kid I knew had a computer in his home, even if it was an old model with a slow Internet connection. But most of us used the computer to send instant messages to each other and play online games. Drew, on the other hand, knew how to take apart and reassemble a PC the way Neil knew how to take apart and reassemble guns. He even wrote his own computer programs for fun, a few of which I had downloaded from his personal web page.

"*You* want to go fishing?" Neil asked.

"Absolutely. I've always wanted to go, and my dad keeps promising to take me one of these days."

"So go with your dad," Neil said. I could see from the look on Drew's face that Neil's remark hurt him slightly.

"Well, if you don't want me along, I won't butt in."

At the top of the stairs, I slowed my pace to allow Drew to catch up alongside us. I looked at him as we walked and said, "It's not that, man. It's just that, well, we had to pay for this fishing trip, so we can't really bring anyone else along for free. Know what I mean?"

Apparently not. "You mean Karen is making you pay to fish on her pond?" Drew asked.

"Well, not literally," I answered. As we walked to class, I tried to give him the short version of how we traded Vic's worms, Neil's tackle, and my dessert for a day of fishing.

"That's pretty funny," Drew remarked. "I can see you're not wanting any freeloaders. So how about if I kick in some payment too?"

"I don't know," I said. "I really don't feel like going through that all over again with Karen."

"You don't have to," Neil interjected. "She did say that if you gave her that strudel, you could bring *anyone* you wanted."

I squinted at Neil. "Are you sure about that?"

"Of course! Remember? 'You give me that piece of strudel, and you can bring anyone you'd like.' Her exact words."

"Yeah, but I'm pretty sure she just meant you and Vic," I protested.

Neil shrugged. He didn't particularly care if Drew came fishing with us or not. Drew looked at me with begging eyes.

"Well…" I sighed, pausing to consider my options. What the heck, I decided. If that's what Karen said, then that's what she said. A deal's a deal. Maybe it wasn't too late to get the best of the bargain. "Okay, Drew, I'll make it easy on you. Make me an offer."

"Um, I don't know," he mumbled. "Let me think. I know! How about the cheat codes for Blood Raiders 4?" Drew was referring to the most popular computer game of the summer.

"Already got it," I replied. "What else do you have?"

Drew snapped his fingers and smiled. "I know. How would you like a free username and password for Penthouse.com?"

I laughed. Maybe I should have been hanging out with Drew all these years. "Penthouse.com? You're kidding!"

"No kidding. I hacked a username and password last week. It's completely untraceable. And…" Drew paused for dramatic effect. "…The things you see on it are incredible."

Neil and I snickered. About two months ago, Vic had showed us a stack of *Penthouses* that he found hidden in his dad's sock drawer, and they were incredible, indeed. None of us was ready to admit that we actually liked girls yet, at least not the flat-chested variety in our grade, but our curiosity was definitely growing as far as the older, more fully developed girls of *Penthouse* were concerned. Mostly, we thought it was funny to look at the pictorials and make rude comments.

And, of course, we loved the joke page and the dirty cartoons.

"All right, Drew. You got a deal."

Drew slapped me on the back. "Thanks, Mark. I'll email that username and password to you tonight."

Neil grinned. "And then you can forward it to me," he suggested.

I scoffed. "Not likely, unless you have something else you want to bargain for. If you play your cards right, I might let you take a peek on my computer."

The rest of the school day passed by uneventfully, if slowly. When the bell rang at 3:00 p.m., I exhaled deeply and pried myself from my seat. As I gathered my books and made my way toward the door, I felt my sapped energy return as it always did when school let out. Unlike other kids, I never required an after-school plate of cookies and milk to recharge my batteries. Just having my freedom back—if only 'til tomorrow morning—was enough to put a bounce back in my step.

I noticed that Neil was talking to Johnny Meyer when we met up in the hallway.

"Hey Mark, I got another customer for you!" Neil said proudly.

I eyed him suspiciously. "What do you mean, another customer?"

"You know, for the big fishing trip on Saturday."

"Yeah," Johnny added, "Neil says you're the one to talk to about buying admission to Karen's pond."

Jeez! I quickly glanced over my shoulder to make sure Karen wasn't in earshot. This was getting way out of control, I thought to myself. "Look, I'm sorry, Johnny, but I can't take on any more 'customers' just now. I'm not running a business. I just want to go fishing, and any more of a crowd could mess up the whole thing."

But Johnny Meyer wasn't going to take no for an answer. "I'll pay you cash."

Now that got my attention.

"Cash?" I gulped.

"Sure," he replied matter-of-factly as he pulled out his wallet. I think my eyeballs must have bugged out of their sockets cartoon-style as Johnny flipped through a large wad of bills. "Neil said you might be willing to trade, but I don't have anything I really want to give up, except cash. How much are you charging, five dollars, ten dollars?"

"Uh, yeah, ten, um, ten dollars will do it," I stammered.

"Cool. Mark me down as paid," Johnny said as he shoved two five-dollar bills in my hand.

"Okay. Do you want a receipt?" It seemed like the right thing to say.

"No, I trust you. Besides, Neil's a witness. Thanks again." He ran off ahead of us to catch his bus, just before its doors closed.

I looked at Neil as we climbed aboard our own bus. "Thanks, I guess."

"No problem! This is turning into a great day for you after all." Neil patted me reassuringly on the shoulder.

I suppose he was right. Despite the run-in with Miss Farkas, things were looking up. I was going fishing on Saturday, and to top it off, I had a little money in my pocket.

"Where do you suppose a kid like Johnny Meyer got that big roll of cash?" I asked.

"Beats me," said Neil. "I think his dad works for the township as some sort of accountant, and his mom is a teacher in the high school."

Huh. I never would have thought those jobs paid very well, but what did I know?

Coming up the aisle of the bus towards us was Vic, tailed by another kid, Harrison Wolfe. Both of them were smiling.

"Hey Mark, guess what?" Vic asked.

I didn't have to guess. "You got me another customer."

Chapter Four

Hook, Line and Stinker

Yes, Vic had gotten me another customer. Two, in fact, since Harrison wanted to bring his older brother David with him. No cash this time, however. Their chosen medium of barter was baseball cards, which they collected by the carton load. After brief negotiations, we settled on a Derek Jeter rookie card to cover both Harrison and David. I was disappointed to discover later that, although the card was in mint condition, it was only worth twelve dollars, according to a website on sports collectibles.

The other thing I discovered when I got home and logged onto the Internet was that I had three more bass fishing customers, one who left an email message and two who contacted me by instant messenger. Sara Berra offered me a Dave Matthews Band CD, while two of her friends offered ten dollars cash and two packs of cigarettes, respectively. I quickly accepted the first two offers and renegotiated the last one, since I had no intention of taking up smoking (yet). To my surprise, the kid immediately accepted my counter-offer of ten dollars.

That made thirty dollars so far today, plus various goods and services—including the bass fishing itself—all for not much effort, as far as I could tell. Oh yeah, I was obligated to give Karen fishing lessons. How hard could that be?

I took on one more customer that evening, or maybe freeloader would be more accurate. Just before dinner, my little brother Sam walked into my room (without knocking, as usual) and asked what time we were going fishing on Saturday. When I told him that "we" weren't going anywhere on Saturday, since this was a fishing trip for big kids only, Sam pointed out that the whole fishing trip would likely fall apart if my mom learned about it and my two detentions at the same time. I never did figure out how Sam knew about my detentions. Anyway, Sam offered his silence on the subject of the fishing trip in exchange for being able to tag along.

What the heck. For a little kid, Sam actually knew how to fish fairly well. He wouldn't be too much trouble, as long as he avoided falling into the water—not the easiest of challenges for a rambunctious eight-year-old.

As the week wore on, the size of the fishing trip snowballed. Gradually, my reluctance to take on new "customers" gave way to my greed. By Friday, I caught myself going out of my way to recruit a couple more fishermen.

"What's the final count?" Vic asked me on the bus ride home Friday afternoon.

"Seventeen anglers, I think," I answered.

"Make that eighteen," Neil said as he joined us. "Adam DeLoof just told me that he wants to go. He'll pay you ten dollars in the morning."

Eighteen. That was eighteen anglers and roughly $160 worth of payments, I figured, including $90 cash. All for doing not much work at all.

I was still a little worried that Karen would get wind of it and cancel the whole thing. If she did know about all the kids who were now coming, she was keeping it to herself, because she hadn't said much more than "hello" and "see you Saturday" to me since we struck our bargain at lunch on Monday. I don't know how she could not have heard about it, since everywhere I went, kids seemed to be talking about it and asking to come. Then again, my customers were mostly boys, so maybe word wasn't circulating as quickly among the girls. She would find out tomorrow morning, of course, when we all showed up at her house, but then it would be too late for her to cancel.

...I hoped.

As much as I liked the money and baseball cards and other payments, the thing that made me happiest was the prospect of fishing with my friends. I had been a little downcast all week with the start of school, but now that the weekend was here, I felt terrific. The forecast for Saturday morning called for overcast skies—perfect for fishing, according to my dad. When I got to the dinner table Friday night, I felt like I was walking on clouds. Even my mother's boyfriend Frank couldn't get to me.

"So how was everyone's week?" my mother asked cheerily as she brought the platter of breaded pork chops and pierogies to the table and sat down.

"Great," I said as I grabbed the tray and served myself a heaping helping.

"Great," Sam echoed.

Frank harrumphed. "It seems to me that if a young man gets two detentions—in the first week of school no less—it should hardly count as a great week."

I looked at my mom and raised my eyebrows in search of an explanation, and she looked back with an almost imperceptible shrug as if to apologize. She knew I didn't want Frank to know about my detentions, not that I cared a bit what he thought of me. I just didn't need his smug attitude.

Attempting to change the subject, my mom asked Frank, "Well, how was your week, dear? Were you able to make any progress on that budget problem?"

"Hardly. Every morning another principal called me to complain that they don't have the supplies or the teachers to make it through the year. This recession has crippled our budget."

"Really?" my mother exclaimed. "I know everybody in Walton is feeling the pinch, but I thought the schools would be exempt."

Frank nodded solemnly. "In a world with the correct values, the schools would be exempt. But our budget relies on property tax revenues. With all the unemployment, people are putting off repairs and improvements to their homes. That drives property values down, which means less money for the schools. Not only that, so many people are leaving Walton to look for jobs down south, there's a glut of houses on the market."

"And with lots of sellers and no buyers, that drives property values down too, right?" my mom asked.

"Right. If the county commissioners don't approve that property tax increase next month, I don't know what we'll do."

I came close to spitting out my milk. Sam, watching me struggle to keep my composure, got milk up his own nose from laughter. A bubbly mixture of Sam's snots and milk sprayed across his dinner plate.

"Boys!" our mom yelled as she stood up to fetch a roll of paper towels.

Frank glared at me from over the top of his glasses. "You think there's something funny about the schools running out of money?"

"Well, yeah, that is funny too," I conceded. "But what I was laughing at is the *stupid* idea of raising property taxes, when you just finished explaining how people can't afford to live in Walton as it is."

"You couldn't possibly understand," Frank condescended. "Government policy is a complex, sophisticated subject. I'm certainly not going to try to explain it to someone who probably won't make it through the seventh grade."

"Frank, please," our mom said as she cleaned up Sam's mess.

I smiled at Frank, mocking the contempt in his eyes. "You're right, Frank. To me, government policy doesn't seem much more complicated than the Mafia deciding how much to shake down the victims it 'protects.' Pay us what we say, and we'll give leave you alone... for now. But then, I'm just a stupid kid, so there must be something more to it than that."

If my mom wasn't standing right there, Frank would have smacked me for sure. As it was, his face turned purple and he clenched his jaw as he spoke. "Listen, you know-it-all little brat. The Mafia extorts people by *force*!" Oops, I forgot Frank was Italian-American and somewhat sensitive to the Mafia thing. Oh well. Tee-hee. "The people they 'protect' don't have any choice in the matter. But our government is elected through the democratic process to provide essential services for society."

"And what if some people don't want those services?" I asked ever so innocently. "The government won't make those people pay anyway? By force?"

"Shut your stupid little mouth!" Frank screamed.

I stuck out my tongue instead.

"Stop it! Both of you!" my mom pleaded. "Can't we ever have a peaceful meal around here without you two at each other's throats?"

"Hey, Oddfather," I taunted, "can I kiss your ring?"

My mom grabbed me by the collar and tugged me away from the table. "All right, mister. You've had enough to eat."

She was right. I knew I better quit before Frank had a heart attack.

Then again...

...Nah. I'd just get stuck escorting my mother to the funeral tomorrow while everyone else went fishing.

When morning finally arrived, I was up before my alarm clock went off. At 7:00 a.m., I knocked on Sam's door, but he was already up and dressed as well. We headed downstairs and startled our mother, who was reading the paper over a cup of coffee before heading over to her dessert shop. No weekends off when you're a struggling entrepreneur. Frank was still in their bedroom and would remain so for several more hours.

"What are you two doing up and dressed so early on a Saturday?" my mom asked.

"We told you the other day," I lied. "We're going fishing over at Karen Thomas's house."

My mom looked up from her paper just long enough to see Sam nod in agreement. "Really? I don't remember that."

"Sure," I continued. "You said fine, and Frank rolled his eyes and said something like kids should spend their Saturdays studying or some crazy talk like that." Well, it sounded like something Frank would have said, if the conversation had happened.

"Well, don't come home too late. And keep an eye on Sam. Make sure he doesn't fall in that pond."

"Aw, Mom," Sam whined.

How was I supposed to prevent him from falling in the pond, I wondered. Nevertheless, I reassured my mother that I would take good care of my little brother. After a quick breakfast of cereal and juice, during which our mother thoughtfully packed us sandwiches and snacks for our excursion, we kissed her goodbye.

I had remembered to fetch our fishing poles and tackle box from the basement before going to bed, so we were able to make a relatively quick departure. We had always taken a car driven by my father on any fishing trip, and I hadn't considered the difficulty of carrying the gear while riding bicycles, which was now our only available mode of transportation. I wedged the large tackle box between the handlebars of my bike and the support bar that is somehow essential to boys' bikes. Hopefully, the tackle wouldn't spill during travel. We each balanced our poles across the top of our handlebars, and we were off.

It was a glorious early September morning. The sun was still low on the horizon and had not yet dried the dew on our lawn. A cool breeze chilled us slightly as we rode, and I momentarily wished I had worn a jacket, but I knew the temperature would rise before long. Normally on the Saturday before Labor Day, there would already be lots of cars clogging Walton Street with families from New York City getting away for one last long weekend of the summer. That was not the case this year, of course, as Sam and I had to dodge only a few cars whose drivers were immune to the recession.

When we arrived at Karen's house just a few minutes before eight o'clock, we saw three other bicycles already parked in the driveway. An old gray Jeep Cherokee pulled in the drive behind us. The front passenger door opened, and Neil jumped down from his seat, lugging an oversized orange tackle box behind him. His father stepped out on the driver's side, and they both walked around to the rear of the vehicle to unload another tackle box, a landing net and Neil's fishing pole.

"You sure you don't want me to stick around?" Neil's dad asked. Most of my friends' parents were a real pain to have around, but Mr. Jones was different. He was like one of the guys. I knew that he didn't ask to stay just to keep an eye on Neil and all that sweet homemade tackle, although that was certainly part of it. More than anything, Mr. Jones likely just wanted to fish. He was a genuine outdoorsman, or at least as much of a genuine outdoorsman as you could be while working full-time—until recently—as a computer guru on Wall Street. I was surprised Neil didn't want him to stay.

"Nah," Neil replied, "that's all right. This is kind of a kids-only thing today. Know what I mean?"

His dad shrugged. "Sure. No problem. Just give me a call when you want me to pick you up."

Just as Neil's dad was about to pull out, Vic and his father pulled in the driveway in their SUV. Vic slid open the side door and pulled out his fishing pole along with two large coffee cans that were probably filled with night crawlers. Two more kids came up the driveway on bikes.

As I watched all the arrivals, I heard someone behind me call out in a vaguely strident tone, "Mark Hoffman."

I turned around to see Karen standing on her front steps with her hands on her hips. The three kids whose bicycles were in the drive when Sam and I arrived were standing behind her.

None of them looked happy.

"Hi, Karen," I said with a smile. "Ready to do some bass fishing?"

"Come here, Mark," Karen replied icily.

Neil and Vic cast wary glances at Karen and then at me. I shrugged and moseyed casually towards the porch where our host was standing.

"What's up?" I asked.

"You know perfectly well what's up!" she whispered angrily. "What are these kids doing in my yard?"

I raised my hands and spread them palms upward, as if not fully understanding the question. "Why, they're here to go fishing of course." Another two kids entered the driveway on bicycle, followed by a van carrying a few more of my customers.

Karen's blue eyes seemed to catch fire as she glared at me. "What do you mean, they're here to go fishing? I said you, Neil and Vic could come, not the entire school!"

Taking a deep breath, I explained, "Well, Karen, technically you said I could bring anybody I want." I half-expected her to hit me, but she held off. For now.

"I most certainly did not."

"Yes, you did," I argued, looking around for support from my Neil and Vic, who not surprisingly pretended to be out of earshot. You said, and I quote, 'You give me that piece of strudel, and you can bring anyone you'd like.'"

Grasping her temples between a thumb and forefinger, Karen shook her head in dismay. "Mark, just how many kids did you invite to go fishing here today?"

"Eighteen. Well, twenty if you count you and me."

"Twenty kids?!" she exclaimed.

"Only if you count you and me," I protested.

Karen opened her mouth, but no sound emerged for several uncomfortably long seconds. Finally she managed to blurt out, "My dad will kill me if he sees twenty kids in our backyard today! No way, sorry. The deal's off."

This time, everybody who was supposedly out of earshot piped up.

"Off? No way!" Vic protested.

"A deal's a deal!" Neil added.

"I want my money back!" several kids yelled.

I turned around to face the mob, waving my arms in the air to try to get their attention. "Everybody just calm down," I shouted.

The kids fell silent faster than I expected. In fact, they were too quiet. The silence was quickly shattered, however, by a booming voice from inside the house behind me.

"What's all the racket out here?!"

Turning around again to face the porch, I saw that Karen's father had joined her. He was a sight to behold. Mr. Thomas stood about six-and-a-half-feet tall, and only a pair of boxers and a sleeveless T-shirt clothed his hairy, muscle-bound body. His military-style haircut was gray around the temples, and the dark tan that covered most of his upper body was a purplish-brown on his face and neck. The sight of his huge chest and arms caused me to gape like an idiot.

He was the scariest-looking man I had ever seen in my life, and he was angry. Angry at me. My pulse raced as I waited for Karen to turn him loose on us. Out of the corner of my eye, I spied my bike and fishing equipment. If we had to make a break for it, I could never gather it all up in time. The best I could do would be to send Sam on his bike for help while I begged for mercy.

"Nothing, Daddy," Karen answered in a sweet, innocent voice. My eyes moved from the swarthy, ultra-masculine Mr. Thomas to his pretty, fair-skinned daughter. They hardly looked like they belonged to the same species, much less the same family.

"Don't nothing me, young lady," he barked. "Too much noise and too many children to be nothing."

"Honestly, Daddy, these are my friends. Please just wait inside for a moment, and I'll come in and explain everything."

Mr. Thomas glared suspiciously at the kids in his driveway, including a few more that were just now pulling in, and hesitated momentarily before opening his screen door and returning to his house.

I breathed a genuine sigh of relief. "Thanks, Karen. I owe you big time."

She smiled at me. "You don't know the half of it, Mark. Now what's all this I heard about them wanting their money back?"

I decided that I might as well come clean. I told her about how the whole thing had gotten out of control, how I just wanted to go fishing but that it had somehow snowballed into this huge enterprise.

When I finished my story, Karen appeared to be satisfied. "So all these kids paid you to come fishing today?"

"That's right," I nodded.

"I see," she said. "I guess I can't blame you. Well I can, but I won't."

What a relief, I thought. "Thanks a million."

"Well, probably not quite a million," Karen replied, her smile growing.

"Come again?" I asked.

"Before we all go fishing," Karen said, "there is the matter of my commission. True, you did put this whole thing together, but it is my pond, and a measly piece of strudel hardly seems like appropriate payment."

"But we had a deal!" I protested.

Karen shook her head. "Look, Mark, let's cut through the nonsense. You know that I never thought you would invite eighteen kids here today. The deal was just you, me, Neil and Vic. So you have three choices. We can forget the whole thing, we can stick to just the four of us, or you can cut me in for fifty percent of your proceeds. That seems fair."

"Fifty percent? No way!"

"You tell her, Mark," Neil chipped in from somewhere behind me.

Reaching for her screen door, Karen said, "Okay now, I have to go in there and tell my father what's happening. Either I go in there and make up something that will allow everybody to stay here and do some fishing, or I tell him you just showed up and refuse to leave. Which will it be?"

Everybody looked at me for an answer, but I was dumbfounded. I didn't know what to say.

"Oh, one more thing," Karen added. "My father is a cop, and this wouldn't be the first time he took a kid to the police station for trespassing in our yard."

"Fine," I said. "I guess we do it your way. But not all my payments were in cash."

"That's okay," she replied. "Take a guess at their cash value."

"I already did. I figured it was about one hundred sixty bucks in cash and other junk."

"Then I'll take eighty," she said. "Cash. Now."

What could I do? Just like in the cafeteria with the strudel, Karen had the advantage and she knew it. I didn't even try to pretend that I didn't have the money with me. I shrugged, dug into my front pocket for the wad of bills, and peeled off eighty dollars. Easy come, easy go.

"Stay right there," Karen said as she took the money and headed into the house. "I'll be right back."

True to her word, Karen returned a minute later and escorted us around the house to her backyard, where we saw the big pond. It was gorgeous. I thought that if I lived in a place like this, I would go fishing every day. After some brief pandemonium in which lures, night crawlers and various trinkets were frantically exchanged, the first fishing lines hit the water.

Not my fishing line, of course. First I had to set up Sam's rod, bait his hook, and give him a refresher course in the proper technique. Once he was in business, I turned to my rod and the extra one I brought for Karen.

"Okay, moneybags," I said to Karen as I handed her a rod, "let's take it from the top, or maybe the bottom. See this round metal contraption going halfway around the reel that looks like a thick wire? That's the bale."

"This?" Karen confirmed.

"Yes, that's the bale. Lift it back—"

Karen pulled back the bale, and her line spewed out of the reel into a tangled mess.

"—but first make sure your thumb is holding the line down on the spool. Otherwise you end up with a bird's nest like that one." I sighed, set my own rod down, took back Karen's rod and proceeded to untangle the bird's nest for the next five minutes.

"All right, let's try it again," I said, handing Karen's rod back to her. "Hold the rod like this in your right hand, just underneath the reel. Now take your right thumb and place it firmly on the spool of line. Good. Now—keeping your thumb firmly on the line—take your left hand and pull back the bale. Okay, now watch me do this first. Lift your right arm up and back over your shoulder, like so, and snap your arm forward again, releasing your thumb off the line toward the very end." As I demonstrated, I cast my line effortlessly about forty yards out.

Karen tried to follow my lead, but she let go of the line too late, flinging her lure into the shallow water about three feet in front of us. Consoling her that it wasn't a bad effort for her first time (it really wasn't; I've done as badly myself when my mind wanders), I showed her how to turn the crank and reel in her short length of fishing line.

"Try it again, but let go just a second earlier, just as your arm reaches two o'clock," I suggested in my most encouraging tone. She still released the line too late, but much better than her first attempt. Her lure landed with a firm plunk about twenty yards into the pond. "Now just reel it in slowly—about one revolution every three seconds—and let the jitterbug do the rest."

"The what?" Karen asked as she awkwardly reeled her line.

"The jitterbug," I replied. "It's the style of lure you're using. You probably noticed it's sort of shaped like a little frog. It jitters back and forth along the surface of the water as you reel it in. I'm using a hula popper, which is similar, except that it bobs up and down along the surface instead of jigging left and right."

Karen paused for a moment as she contemplated her lure, which approached the shore and popped out of the water towards her. She seemed vaguely disappointed that there wasn't a fish attached. "Oh. Why aren't we using worms like Vic and your little brother?"

"We will, later," I said. "I wanted to start you off with a surface lure, because I thought you might be squeamish about live bait." Karen cast a disapproving look at me to show she was mildly insulted. "Plus, I prefer surface lures first thing in the morning and late in the evening. The fish usually look for food along the surface of the water in the morning, when the bugs are out. We'll switch to worms later when it warms up a little and the bass go deeper in the water to stay cool."

Karen shrugged. "Makes sense to me, I guess."

"Good. Now on this next one, see if you can aim your cast a little bit. See this dark area to the left of us, where the weeds end and the water turns from green to gray? You don't want to cast into the weeds, although even if you do, you shouldn't get snagged, since you're using a surface lure. But try to cast just along the edge. Lots of times that's where bass like to feed."

Karen's cast was even better this time, getting out about thirty yards, and right along the edge of the weeds as I had instructed. I cast in the opposite direction into the deep middle of the pond, just so our lines wouldn't cross. Glancing over to the small dock where Neil, Vic and Sam were fishing, I noticed that little Sam had already caught the first fish of the day. It was just a tiny sunfish, but you would think he had caught a marlin the way he shrieked with glee. I watched as Neil helped Sam unhook the fish. Neil was about to throw the sunfish back when Sam started whining in protest. Not wanting to waste good fishing time explaining to Sam why his fish was too small to keep, Neil good-naturedly filled a bucket with water and dropped Sam's fish inside. That was a smart move. Sam forgot all about fishing as he sat down and studied his catch swimming around the bucket. That was one less line in the water to get tangled up with, as far as Neil and Vic were concerned.

But I had bigger fish to fry—or catch, as the case may be. I tried to settle down for some serious fishing. Every so often, I had to stop what I was doing to tend to Karen, but otherwise I was able to focus on my own rod. I loved getting into that zone where nothing else existed but the pond and me. My usual fishing experience was that after taking a few dozen casts, I would forget myself altogether and become the lure. This morning was no exception, as I saw myself in my mind's eye popping across the surface of the pond, enticing any smallmouth bass nearby to action. The cool fall breeze blowing across my face became ripples of water, carrying my plastic green-and-yellow-colored body toward shore.

Suddenly, my pole jerked forward.

Chapter Five

Dopey Dads

I tugged back on my pole to set the hook—quickly and firmly, but not so hard as to yank the lure from the fish's mouth.

"Got one!" I yelled, as I cranked the reel furiously.

"Make up your mind—are you going to talk all day or fish?" Neil yelled from the dock fifty yards away. It was one of our long-running jokes. Each of us had been reprimanded separately by our fathers on previous fishing trips for disrupting the serenity of the sport with unwelcome chatter. Somehow old fishermen took it as indisputable fact that any conversation on shore (or especially in a boat) would somehow scare away the fish in the water below.

The bass gave me a good fight, zigging and zagging across the section of pond in front of me. I had to yell (as sweetly as I could manage) at Karen not to cast her line back out until I got my catch ashore.

About twenty yards out, the bass jumped out of the water in an acrobatic spinning flip—one final attempt to pop my lure from his mouth. Thankfully the treble hook held fast. That was always the most fun—and frustrating—part of fishing for smallmouth bass. They're called smallmouths for a reason, and many a fisherman has lost a trophy catch at that moment when the fish leaps into the air, seeming to wink at the angler before spitting out a large lure that didn't quite fit in that tiny jaw.

As my fish came within reach, I carefully held my rod in my right hand, keeping the tip down and the fish submerged until I could pick up my landing net in my left. I've seen too many over-eager fishermen—myself included—hastily try to yank a big fish out of the water and onto land, only to yank the hook from the fish's mouth instead. Swooping the net underneath, I swung around and gently set the net, rod and flip-flopping fish on the firm ground behind me.

"It's a beauty!" Karen marveled.

It was indeed—a beautiful three-pound smallmouth bass. Its compact muscular body shimmered with golden-green scales accented by broad dark-green vertical stripes. Red gills flared open as the fish struggled to extract oxygen from the strange dry atmosphere. I bent over to unhook it, which proved to be unnecessary, as the fish quickly freed himself from my hula popper's treble hook with two quick flip-flops. Pulling him from the net, I threaded the metal end of my fish stringer through his left gill and out his mouth.

"Thanks," I said, as I tied the loose end of the stringer to a tree root along the pond's edge and tossed my secured bass back into the water.

Karen looked glum. "What do you suppose I'm doing wrong?"

"You mean, aside from not having your lure in the water?" I replied. "This is like the lottery. You can't win if you don't play."

She cast her line again and again. About five minutes later, she screamed, "I've got something! I've got something!" However, she didn't set the hook right away, and when I told her to do so, she panicked and pulled back too hard. The taut line fell limp, and I didn't have to tell her that the fish was gone. That led to accusations that I gave her bad instructions, a defensive outburst on my part, and finally about twenty minutes where neither of us spoke to the other.

I got another fish soon after that, and after I landed it and added it to my stringer, Karen announced that she wanted to swap poles and lures. That was fine with me, and I even suggested switching spots for good measure, to which she quickly agreed. I was almost relieved when I didn't catch another fish right away. No need to run up the score, I thought. Not that I was keeping score, but I had the feeling Karen was.

Around eleven a.m., I asked her if she was hungry.

"What do you want to trade for this time?" Karen asked with a coy smile.

"Nothing," I assured her. "This time it's every man or woman for him or herself." As I set down my fishing pole and picked up my lunch bag, I added, "Unless you have a soda you'd like to give up. I'm dying of thirst."

Karen laughed. "I'll see what I can do. We might even be able to give you a complimentary soft drink to show our appreciation for your business. Just don't tell the other customers."

"Deal," I agreed.

We walked back towards Karen's house, making a detour to the little boat dock to get Sam. As I suspected, he hardly fished at all for the past few hours, although he still managed to catch two more sunfish. Vic had two nice-sized smallmouths, but Neil had nothing yet to show for his efforts.

"See, Karen," I said. "Not everyone catches a fish right away. Sometimes it's just a matter of luck."

"That and Neil fishes like a girl," Vic added.

"Eat me," Neil retorted with a grin. Like any true fisherman, Neil was content just to be fishing. Whether he actually caught anything was secondary.

The five of us walked together towards Karen's backyard patio. Several of the other kids must have had the same idea and were already settled into the patio furniture, enjoying their early lunches. It was also apparent that sodas were indeed complimentary today, as Mrs. Thomas cheerfully brought around a tray of soft drinks to offer the young anglers.

I took a Coke for myself and a juice box for Sam, and not seeing any empty chairs or benches, spread out our lunch on the neatly manicured lawn just off the patio.

As I bit into my sandwich, I noticed that Mr. Thomas, Karen's father, was looking at me. At least, I thought he was looking at me, but I couldn't be certain as he was wearing reflective aviator-style sunglasses. He had been mowing the lawn, and bits of fresh-cut grass stuck to his sweaty, burly legs and arms. His clothes were the regulation-issue dad's summertime uniform in our town—khaki shorts, a sky-blue golf shirt that was too tight around the neck (especially *his* neck), and old brown-leather deck shoes with no socks.

I tried to ignore his intimidating presence, but it was difficult. Taking a sip of my Coke, I turned to my brother and asked, "Having fun, Sam?"

"Sure, I guess," he said. I knew better than to read anything into his indifferent response. He would have had the same answer if he had spent the morning in a free candy store playing video games while sitting on a pony.

"Good. Maybe after lunch you and I can take a few casts together and see if you can catch a bass to bring home."

"Whatever."

This touching exchange of brotherly emotion was interrupted by a large shadow cast over our lunches. I didn't even have to look up to see who or what caused the shadow, and I didn't particularly want to look up either. Nevertheless, Sam certainly wasn't going to be the assertive one, so the job fell to me, the big brother.

"Hi, Mr. Thomas," I squeaked, squinting at the bright sunrays reflecting off his mirrored lenses. "We were just saying what a swell time we're having here. Thanks for letting Karen invite us over."

Mr. Thomas stared at us, but no words passed through his taut lips. I smiled weakly, wracking my brain for something intelligent to say.

"How about those Yankees?" I offered, then quickly remembered to add, "Sir."

Still nothing.

After an eternity (okay, maybe ten seconds or so), Mr. Thomas finally said in a deep, quiet voice, "Aren't you two Dr. Hoffman's boys?"

I gulped. "Yes, sir. I'm Mark Hoffman, and this is my brother Sam."

Now he stooped down over us, his inscrutable sunglasses no more than a foot from my face. At this close range, I thought I could almost see eyes behind the lenses. Mr. Thomas's breath was hot and smelled of the boiled knockwurst sandwich he had been eating.

"You don't know who I am, do you, boy?" he asked in an unmistakably unfriendly tone.

"Um, other than Karen's father, no, I guess I don't," I answered. Out of the corner of my eye, I could see that Sam looked pale as a ghost and his eyes were bulging with terror.

"I'm Lieutenant Anthony Thomas," he said, as if that would clear up everything. When he saw that his name and rank made no impression on Sam and me, he added, "I was the arresting officer when we busted that dirtbag father of yours and shut down his little marijuana distribution ring."

"Oh."

I didn't know what else to say. To my surprise, I didn't want to punch him. Okay, maybe I did want to punch him a little bit, but total fear overwhelmed the desire.

"What's the matter, boy? Didn't your mother tell you what happened to your old man? Can't say I blame her. I'd be ashamed too."

Shaking my head, I rose to my feet. My intention was to look him in the eye—or sunglasses, as the case may be—but even with my above-average height for my age, I was still a good six inches shorter than Mr. Thomas.

"No, sir, our mother and father told us everything," I said. "In fact, we attended every day of my dad's trial. We watched the state ruin his life for obeying his Hippocratic oath."

Mr. Thomas harrumphed. "I didn't know drug dealers took Hippocratic oaths."

Nearly in tears, Sam blurted out, "My dad is not a drug dealer! He's a doctor!"

I put my arm around my brother. "That's right, Sam, and don't let anybody"—I looked up at Mr. Thomas—"tell you otherwise. Daddy is an oncologist, and he gave marijuana to his cancer patients who would have *died* without it."

"That may be what he told you and told the court," Mr. Thomas said, "but the fact is that so-called medical marijuana is illegal in the state of New York. Your father took the law into his own hands."

I looked straight at Mr. Thomas and replied calmly, "And you took his patients' lives into yours. Did you know that most of them have died since my father has been in jail? Some of them just choked on their own vomit because of the nausea caused by their chemotherapy."

Now Mr. Thomas removed his shades, exposing eyes filled with fury and contempt. "You smart-mouthed little punk. How dare you come onto my property and speak to me like that?"

Before I had a chance to reply, Karen and her mother appeared out of nowhere and stood between us. "Anthony, stop that this instant!" Mrs. Thomas exclaimed. "You're embarrassing our daughter and behaving terribly toward her guests."

"Stop it, Daddy!" Karen pleaded.

"Stay out of this, Karen," Lieutenant Thomas scolded her. "You too, Sharon. These disrespectful punks are no good. The apple doesn't fall far from the tree, I always say."

"Please!" his wife begged.

Mr. Thomas pointed at Sam and me and continued. "For all we know, they're here to deal their pot to the rest of these kids, including Karen. Maybe I'd better frisk them."

"What pot?" I asked. "I wouldn't even know where to get it." That wasn't entirely true. There wasn't a kid in the seventh grade, at my school or any other school in the country, who didn't know where to get marijuana if he or she were so inclined. But I simply never had the inclination.

Sam, meanwhile, decided to do what he did best when scared out of his wits. He ran as fast as he could, screaming as he went. Apparently, he was too scared to remember that his bike was parked out front, and he took off toward the woods behind the pond. Realizing that getting lost in the woods was possibly scarier than getting frisked, he turned around after about thirty seconds and headed back towards us.

"Get back here, Sam," I said as he came within range. "Let's grab our stuff and get out of here."

Karen shook her head. "Oh no you don't. You're not going anywhere. Daddy won't bother you. Will you, Daddy?"

"Karen, I already told you to stay out of this," Mr. Thomas snarled.

Mrs. Thomas stepped between her husband and me. "No, he won't bother you anymore. That's a promise." Then she turned toward her husband and gave him a look that was at least as scary as the one he had given Sam and me. This was a family that thrived on intimidation.

Lieutenant Thomas took one step towards the house before looking back at us. Pointing at me again, he said, "You just watch your step, boy. I have my eye on you."

Pretending to ignore him as he stormed off, I looked at Karen and said, "It's all right. We had enough fishing for today. We'll just go."

"I said no," she said firmly. "A deal is a deal. You're not going anywhere until I catch a fish." The serious look on her face turned to her usual pretty smile, and she winked at me.

Looking around me, I noticed that all the kids were watching, which shouldn't have been too surprising, considering the scene we just made. Remembering to take a long overdue breath, I exhaled deeply and said, "Okay, let's do it."

Sam wasn't having any of it, however. "I want to go home!" he wailed, tears streaming down his cheeks.

"Just give me a couple of minutes," I assured Karen quietly. Taking Sam by the hand, I walked with him (okay, I dragged him) toward the little dock where he had been fishing. He continued to howl relentlessly. His stamina when crying was really quite impressive.

Digging around in my pockets, I pulled out half a roll of fruit Lifesavers. I stuck a piece of candy in Sam's mouth, which caused some momentary confusion as his instincts veered between sucking on the sweet treat or continuing his hysteria, but the candy won out and he began to quiet down.

"Now look," I said as we arrived at the little dock, "just forget about that creep. There is nothing to be afraid of here. We can still have a good time today."

"But... (sob)... he... (sniff)... sent... Daddy... (gasp)... to... jail!"

Glancing back toward the house, I said, "I know, Sam. I hate him as much as you do. But the thing is, we can't let him win. See, a bully like that, they get their jollies out of scaring people like us. And we have to show him that we're not scared. Because there's nothing to be scared of, right?"

Sam shook his head. "That's what Daddy always said. And now he's gone!" The tears were flowing again.

I wrapped my arms around my brother and gave him an uncustomary hug. We generally weren't the hugging types. "I know, Sam. I know. Lieutenant Thomas really did a rotten thing to our family. But like Daddy tells us whenever we visit him, you and I are the men of the family while he's away. Remember? As the men of the family, we have to show Karen's dad that he hasn't licked the Hoffmans, that he'll never beat us. Karen's dad wants us to leave, because that way he'll know he beat us, and he can sneer at us while we get on our bikes and pedal home. That's what guys like him do. You know those kids who were picking on you last year and wouldn't let you play in the sandbox by the playground?"

Sam smiled and nodded. "Uh-huh. You beat that one kid up real good!"

I nodded in agreement. It was all part of the big brother job description. "Yup. Well, most of those kids will probably grow up to be cops. Or maybe Mafia enforcers, which amounts to the same thing. I'll bet you Mr. Thomas was one of those playground bullies himself. Now we're in his sandbox, and he's doing his best to scare us off. But we're not going to let him. Right?"

"Right," Sam agreed. "Hey, Mark? Will you stay here on the dock and fish with me?"

What the heck. I could help Karen not catch fish from the dock just as easily as where we were this morning.

"Sure," I said. "Just let me go get my fishing pole, and I'll be right back." Pausing for a quick peek in Sam's bucket, which contained three sunfish that surprisingly weren't floating on top yet, I ran off to fetch my equipment.

Karen was waiting for me when I arrived at our morning fishing spot.

"Mark, I'm really, really sorry about that," she said as she looked at me through big, dewy eyes. I wondered if she had been crying too. "Is Sam okay?"

Shrugging, I answered, "Yeah, I guess. He'll live. But if it's all the same to you, I'd like us to fish with him from the dock over there."

She nodded. "Of course." As we gathered up our gear and made our way back toward the dock, Karen asked, "Sam, do you think your father really distributed marijuana?"

"Sure," I said with another shrug. "He never denied it. He's a doctor, and he does whatever it takes to save his patients' lives."

"Even when it's illegal? Do you think he has the right to make that kind of decision?"

I laughed. "If you were dying of cancer, Karen, who would you rather have making the decisions about your medicine, doctors or politicians?"

Karen didn't say anything for another minute or so. After careful consideration, she finally said, more to herself than to me, "All I know is that people should obey the law. My dad says lack of respect for the law is what's ruining the country."

"Maybe," I said. "Or maybe this country just has too many bad laws to respect."

As we approached the dock, Karen struggled to find words to make things better. "Well, if it was his first offense, he'll be out soon, right?"

"No, Karen, he won't. This is New York. Haven't you ever heard of the Rockefeller Drug Laws? The judge had no discretion in sentencing my dad. He got fifteen years."

"Fifteen years?" she gasped. "But how is that possible? He must have sold an awful lot of marijuana—"

"He didn't *sell* anything," I interrupted. "He distributed it to his patients for free. And they only busted him for distributing two ounces. The mandatory sentence for that is fifteen years to life. I'll probably have kids of my own by the time my dad gets out."

"But—"

We were now about ten yards from Sam, and I lowered my voice. "Look, Karen, I think we'll all have a much better time this afternoon if we just drop this subject."

"No problem," Karen answered. She waved to my brother and with a big smile said, "Hey, Sam. I hope you're having fun."

Sam said nothing, which wasn't too surprising. He was usually a quiet kid to begin with, particularly around people he didn't know well. The morning had gone all right because he was with Vic and Neil, whom he had known his entire life, but the lunchtime confrontation with Lieutenant Thomas sent him back into his shell.

Pressing ahead with the business at hand, I announced, "All right, boys and girls, it's getting warm. That means the fish are likely to be lurking deeper in the water to stay cool, instead of feeding on the surface. So I think we should switch from surface lures to leadhead jigs."

"Whatever you say," Karen said. "I couldn't do any worse than I did this morning."

"You did fine this morning," I assured her. "You just need to change your bait to change your luck." As I set my stringer of bass in the water, I turned toward Sam and asked, "Are you going to try to catch one of these nice smallmouths, or are you going to play with that bluegill all day?"

"I don't care," Sam answered with a shrug.

I decided to interpret that as "yes, I'd love to catch a smallmouth bass," and I removed his simple hook, sinker and bobber rig, replacing it with a lead-weighted jig and a fresh night crawler. A brief struggle ensued as I lifted the pole to cast Sam's line for him. He insisted on doing it himself. To my surprise, Sam cast it quite well for someone his size, hurling the jig about twenty yards directly in front of him.

To my even greater surprise, Sam hooked a smallmouth on his second cast. I had just changed Karen's tackle and was about to take care of my own, but I had to drop my pole and fetch the net.

All I needed was to listen to Sam shriek if his big fish got away. Thankfully, we landed the bass without incident, and it was a nice three-pounder.

"Okay, Karen," I said with as much encouragement in my voice as I could manage, "it's your turn to catch a fish. Let's see some action."

Karen turned and glared at me. "Don't you think I'm trying?" she snapped.

"Of course," I said meekly. I had never seen that look on her face. In fact, I had rarely seen Karen not smiling. "Sorry. I was just trying to be supportive."

"Hmmph." She turned toward the water and jerked her rod forward in a hurry, casting the lure five feet in front of her, just as she did when I first showed her how to cast earlier in the day. Not saying a word, I tried to ignore the tension in the air as I finally turned my attention to my own rod.

Karen never did catch a fish that afternoon, although she did get one nice bite. She lost the fish when she jerked too hard while trying to set the hook. I took the blame for that one, since I had been yelling at her to set it.

Nevertheless, Karen's mood picked up towards the end of the day, as various kids stopped by on their way home to thank her for her hospitality.

"You're welcome," Karen said sweetly to the first group of departing anglers. "Come back anytime. Even if I can't catch fish, I can always make some money."

Neil overheard her and raised his eyebrows. "Are you serious, Karen? You would let us come back here again? That's great!" Needless to say, Neil had broken his morning dry spell by catching two nice-sized bass in the last hour of fishing.

"It sure is!" Vic agreed.

"Yep," I added happily, "just pay me, and I'll give Karen her share, just like this morning."

"Oh, but that's the good news," Karen said. The corners of her mouth turned up into a big, dimpled grin. "You don't have to pay Mark to fish here anymore. You can pay me directly. In fact, I'll be cutting the price for my repeat customers."

I was steamed. "But that's not fair," I whined. "I'm the middle man!"

Karen shook her head and patted me on the arm. "You mean you *were* the middle man. Don't get mad, Mark. You're still welcome to come here as a customer, but to be honest, you stink as a fishing instructor."

At Neil's suggestion, Karen walked back to her house to fetch some plastic freezer bags for the fillets, while Vic, Neil and I pulled up our stringers and started to clean the day's catch.

I tried to concentrate on the task at hand, but my mind kept wandering to my frustration with Karen. Maybe nothing would come of it, I tried to convince myself. After all, how many times are these kids going to come here to fish? Especially if they have to pay for the privilege?

That wishful thinking vanished as I listened to my friends enthusiastically discuss their plans to return the very next Saturday. Vic and Neil both lined up customers for their bait and tackle, respectively, from each group of kids who passed by the dock on their way towards their parents' waiting cars. In fact, a few of my former customers returned a few minutes later with their parents' loose change in order to buy some of the day's more successful lures from Neil. Others were striking barter deals similar to the strange bargains they had made with me to fish here in the first place.

I was lost in thought and self-pity when Sam tapped me gently on the shoulder. "What's the matter, Mark?" he asked wide-eyed.

Dumb kid, I said to myself. He wouldn't understand. "Nothing," I said as I hacked away at a fillet. Normally I was a half-decent fish cleaner, but in my distraction I was making a mess. "Keep your hands away from the knife. It's sharp."

"I figured you'd be happy," he said.

"Yeah, I know," I conceded. "You're right. I got what I wanted, which was to do some fishing. But listen to all these guys. They all have these little rackets and mini-businesses going. I'm the one who started the whole thing, and I'm cut out of it."

"Why are you cut out?"

I shook my head. "You're such a dummy, Sam. Everybody else has something to sell or trade for. Vic has his worms, Neil has his tackle, and the other kids have something else to trade or their own money. Karen just cut me out of the one thing I had, which was access to her pond."

Sam shook his head. "You never had that in the first place. You traded for that too."

"Oh yeah," I replied. "Well, that won't be happening again either. You heard Karen. I stink as a fishing instructor."

More head shaking from Sam. "You're the dummy, not me!"

"Whatever," I answered dismissively as I tossed a bony fish carcass into the weeds and removed another bass from the stringer for cleaning.

"The fishing instructions got you here, but it was *Mom's dessert* that got Neil, Vic and me in."

I dropped my knife.

"Are you saying what I think you're saying, Sam?" Maybe I was the dummy after all.

Sam grinned and whispered, "Let Karen have the pond. It will freeze up come winter anyway. We have the desserts, and everybody knows they're the best desserts in town."

"You mean—"

"I mean," said my brilliant eight-year-old brother, "that you and I are going into the dessert business!"

Chapter Six

Making Some Dough

The whole bike ride home was a blur. I tried to think through Sam's proposal. It sounded brilliant. Every kid in Walton knew about my mom's great desserts. They would sell themselves, I thought.

How much should we sell them for, I wondered. We couldn't just sell them for the same price as my mom's store. Our potential customers were just kids; they didn't have the income level of my mom's yuppie customers. (For that matter, my mom's yuppie customers no longer had the income level they once did, but that was her problem.) Also, we didn't have any overhead—no storefront, no rent, no insurance and whatever other bills my mom had to deal with to make her business run—so we could afford to charge lower prices.

On the other hand, we couldn't just expect my mom to give us an infinite supply of free desserts to sell. For one thing, she just wouldn't. Any baking she did for people outside her immediate family was on a for-profit basis... for her profit, that is.

As Sam and I turned onto Walton Street and approached our home, we saw the front of Ellen's Pastry Place, my mom's little shop that was attached to the side of our house. It was a quaint, clean store painted in pastel colors and decorated inside with all sorts of old-fashioned knick-knacks. Our mom told us that it was supposed to look like the old country bakeries that she grew up around in Vermont. I noticed that the "open" sign was still showing in the front window, along with an assortment of wonderful baked goods that had gone unsold.

"I guess we should go in and say hi to Mom," I told Sam as I stepped down on my kickstand and dismounted my bike.

"Okay. But we're not telling her about our business, are we?"

"No, I don't think so. Let's just look around casually and see what's what."

A little cowbell over the door rang as we entered the store. Our mother looked up from the tarts she had been wrapping in cellophane and smiled.

"Well, from the way you two smell, I take it you had a good day of fishing," she said.

"Yeah, Mom, we did great!" Sam exclaimed. "I caught three sunfish and a bass. Mark caught some bass too." I nodded in agreement.

"That's wonderful, boys," Mom said. "Why don't you take the fillets inside and put them in our refrigerator before they go bad out there in that heat."

"The fillets are fine," I replied. "They're on ice. Are you coming home soon?"

Mom nodded as she placed the tray of tarts under the display case. "No point in keeping this place open any longer today. I just have to get a few things prepared for the after-church crowd tomorrow."

Removing a tray of walnut brownies from the case, she placed two on paper plates for Sam and me. I fetched us two small cartons of milk from the glass-fronted refrigerator by the entrance and brought them to the table where my mom and brother were now sitting. As we enjoyed our snack, Sam and I found ourselves looking the store over as if for the first time, although we had both spent nearly as much time in Ellen's Pastry Place as in our own home next door.

"Hey Mom, how hard is it to bake all this stuff?" I finally asked through a partial mouthful of brownie.

The question caught her by surprise. "How hard is it?" Mom paused for a moment and studied her store herself. "Not too hard, I suppose. I love to bake, and Mrs. Whitney works a few hours in the morning when we're busiest making everything. The hard part is selling everything, especially lately, and doing all the other things that make this store run."

"Like what?" Sam asked.

Mom gaped at us in mild astonishment. "I never knew you two took an interest in what I do." Sam and I did our best to look hurt, but I'm not sure she bought it. "There are all sorts of things I have to do besides bake pastries. I have to clean the store and the kitchen several times a day. Nobody wants to buy desserts from a filthy store, and the Walton Board of Health is brutal on businesses that sell food, especially when the business owner doesn't pay bribes to the health inspectors. Then there are bills to pay. The taxes alone take me hours a month just to fill out the forms. When you own a small business, the government is always sending you lots of complicated, maddening forms, and they're all very important for some reason and have to be filled out just right, or they make your life heck."

The looks on our faces must have been complete blanks, and I think our mom momentarily doubted whether we were genuinely interested in her shop. If only she knew just how interested we were.

"But the baking itself, that's easy?" I asked impatiently, wanting to steer the conversation back to the essential information.

"Yes, Mark, I suppose it is," Mom answered. "At least, it's easy for me. And certainly it's the most enjoyable part of the job."

Sam had a good question. "How do you remember all those recipes? Do you just remember everything in your head, or is it all in a cookbook?"

Mom laughed. "Well, they're not in a cookbook, although one of these days I am going to write one. But I don't totally rely on my memory either."

She stepped back around the display case, and Sam and I followed her into the shop's large kitchen area. My mom wasn't kidding about the frequent, diligent cleaning she did. Bright, sparkling appliances and countertops surrounded us. Taped to the wall were yellowing copies of various handwritten recipes.

"These recipes that you see displayed are the ones I use all the time," Mom said. She pulled a large three-ring binder from under one of the countertops and added, "I mix in a few of these special recipes occasionally, just to keep things from getting dull for me or my regular customers."

I did my best to look calm as I read the recipes taped to the wall. They didn't look too hard to me, just lists of ingredients, oven temperatures and cooking times.

"Pretty neat," Sam said.

Our mom arched an eyebrow as she cast a suspicious glance first at Sam and then at me. "If you say so," she said. "But if I didn't know better, I'd think you two were up to something. Now I really need to get some work done before I can leave for the night. You two go on home and put that fish in the refrigerator, and I'll cook it for dinner as soon as I get there."

True to her word, our mother arrived home about an hour later and quickly made a delicious dinner of grilled bass, potatoes au gratin, asparagus, and concluded with an incredible peach cobbler. After dinner, Sam and I adjourned to his bedroom for video games and strategizing.

"I still don't understand why we don't just make Mom a partner and have her bake the desserts while we sell them," Sam said, as his on-screen ninja fighter threw one lame punch after another at my fighter.

I absent-mindedly blocked Sam's attack with one virtual arm as I delivered a vicious roundhouse kick to his head. Sam stared at the screen in disbelief, pumping his controller in a futile attempt to reinvigorate his weakened ninja. I backed off just enough to keep him in the game while we talked.

"You heard her," I answered. "Mom's way of doing business means we lose a big chunk of our profits to taxes, plus we have to follow all those stupid regulations that have nothing to do with selling desserts. It would be a huge pain in the butt. We have to avoid all that nonsense to make the business worthwhile."

"Yeah, I guess, but do you really think we can make the desserts ourselves?"

Nodding as my ninja ducked and jumped to avoid an assault from Sam's sword, I said, "Yeah, we'll manage. Luckily we have the rest of a three-day holiday weekend and nothing much going on, so we have time to prepare."

On Sunday afternoon, Sam and I told our mom we were going to Neil's house, but we rode our bikes to the supermarket instead. Sam and I had put together a shopping list from our memory of one or two recipes posted on the dessert shop's kitchen walls. We figured that while our mom might not notice raw ingredients missing right away, she would get suspicious eventually, especially if we were successful and used a lot of supplies. Also, we agreed that there was no point in stealing the ingredients from our mom's business. We weren't thieves, and even if we were, it would be more efficient just to steal money outright, rather than flour and sugar.

Steering our rickety shopping cart up and down the supermarket aisles, with Sam straggling behind me, I found the baking supplies. I glanced at the list. The first item was flour. Let's see… flour, flour, flour. I selected a ten-pound bag of Gold Medal Easy Bake, eased it off the shelf and dropped it in the cart. That was my first mistake. The paper bottom of the bag split open on impact, and white flour sifted through the wide mesh of the cart onto the floor below.

"Man," I muttered as I lifted the broken bag out of the cart and placed it back on the shelf, flour streaming onto the floor and my shoe the entire way. Sam grabbed his stomach and doubled over in childish laughter. "Come here," I said. He stopped laughing only briefly when I put a handful of flour down the front of his shorts. His quick little hands scooped some spilled flour from the floor and flung it in my face, which made me laugh in spite of my frustration.

"Okay," I said as I coughed up flour, "we need to behave or we're going to get kicked out of here before we get what we need."

After replacing our broken bag of flour with a sealed one, we continued down the aisle and found a bag of sugar, a box of baking powder, a box of baking chocolates and a bottle of vanilla. Then it was over to the dairy section for milk, butter and eggs. That would do for now. If we forgot anything, we would have to borrow it from our mom's supplies and replace it later.

We paid for our groceries out of my profits from the fishing outing. Slinging the handles of the plastic bags across our bike handlebars, Sam and I headed for home. Lucky for us, and unlucky for our mom, business was so slow this holiday weekend that she had closed her shop earlier than usual. Glancing around to verify that we weren't being watched by our mom or her stupid boyfriend Frank, I hoisted Sam up to an unlocked window on the far side of the shop, which he scurried through before falling to the floor. He ran to the front entrance, disabled the burglar alarm, and let me through with our groceries.

Sam and I didn't linger long in the shop; it was too risky in the middle of the afternoon. I just tossed the groceries into the refrigerator, and we made a swift departure. Knowing that we would need to return later that night, we didn't re-set the alarm or lock the front door on our way out.

A driving rain began shortly after Sunday dinner, and it hadn't stopped by the time Sam and I went to bed. I thought the bad weather was a mixed blessing. On the one hand, the noisy wind and rain would provide good sound cover when the time came to sneak out of the house. On the other hand, we would have to be very careful not to leave telltale wet, muddy footprints leading to and from the dessert shop. Of course, we would also have to get the desserts out of the shop without getting them soaked.

A few minutes after midnight, when I was certain that our mom and Frank would be asleep, I tiptoed out of my room to fetch Sam, who was up and waiting for me. Together we crept down the stairs and out the side door closest to the dessert shop entrance.

The rain was heavy and cold, and we did our best to cling to the side of the house underneath the gutter as we made our way to the shop, not only to keep ourselves dry and warm, but also to avoid being seen. Slowly turning the knob, I pushed the door open. Sam reached for the light switch, but I blocked it with one hand while I closed the door with the other. We made our way to the kitchen by the glow of the display case lights, which my mom left on for security purposes. Once inside the cooking area, I closed the door that separated it from the main shop and switched on the light. Since there were no windows in the kitchen, the light would not be seen from the outside.

"Okay, partner," I enthused as I clapped my hands together, "where do you want to start?"

Sam yawned and stretched. "Let's start by going back to bed for a few hours."

"None of that," I said with my head in the large commercial refrigerator. I removed our grocery bag and set it on the counter. "There's no time for rest when you're an entrepreneur. Hand me that large baking pan over there. Better yet, take this shortening and grease the pan while I find a mixing bowl. I figure we'll start with some brownies, since that looks like the easiest recipe."

"Brownies?" Sam winced.

"Now you don't like brownies?"

"Well, no, I like them," he replied. "But they're so… ordinary. Mom's desserts are incredible. How about some raspberry tortes or chocolate éclairs?"

I shook my head. "That would be great, except for one problem. We don't know what we're doing."

"We just have to follow the recipes," Sam protested.

"I'll tell you what. Let's start with something easy, like brownies, just to get our feet wet."

"I thought we were trying to keep our feet dry tonight."

"Hyuck, hyuck, hyuck," I laughed sarcastically. "I thought you had a brain. We'll save the fancy stuff for later, if there's time."

We looked at the recipe for brownies, which was posted on the front of one of the storage cabinets. Of course, since it was our mom's recipe, it wasn't a recipe for ordinary brownies, but rather Wild Walton Walnut Brownies.

The first ingredient was two cups of flour. I tore open the bag of flour and tried to pour it carefully into a measuring cup. At first, the flour clogged the small opening I made in the bag. Sam stuck his hand in the opening to help it along, which worked too well. I jerked the bag back to stop the flow, but not before several small mountains of flour found their way into the measuring cup and onto the countertop and floor.

"What did you do that for, you idiot?" I yelled.

"You were the one holding the bag!" Sam whined.

"Aw man, quit stepping in it, will you! Go find a broom and a dustpan and clean the mess up."

Sam folded his arms defiantly. "*You* go find a broom. You're not the boss of me."

Tempting as it was to smack my little brother upside the head, I restrained myself and went to the closet to fetch a broom. Something was starting to tell me that this whole thing was a mistake.

I returned with the broom to find Sam opening the carton of eggs. "Don't touch those!" I yelled.

"Why not? The recipe says we need six eggs."

"Yeah, well I'll break them when we're ready. You'll just make more of a mess. Why don't you start chopping the walnuts? Just *please* be real careful with the knife."

"I *know*," Sam groaned while rolling his eyes.

I gave the area a hasty sweep and disposed of the excess flour. Then, grasping an egg between my index finger and thumb, as I had seen my mom do hundreds of times, I cracked it against the rim of the mixing bowl. The yolk ran down the outside of the bowl and slid along the countertop before flopping onto the floor.

"Good thing you're not making more of a mess," Sam smirked.

I shook my fist at my brother. "I swear I'm going to pound your head into the ground if you don't shut up." Taking another egg, I tried to crack it on the inside rim, but the previous attempt apparently made me gun-shy. I tapped the egg so gently that it didn't crack. When I increased the force, the entire egg smashed in my hand, sending shell fragments, as well as egg yolk and whites, into the mix. I cursed under my breath as I picked out the shell bits.

"Ow!"

"What now?" I yelled, as I turned to see Sam holding a finger that was bleeding badly.

"Ow!" Sam repeated in a shrill scream. "It hurts! It hurts!"

"Quiet! Quiet!" I stage-whispered as I ran frantically to his side. "You're going to wake up the whole neighborhood!"

"I don't care!" Sam yelled just before bursting into tears.

Feeling a bit panicked myself, I turned on the cold water in the sink and stuck my brother's hand under the flowing water. Then I wadded up some paper towels and pressed them on the center of the wound.

"You're hurting me!" Sam blubbered.

"Sorry. You do it. Try to keep some pressure on the cut so it stops bleeding."

Sam's loud crying gradually turned to a quiet whimper. I wasn't sure what I wanted to confront less—Sam's injury or the mess in the kitchen. Since my brother appeared neither to need nor want my help at the moment, I reluctantly chose the latter. I grimaced as my eyes took in the horrible sight. A trail of drying blood that started on the walnuts Sam was chopping followed us across to the floor to the sink where Sam stood. At my workstation, globs of hardening egg yolk lay on the countertop and on the floor among wisps of flour. (I guess I didn't do too good a job sweeping.) I felt physical exhaustion beginning to overtake my body. What time was it, I wondered? Neither of us had brought a watch, and the clock above the ovens was stopped. My guess was that it was at least one a.m., maybe later, and we hadn't made any progress. If anything, we were further behind than when we started.

I decided that the best course of action was to press on. Finish the brownie mix, I told myself, and take care of the cleanup while the brownies are baking. Leaving Sam to nurse his wound on his own, I returned to the mixing bowl and resumed my struggle to break six eggs in the bowl without worsening the mess. To my surprise, I had much better luck this time. The next four eggs broke and plopped into the mix without shell fragments. I got a few bits of shell on the last egg, but I quickly picked them out.

The next ingredient was five ounces of unsweetened chocolate. I looked at the chocolate we bought; it was labeled "semisweet". Hmmm. Reading the recipe again, I noticed that I had missed something in writing my shopping list from memory. The base of the brownies called for unsweetened chocolate, but the frosting called for semisweet. We had only bought the latter. Oh well, how bad could extra sweetness be in a dessert? Let's use the semisweet in the base and the frosting, I decided. Unwrapping the chocolate bar, I noticed that unlike an ordinary candy bar, this "baker's chocolate" was marked and partially separated into one-ounce segments. I broke off a five-ounce chunk and dropped it in the mix.

Somehow I managed to add the sugar and butter to the mix without incident. That just left one ingredient to go. Moving to Sam's workstation, I rinsed off his blood-splattered walnuts. Good thing the health inspector doesn't work the night shift, I thought as I resumed the chopping where Sam left off. Sam was now hunched over on the floor next to the sink, fast asleep. Although the paper towel he held tightly over the wound, even while sleeping, was soaked with blood, I hoped that the bleeding had stopped.

I added the chopped walnuts to the mixing bowl and placed the concoction under my mom's large industrial-strength mixer. As I tried to insert the mixing blades, I came very close to knocking the bowl onto the floor, but I was able to grab it by its slippery rim at the last second. Finally, with everything in place I flipped the power switch on the mixer. Chunks of butter and chocolate pinged violently against the blades and flew out of the bowl. Reducing the power setting with one hand, I scooped up the escaped ingredients with my other hand and returned them to the batter. I slowly rotated the bowl by hand while the mixer did its thing.

After three minutes, I turned off the mixer and examined my creation. It wasn't pretty. The chunks of butter and chocolate never did get thoroughly beaten. As a matter of fact, long streaks of egg yolk never quite made it to the batter stage. The batter was more of a collection of separate ingredients loosely mixed together in a chunky jumble. It certainly didn't resemble anything that would eventually be brownies. I gave it another one-minute ride in the mixer, but that didn't help.

Maybe some sort of transformation would happen during the baking process, I told myself. The chocolate and the butter would melt together, and the whole thing would morph into one of my mom's famous desserts. There was only one way to find out. Searching the countertop for a moment, I found Sam's greased baking pan and poured the lumpy mixture.

Now for the fun part. I turned the control on the oven to 350 degrees, slid the would-be brownies onto the lower rack, and closed the door. In thirty-five minutes, we would have the results of the Hoffman Brothers' first entry into the world of professional dessert making.

Actually, we would have half the results. There was still the matter of the frosting. Glancing at the recipe again, I saw that the frosting consisted of only two ingredients, whipping cream and chocolate. That looked easy enough, I thought. The spilled eggs and blood were starting to dry and harden on the floor and other surfaces, so I decided to take a break from cooking to do some cleaning.

As I stepped over my sleeping brother to retrieve the roll of paper towels, a wave of fatigue—and jealousy—hit me. I could really use some sleep too, I decided. Not too long, just a few minutes to refresh, and I would have the energy to finish cooking and cleaning. With a vicious twisting stretch of my upper body and a long, gaping yawn, I sat down on the floor next to Sam to rest my tired eyes.

I'm not sure how long I was asleep. The first thing that woke me was the cold spray of the overhead sprinklers. Since it was still raining hard outside, I imagined momentarily that I must be near an open window. That was followed instantaneously by the shrill, pulsing sound of the smoke alarm.

That was followed by a scream and sobbing from Sam. I finally opened my eyes to a thick, smoky haze.

The kitchen was on fire!

Chapter Seven

Out of the Baking Pan, Into the Fire

Sam and I jumped to our feet. "Let's get out of here!" I yelled.

"What about the brownies?" Sam whimpered.

I grabbed him by the arm and darted out of the kitchen. "Sam, I think we can safely assume the brownies are now blackies."

We both began to cough violently, so I pressed my hand to the back of Sam's head and pushed him toward the ground, below the smoke. Crouching low, we made our way to the front door. I flung open the door, and we ran out into the rain.

Seconds later, we both almost wished we were back inside with the smoke and fire. Our mother and Frank were huddled together under the awning on the back porch, and when they saw us emerge from the dessert shop, looks of alternating shock, confusion and anger swept over their faces.

"Hey, two kids just came out of there!" shouted one of the firefighters who had just arrived on the scene.

"Don't worry, we'll see if there are any more inside!" replied another firefighter who was running with an axe into the shop.

I closed my eyes and clutched my head with both hands, wishing I was anywhere else.

"Mark! Sam! Get over here this instant!" my mom shrieked at the top of her lungs. That snapped me out of my self-pity for the moment. Sam and I looked at each other, shrugged, breathed deeply, and walked towards the back porch. I felt like I was on my way to my execution.

Sam started bawling before we reached my mother. I think I was the only one who noticed his tears in the rain. My mother either didn't notice or was too possessed by hysteria to care.

"Are you boys okay?" she shouted, even with us now standing inches from her on the porch. Stooping down and wrapping a loving arm around each of us, she continued her interrogation. "What were you doing in my shop? Is there anyone else in there? How did the fire start?"

Not intending to cause my mother even more anxiety than we already had, I nonetheless gave the one answer she despised above all others. "I don't know," I said.

"What do you mean, you don't know!" she screamed, her arm still wrapped around me but squeezing harder than a mother-child hug traditionally requires.

"I don't know!" I repeated, sounding somewhat hysterical myself. "We're sorry, Mom! Really! It just happened! We're sorry!"

One of the firefighters approached us. "Mrs. Hoffman?"

"Yes," our mom answered, standing up and loosening her grasp on Sam and me. "How bad is it?"

"Just some smoke damage," he said. "Everything is under control. There was no one else inside."

In his rubber-gloved hands, the firefighter held a baking sheet that was coated in white fire-extinguisher goo and black soot. Our mom looked down at it and asked, "What's that?"

"It looks like they were once cookies, if you ask me," replied the firefighter.

"No, they're not," Sam sniveled. "They're brownies." I closed my eyes again, wishing I would wake up in my bed from this bad dream when I opened them.

"Brownies?" our mom and Frank exclaimed simultaneously.

I nodded. Sam started to bawl again. To be honest, I thought I might cry myself.

Mom reared back and stared at Sam and me. Her mouth hung open in awed silence. When she spoke again, her voice was barely audible. "You were making brownies? Alone? In the middle of the night?"

"Uh-huh," Sam and I both replied, struggling to avoid our mom's piercing green eyes.

She just continued to stare at us in disbelief. Finally she stood up, released her grip on Sam and me, and addressed the firefighter. "I don't know what to say."

"That's all right, ma'am," the firefighter said. "These things are traumatic. The important thing is that no one was hurt. You'll want to call your insurance company in the morning about any damage."

Our mom nodded.

"That's really it for tonight," he continued. "We're just going to put away our hoses, and we'll be on our way. You should try to get some sleep. You have a busy day ahead of you cleaning up your store."

Frank walked toward the dessert shop with the firefighter as they talked quietly. A cop who had just pulled up in a patrol car joined them. We briefly watched them from the porch before our mom took us inside and up to bed.

I don't think anyone in our house got any sleep that night—at least not me. Monday morning I dragged myself down to the kitchen, anticipating a big confrontation with my mom at the breakfast table, but she wasn't there. I poured myself a bowl of cereal, but only ate about half of it, as my stomach was twisting in on itself.

Dumping the soggy cereal down the garbage disposal, I figured out where my mom was. I walked out to her store and found her in the kitchen, scrubbing the soot and fire extinguisher foam from the oven. She looked much older than usual. Her face was drenched in sweat and grime, her eyes had dark circles under them, and she wore an old bandana on her head and yellow rubber gloves on her hands.

"Good morning," was all I could think to say.

No response.

"I'm really sorry about last night."

Still nothing.

After several minutes of my standing there, looking and feeling like an idiot, my mom finally grumbled, "Well, what are you waiting for? You and your brother made this mess. Grab a sponge and get to work."

At least she was speaking to me. I found a sponge in her soap bucket and went to work on the surfaces around the oven. About a half hour later, Sam joined us.

Around noon, our mom gruffly announced that we should break for lunch. We went back to the house, and mom slapped some cold leftovers on three plates. She would probably not be in the mood to play doting mother anytime soon.

Mom sat down, and the three of us glanced awkwardly at each other. "Well?" she asked.

"Well what?" I replied.

"Do you want to tell me what got into you two last night?"

"Not really," Sam answered.

"Too bad," our mom said. "That wasn't at all like you boys. I'm used to you getting in trouble at school, but I thought you had more respect for me."

I replied with that standard, "Awww, ma…"

"Don't 'awww ma' me," she snapped. "You tell me this instant what I did to deserve this."

She was taking this much too personally. Sam and I looked at each other and shrugged. No point holding back now, I figured. Our business plan was dead in the water.

So for the next twenty minutes, we told our mom everything. We told her about the deal we had to cut with Karen to go fishing, and about all the other deals that followed, which put me in the fishing-broker business. Then we told her about Neil's tackle business, Vic's bait business, Karen's fishing and hospitality business, and all the other enterprises that fishing trip spawned among the kids of John Dewey Elementary and Middle Schools.

"Everybody had their own business but us, because Karen decided to sell direct," I concluded.

"And then I told Mark that we should be in the dessert business, because it was your great strudel that got Karen to let us go fishing in the first place!" Sam added triumphantly.

I nodded. "That's true. If it weren't for Sam…"

"You wouldn't be in the dessert business?" our mom asked.

I opened my mouth to agree, but paused. "Except that we're not in the dessert business anymore, because of last night, right?"

"Yeah, you ruined three businesses in one week—your fishing business, our dessert business, and Mom's dessert business," Sam observed. "Maybe you'll set a world record."

I was about to slug my brother when my mom's next comment caught my attention. "Not necessarily," she said.

Sam and I both looked at her. "What do you mean, Mom?" Sam asked.

Our mom smiled (something I thought I might never see again after last night) and clasped her hands together under her chin. "Don't get me wrong. I'm still furious at both of you for what you did to my store, and if you think you won't be punished, you're sadly mistaken. But that aside, I think I know how we can make this work. Do you two still want to go into the dessert business?"

"Yeah!" we exclaimed in unison.

"And you concede that making the desserts is outside your area of expertise?"

"No, well um, yeah, um maybe," we muttered sheepishly.

Our mom stood up. "Then I have a business proposal for you. It's no secret that my business has been slow. If you think you can sell my pastries better than I can, then go for it. I'll do the baking, you do the selling, and we'll split the profits."

I couldn't believe my ears. Sam and I looked at each other and then back at our mom. "Are you serious?" I asked.

"Sure," she said. "You'll work for me."

"You mean, you'll work for us," I corrected her.

"I beg your pardon, young man," she snapped. "Don't you think you're pushing your luck?"

I shook my head as I stood up. Pacing the room, I said, "Think about it, Mom. It's the only arrangement that makes any sense. You can't hire us as employees, because you have a legitimate, licensed and regulated business to worry about, and the state doesn't like businesses employing twelve-year-olds and eight-year-olds. And after last night, you're probably not ready to make us co-owners of Ellen's Pastry Place."

"Not likely," she huffed.

"That's fine, Mom," I continued. "That just means the only way this will work is for us to hire you."

"What?!"

"Well, then you'd be an independent supplier. You'll be our vendor."

Our mother looked at us and said nothing for several seconds. She eventually shook her head and said, "No. Absolutely not. I love you two boys more than anything in the world, but I'm still the parent around here. Until you're adults, you answer to me."

"You'd still be the Mom at home," Sam protested. "This is just business."

"Really, Mom," I agreed. "You're letting your adult pride get in the way of your business sense."

"And you, young man—both of you—are getting way to big for your britches," she said. "This was a bad idea. Let's just forget the whole thing and get back to work."

Sam and I stood up and grabbed our sponges. "I'm sorry to hear that, Mom. But if you change your mind, the offer is still on the table."

Our mom shook her head. "Negotiations are over. Meet the new boss, same as the old boss."

Sam and I scrubbed the soot off the kitchen surfaces for a few more hours, while our mother tried to reach her insurance agent on the phone. Of course, no one picked up at the agent's office, since it was Labor Day. Everybody but us was enjoying one last bit of summer.

At sunset, our mother finally had mercy on us and let Sam and me go while she stayed behind to put away the cleaning supplies. As my little brother and I dragged ourselves back to our house, we discussed our business situation.

"We were so close," Sam whined. "Maybe we shouldn't have refused her offer. At least we'd be in business."

"No, Mom would be in business," I corrected him. "We would be just a couple of working stiffs."

"So?"

"So, I want to be an entrepreneur. Don't you?"

"No, but I do want us to run our own business," Sam said.

"You dumb little kid," I laughed. "That's what an entrepreneur is. What a dope!"

With that, Sam punched me hard (I mean, hard for a little kid) in the stomach and ran inside the back of the house. I chased after him, but he quickly locked the screen door behind him.

While I rattled the door handle in frustration, he smugly stuck out his tongue at me.

"I will kill you!" I bellowed. "Open this door! You're dead meat! Dead meat!"

Sam repeated "dead meat" at the same time I was yelling it.

"Cut it out!" we said in near unison, Sam just a half-second behind me. "Stop repeating—hey! I'm serious! Stop it!"

Now Sam was not only repeating everything I said, but copying my motions as well. When I rattled the door handle, he rattled the handle from the inside. When I held my index finger in warning, he mirrored me from the other side of the screen.

"You are so dead," I told him, and he told me with a smile.

I slowly turned my back and faced away from the door. Sam did the same, but a moment later he realized he could no longer see me to copy me. He would have to twist his neck around to glance at my next action. That moment of distraction was all I needed. By the time he looked back for me, I was gone.

It only took Sam a few seconds to figure out what I was up to, but it was too late. He made a mad dash through our house for the front door. Just as he was reaching for the lock, I pushed the door open. Sam tried to back up and flee in the opposite direction. I grabbed him by the arm and flung him onto our living room sofa. As I pounced on him, he tried to squirm away, and we both ended up in a pile on the floor.

"Hold still so I can kill you!" I hollered as Sam writhed around.

"I'll tell Mom!" Sam yelled.

"Dead men tell no tattletales!" I replied. Sam let out a yelp as I tried to put him in a headlock. He slipped his head out and somehow gave me a Vulcan sleeper grip (a pinch to the base of the neck). To be honest, it hurt quite a bit.

I spun around and grabbed his big toe. "The secret deadly toe hold!" I declared, squeezing Sam's toe as hard as I could while he screamed. "Say uncle!"

Nothing but more screams.

"Say uncle!" I repeated. "Say it!"

He still refused to say it. After about a minute, I turned around again and administered a pink belly, then an Indian burn, and finally a severe noogie. His stomach, his left forearm, and the top of his head were all bright red. Sam got in a few ineffective blows, but he took the brunt of the beating, by far. Despite my repeated commands and ruthless wrestling tactics, the little guy would not say "uncle."

In all the times we had wrestled, I don't think I ever once got Sam to say it. Most of the times, our mother or father heard the ruckus and broke up the match before a victory could be decided, but in those few instances where we went the distance, we always battled to a draw. I had to admit (to myself, of course, not to Sam) that my brother was tough. I tried not to think about what might happen to me if he ever caught up to me in size.

Eventually I rolled off Sam, and we both lie there on the floor for several minutes, catching our breath.

"I win," Sam panted.

"Whatever," I said as I stared at the ceiling.

Neither of us was in a hurry to get off the floor. With some of our recent frustration worked out of our systems, our minds returned back to business.

Sam said, "Well, if we're anti-pin-yours—"

"Entrepreneurs," I corrected him.

"Whatever," my brother continued. "Then we're entrepreneurs without a product."

I thought about that for a minute. "No," I said. "We have a product. What we're missing is a supplier. And I think I know where we can get one."

Sam gave me a puzzled look, but when I jumped up and raced up the stairs to my bedroom, he tailed right behind me. I turned on my computer and waited impatiently for it to initialize and then again for my dial-up modem to connect to the Internet.

The instant messenger screen popped up, and I scanned through my "buddy list" to see which of my friends were online who might be able to help. I saw Karen Thomas's screen name highlighted next to an open-door icon and clicked on it.

Burpmaster7: hi karen
Karent32: Hi, Mark!
Burpmaster7: how r u
Karent32: OK. How r u? My daddy says there was a big fire at your mom's store last night!!
Burpmaster7: no big deal
Burpmaster7: just a little fire in the kitchen
Karent32: Was anyone hurt?
Burpmaster7: yeah the brownies burned to death
Karent32: LOL
Burpmaster7: hey do you know anyone in our class who knows how to bake?
Karent32: ???
Burpmaster7: I'm looking 4 someone who can bake desserts and wants to make some $$

There was no response for about a minute.

Burpmaster7: u still there?
Karent32: Yes, I'm thinking.
Karent32: Well, there's Wendy. She made cookies one time when we had a slumber party.

I wasn't sure I wanted to go into business with Wendy Siegel. She was a nice enough girl, I guess, but she would be likely to do the same thing Karen did with my fishing business. Cut out the middle man once the business proved successful.

Burpmaster7: anyone else?
Karent32: Well, there is Celeste Szuck…
Burpmaster7: szuck the truck?!? (vomit)
Karent32: You're a jerk, mark. Celeste is such a sweet girl.
Burpmaster7: LOL! how come u never hang out with her?
Karent32: I talk to her sometimes.

86

Burpmaster7: yeah right

"Who's Celeste Szuck?" asked Sam, who had been reading over my shoulder.

"Szuck the truck," I answered. "She's this fat pig in my grade who everybody hates."

"Oh," said Sam. "Is she that girl with the huge birthmark on her cheek?"

"Yep."

"Why does everyone hate her?"

"Because she's a truck," I replied impatiently, as if the answer should have been obvious.

Sam sat down on the floor while I continued to pump Karen for more names. She wasn't coming up with any.

"Well," Sam observed, "if she's that fat, she probably does know how to bake."

Hmmm. The kid had a point.

Burpmaster7: do you have the truck's i.m. alias?
Karent32: Yes, but only if you stop calling her the truck!
Burpmaster7: fine! Do you have celeste's i.m. alias?

A minute passed without a reply.

Burpmaster7: ???
Karent32: Hold on, I'm i.m.'ing Wendy for it.

After another long pause during which Wendy i.m.'ed another girl, and that girl i.m.'ed yet another girl, somebody finally had the Truck's screen alias and sent it back along the chain to Karen.

Karent32: It's hersheykiss3.
Burpmaster7: LOL! Why am I not surprised?
Karent32: Whatever. What makes you think she'd even want to help a mean person like you?
Burpmaster7: because business is business
Karent32: You're hopeless. Bye.
Burpmaster7: bye

I typed "hersheykiss3" into my buddy list and hit enter. My computer showed me the open-door icon next to her alias and played the sound effect to let me know she was online. I clicked on her name and sent her a friendly greeting.

Not surprisingly, she didn't know who I was from my screen name, and even when I identified myself, Celeste didn't believe it was me. For some reason, she kept insisting that I was somebody pretending to be Mark Hoffman. When I said that I wanted to talk to her about something important, Celeste got even more suspicious. I guess I couldn't blame her for having her defenses up. Pretty much the only time I had ever seen any kids talk to her was to tease her or play jokes on her.

Finally, I told Celeste to just call me on the phone if she didn't believe me, and I gave her my phone number. She countered that the number would turn out to be a pizza place or a truck stop or some other mean trick. Man, this girl was paranoid. I thought about it for a few seconds, and then I suggested that she do a "reverse look-up" of the phone number on the Internet to verify it.

When my mother's name came up on the reverse look-up, Celeste conceded that it was really me. I asked her again to call me, and she said she would. I quickly got off-line to free up the phone. Seconds after the modem disconnected, the phone rang.

I didn't want to give away too much over the phone, because I was afraid her first reaction would be to say no and hang up. Instead, I made small talk for as long as I could manage, and then I asked if I could stop by her house. Once again, she was suspicious that a vicious practical joke was in the works. I reassured her that my intentions were good, and that she could look through the peephole to check that I was alone and empty-handed before letting me in.

After dinner, I rode my bike over to the Truck's—I mean Celeste's—house. Sam didn't want to come, which was just as well.

"Hi, Celeste," I said with as sincere a smile as I could muster. It was hard not to stare at the gigantic oval birthmark on her left cheek. To tell the truth, it would have been easier not to look at her at all. As I mentioned, Celeste was fat, and she had short, greasy hair that combined with her rough features to make her look very masculine. She also had a bunch of zits along the sides of her nose and a big whitehead on her chin.

"Hi Mark," Celeste said with a suspicious expression on her face. She was still having trouble accepting that someone had sought her out for reasons other than cruel humor. "Come on in."

We went down to her basement rec room, which was furnished with old couches and chairs. After some awkward small talk about school, I got down to business.

"Celeste, I'm not sure if you noticed, but last week I organized this little fishing outing that sort of got out of control."

"I know all about that," Celeste said. "Everybody was invited to Karen Thomas's house except me, as usual."

"That's not exactly true," I replied defensively. "Everybody bought admission to Karen's backyard, either through cash or barter. Nobody went for free. If you wanted to go, all you had to do was buy your way in like anybody else."

"Hmm, nobody told me that."

I then proceeded to tell her the rest of the stuff she didn't know, including the various trades and deals I had to make to go fishing, our short-lived fishing business, and our plans for the dessert business. I left out the part about our failed negotiations with my mom to be our supplier.

"So why are you telling me all this?" Celeste finally asked. "Do you think I'm going to buy all your desserts and make you rich?"

"No, not all," I said. "We need a head dessert chef, and I was wondering if you were interested in the job."

Celeste gaped at me. "Me? You want me to be part of your business?"

"Sure," I said. "That is, if you can bake as well as everyone says you can."

She arched her eyebrow (her two eyebrows joined together into one) warily. "Who told you I can bake?"

I shrugged. "Some girls. Is it true?"

Nodding gently, Celeste answered, "I can bake all right. I'm pretty good at it too. But your mother has the best dessert shop in Walton. Why not just get your desserts from her?"

"We could if we wanted to," I said, which was true. We just couldn't get them on the terms we preferred. "But she's busy, and she's expensive. Plus, I'd like to keep this an all-kids business. Adults have a way of complicating things and slowing us down. We need a supplier who isn't too set in her ways."

Celeste rubbed her chin and considered the offer. "Okay, then let me ask you this. If this is such a great idea, why do I need you? Why shouldn't I just sell my desserts directly to the kids at school?"

Jeez, I thought. Here we go again. Why was the first thought of every girl in Walton about how to cut out the middleman? It must be all those factory-outlet stores they shop at.

"That's a good question, Celeste. The thing is, I *know* I can sell these desserts if they're as good as you say. I'm really motivated to do this, and for the most part the other kids like me. But let's be honest here. You may be a great cook, but you're, you know..."

"Unpopular?" suggested Celeste. "Everybody at school hates me? They would just as soon throw a pie in my face as buy it from me?"

I winced. Everything she said was true, but man, she was really depressing me. Maybe I shouldn't be encouraging her to spend more time at the oven, because she seemed ready to stick her head inside and turn on the gas.

"The kids at our school can be real jerks," I said in sympathy. "I wouldn't even waste my time with most of them, except that the truant officer keeps dragging me back there."

Celeste nodded in agreement. "Tell me about it. I've begged my parents to homeschool me. My mom said yes, but my dad thought I needed to stay in school for the socialization."

I shook my head. "I know. I get the same thing. Like being miserable for seven hours a day is an essential part of growing up."

"Unless you're too miserable," Celeste added. "Then they drug you to keep you from fighting back. I guess the really important thing is to teach you how to submit to authority and fit into the group, no matter how screwed up the group is."

I couldn't argue with that. "Look, Celeste. The way I see it, we can help each other. You can make desserts, but can't sell them. My brother Sam and I can sell desserts, but can't make them. If we cooperate, we can all get rich."

Celeste laughed. "We're going to have to sell an awful lot of pies to get rich."

I laughed too, but I was beginning to believe it. "You'll see. But before we go any further, I need to taste these desserts for myself. If they're lousy, then no deal."

"Come with me," Celeste said. We stood up and walked upstairs to her kitchen. Celeste removed the cover from a cake holder on the counter and sliced off a piece of German chocolate cake, plopped it on a plate and handed it to me with a fork.

I was about to dig in, but then I saw her reach for a second cake holder. This time she cut me a nice hunk of pineapple upside-down cake. I carried my two plates to the kitchen table and started to eat, when I noticed Celeste reaching on top of the refrigerator and pulling down a tray with an assortment of cookies and tarts. I thought my house had the most desserts in town, as a consequence of my mother's business, but the Szuck kitchen matched up crumb for crumb.

"Did you make all these?" I asked.

"No, the Keebler elves made them," she droned while rolling her eyes.

I bit into a forkful of German chocolate cake. It was delicious.

The pineapple upside-down cake was tremendous.

The cookies were incredible.

Szuck the Truck could bake!

Chapter Eight

Desserts Express

"These aren't bad, Celeste," I said, trying to disguise my enthusiasm. We still had to negotiate a price, after all. "Not bad at all."

"So now what?" she asked. Good question.

I looked over her inventory and performed some quick calculations in my head. There were maybe fifty cookies, enough German chocolate cake for six good-sized slices, and maybe ten slices of pineapple upside down cake.

"I'll tell you what, Celeste. I'll give you ten bucks for the cookies and five bucks apiece for the two cakes."

Celeste quietly considered my offer. She must have been reviewing her own expenses and potential profits, as well as how much leverage she had.

"Make it fifteen for the cookies and ten each for the cakes," she countered.

"Thirty for everything," I replied.

"Deal," said Celeste. "And no refunds. If you don't sell it, you eat it."

"With pleasure," I said. "Now, do you have anything that I can use to carry these desserts home without ruining them?"

Celeste found some Tupperware containers for the desserts and carefully placed them in a large shopping bag with a sturdy handle. I would be able to loop it over my bike's handlebars and get the desserts home intact, if I rode carefully. I hastily said goodbye, assuring her that I would be in touch very soon with our next order.

After stopping at a closeouts store along the way for a few supplies, I pedaled home as fast as I could without endangering my precious inventory. Quietly opening the backdoor of our house, I tiptoed up the stairs into my room with the bags.

Neither my mother nor Frank saw me come in, but my brother Sam did. He bounded into my room without knocking and yelled, "What do you got there?"

"Shhh," I said. "Close that door behind you and lock it."

Sam did as he was told while I unpacked our inventory. I briefly relayed the details of my negotiations with Celeste. We agreed to hide the stash for now and regroup after the adults were asleep. My mother would probably be lying awake listening for anything unusual after last night's events at her dessert shop, so we would have to be extra quiet.

About 10:30 p.m., Sam sneaked back into my room. I had already taken the desserts back out of hiding, along with some small Styrofoam containers that I picked up at the closeouts store on my way home from Celeste's house. We cut the cakes into slices and carefully placed them into individual packages. Sam started sorting the cookies by variety and dividing them into stacks of four. As he placed the stacks into their containers, I opened the word processor on my computer and designed the labels.

We had a brief discussion about what we should call our company. Sam proposed Sam and Mark's Sweets, and I of course countered with Mark and Sam's. Hoffman Brothers was under brief consideration, but neither of us really cared for it.

"How about Desserts Express?" Sam suggested.

"Hmm, that might work," I said. "And it kind of makes sense, if you think about it. We won't have a store to visit, so we'll be delivering the desserts express to our customers. I like it." We also realized that it was getting late, and we didn't want a repeat of the previous night's disastrous napping, so we hastily agreed on Desserts Express and moved on.

I printed out a set of labels that read "Desserts Express—1 slice German Chocolate Cake." Sam stuck them to the packages while I printed the labels for the rest of our inventory. Next, I typed up a list entitled "Desserts Express—Today's Selections" and listed all of our dessert varieties and prices. My brother and I dickered a bit over how to price everything; we had to make them cheap enough that we would clear out most or all of our inventory, but we also wanted a decent profit margin.

We each gave the menu a final read-through and emailed it off to all the kids we knew, along with instructions for ordering. I thought Sam and I were the only kids up at that late hour, but within minutes some replies started trickling in. By morning, my inbox was full of orders.

After breakfast, Sam distracted our mom while I sneaked the large shopping bag of desserts out onto the front porch. At the bus stop, we encountered some of our customers who had placed orders. Sam crossed their names from our list as I handed out desserts and collected money.

The bus came, and as we took our seats, I realized that Sam and I weren't the only ones doing business that morning. Neil had brought with him some of the homemade fishing tackle that the kids had ordered when we were at Karen's pond on Saturday. He took some additional orders on the way to school. Some of the kids were disappointed to learn that their lures were on back order, as it would be several weeks before Neil and his father could produce all the hand-crafted tackle their customers demanded.

To my surprise, the scarcity of Neil's flies and lures seemed to make them even more popular, and he took additional orders.

Once the bus dropped us at school, Sam and I distributed the rest of the orders we had received and quickly sold our remaining inventory. We also took new orders for the next day, although we had to hedge on those requests, since we didn't know for sure if Celeste would be able to fill them. I noticed Celeste standing off by herself on the playground, as she usually did, but today she was intently watching the commotion that her desserts caused. Although neither Sam nor I said a word about the source of the delicious treats, everybody probably assumed our mother baked them.

The school bell rang and the crowd around us broke up as we headed for our classrooms. I caught up with Celeste on the stairs.

"Looks like you guys did well today," Celeste said.

"Hey, you did great today too," I assured her. "What can you get us for tomorrow?"

"I'm not sure. You pretty much cleaned out my inventory. What do you want?"

I tore the list of dessert requests from my notebook and handed it to her. Celeste read it over and nodded. "This is going to take me awhile, and I only have one oven. If I'm home by four p.m. and start baking right away, I could probably have it all done by ten."

"Jeez, Celeste. That's gonna mean another all-nighter for Sam and me to package everything. Can you make it nine p.m.?"

"I'll try," she said with a shrug. "I'll work out the prices and show you an estimate at lunchtime."

"Excellent. Thanks again." The second bell rang, and I was late for class yet again. At this rate, I might break the school record for tardiness in a single academic year. It was a record I already held, by the way. Maybe they would retire my jersey and hang it in the detention hall when I graduated.

As usual, I tuned out Miss Farkas, our teacher, shortly after I took my seat. My mind was too preoccupied with Desserts Express. We finally did it! We were in business. I pulled my wallet from my pocket and—standing a spiral notebook open vertically on my desk to conceal my actions—I counted the money we had collected that morning. It came to one hundred ten dollars in gross revenue. Subtract the thirty I paid Celeste, plus five bucks for the paper containers and labels, and we had seventy-five dollars in profit. Not bad for our first day of business.

Best of all, it was completely tax-free.

Neil and Vic were surprised when I blew them off at the start of our lunch period to seek out Celeste. The head chef of Desserts Express had prepared a price quote for me on the requested goodies, and we quibbled briefly and cordially over some of the numbers before reaching agreement. I folded her price sheet and stuck it in my shirt pocket before walking back to Neil and Vic's table.

"What are you doing talking to Szuck the Truck?" Neil asked.

I shrugged. "We just had some business to discuss."

"Yeah," Neil snorted. "That fat pig must be one of your best customers."

Neil was a fine one to talk about fat. It's not like he would be passing the Presidential Fitness Challenge anytime soon. But I held my tongue, since Neil was my good friend, not to mention one of my best customers.

Vic had a wry grin on his face. He may have guessed the truth about Celeste's relationship with Desserts Express, but he wasn't saying anything. I didn't really care if everyone knew that Celeste was our supplier. They were bound to find out sooner or later, since Wendy Siegel had recommended her, and Wendy wasn't the kind of girl who kept her mouth shut about anything for very long. Still, I knew that Celeste wasn't exactly Miss Popularity at John Dewey Middle School, and I wanted our customers to decide they really liked our product before they started associating the desserts with her.

I decided to change the subject. "Yeah, business is doing great so far. How about you guys?"

They both nodded while chewing their sandwiches. "Neil's selling lots of lures, and I got a bunch of worm orders for next weekend," Vic said. "We're thinking of merging our businesses. We hired Drew Baxter to set us up with an e-commerce website where kids can place orders for tackle and bait. We'll probably be expanding into maggots and leeches once ice-fishing season starts."

I arched an eyebrow at Vic. "Where are you going to get maggots?"

Vic tried to sound mysterious as he answered. "I have my sources."

"Yeah," Neil laughed. "He grows them in his underwear."

"You're real funny... smelling, that is," Vic retorted.

There wasn't a whole lot Sam and I could do until Celeste finished her baking, but we prepared as much as we could. After school, we rode our bikes over to the odd-lots store to buy some more Styrofoam containers. Sam wanted to buy them on an as-needed basis, but I knew these discount stores changed their inventory constantly, and there was no telling when they would get more in stock. We took all the money we made that morning, plus what we had earned from the fishing trip to Karen's, and bought out the store's entire supply of disposable food containers. They filled twenty large shopping bags. Only after we bought them did we realize that we couldn't possibly carry all of them home on our bikes in one trip, so we convinced the store manager to hold onto some of them until we could return an hour later.

Dinner turned into another verbal sparring match with Frank. The news about the economy grew grimmer by the day, according to our mother's boyfriend. Unfortunately, Frank's remedy was more government meddling that, from my point of view, would only make things worse for working folks and businesses. I told him as much, of course, in my uniquely snotty way, which inevitably threw Frank into another rage. Our mother concluded dinner by announcing that further discussion of current events was forbidden at dinner and breakfast. We would have to find some other way to drive each other crazy.

A few minutes before nine, I told Sam to keep our mom distracted while I sneaked out to pick up our desserts. When I arrived at Celeste's house, she was just pulling the last batch of cookies out of the oven. We hastily put everything into empty Tupperware containers, placed the containers in a couple of large shopping bags, and I headed for the door.

"Aren't you forgetting something?" Celeste asked as I hooked the bags over my handlebars.

"Oh yeah, thanks," I said.

"No, think again. This isn't a charity."

"What do you mean?" I asked.

Celeste held out her hand. "Payment. Now, as we agreed."

Shoot. I forgot all about the money we owed her. "Look, Celeste, we had a little cash flow problem today. I'll pay you first thing in the morning, as soon as we get paid by our customers."

She shook her head. "That wasn't our agreement. I knew you would try to pull a fast one. Pay me now, or give back those desserts."

I thought about making a break for it. Even with the extra baggage, there was no way Celeste could run faster than I could pedal. But this was a bad way to start a business relationship.

"Celeste, you're absolutely right. I should have set aside the money we owe you, but I messed up and spent it all this afternoon. It will never happen again. If you really want me to set down these desserts, I will, and no hard feelings. But let's try to make this work. How about a late-payment penalty?"

She looked like she was considering my offer. "Ten percent extra, plus the original amount, by the time the first school bell rings tomorrow."

"Five percent by the second bell," I countered.

"Okay," she grunted. "Now get out of here. I have cookie sheets and cake pans to wash, and you have desserts to package and orders to take."

I rode off into the sunset, weighed down by bags of sweet delicacies. The hard part was over, I thought. Little did I know the worst was waiting just around the corner... literally.

Chapter Nine

Brownies for Bullies

The next few weeks were a blur of pastry and profits. Desserts Express was turning into a huge success. In fact, Celeste soon found herself unable to keep up with demand, and we had to limit the number of orders we could accept each day. Sam and I started taking advance orders for Celeste's incredible, delectable treats, and before long we were booked solid weeks in advance.

It wasn't exactly a cakewalk—pardon the expression—for Sam and me either. We were shuttling hundreds of desserts between Celeste's house, our house, and the schoolyard each day, requiring multiple trips in each direction. We would stay up late into the night secretly packaging and labeling the desserts. The whole enterprise was exhausting, and we often caught ourselves—or rather our teachers caught us—dozing off in the middle of class.

The funny part is that we weren't the only ones. Neil and Vic's bait and tackle operation was doing brisk business. They didn't have the high daily volume of Desserts Express, but handcrafting flies, jigs and other lures was a painstaking process that also kept them up well past the customary bedtimes of twelve-year-olds.

Karen's fishing hosting business started to slow down with the cooler weather, and I figured that would be the end of it for her. But to my surprise, she expanded into other events that took advantage of her parents' beautiful property. She owned her own horse and had spent a good part of the summer at riding camp. With the money she made from the first few fishing parties, she invested in a flatbed wooden wagon and was soon hosting hayrides around her property. Apple-picking and pumpkin-carving parties followed, and each weekend her backyard was filled to capacity with kids eager to part with their money. It helped that Karen was pretty and popular, and our seventh-grade class was becoming very clique-conscious. If you weren't exactly welcome at the lunch table where Karen Thomas, her friend Wendy Siegel and the other popular kids sat, you were always made to feel welcome at Karen's weekend parties, for a modest admission charge.

The Wolfe Brothers—Harrison and David—had purchased admission to the original fishing party at Karen's place with a few good baseball cards. From that one-time deal, they quickly grew into a full-blown sports card, comic book and collectibles shop. Theirs was not the first such shop in Walton, New York, but in many ways it was superior. The Wolfe Brothers established a competitive advantage by trimming their margins—matching or beating the prices offered by the old, established card and comic book store—and personal service. Like our dessert company, the Wolfe Brothers filled their order immediately, usually by getting on their bikes and carrying their merchandise to their customers. Unlike our dessert company, they were able to do business outside Walton by mailing Internet orders anywhere in the country.

All of our businesses had an Internet presence, of course, but unlike other start-up websites that had come and gone, all of ours were making real products and real profits. For most of us, the web was just one more way to sell our stuff, but we did in-person sales just as often. Most of us young entrepreneurs designed our web pages ourselves, at least at first, but Drew Baxter, the eleven-year-old computer whiz, was pulling in some good money doing professional web design and maintenance when the rest of us got too busy running the other parts of our businesses. Drew even hosted many of our web pages from a server located in his bedroom. Two of the other computer nerds in our neighborhood soon went into competition against Drew, but there was more than enough business to go around.

Business was booming everywhere in Walton—that is, if you were twelve or younger. The old economy run by the adults was rapidly going down the tubes. The only growth was in the reporting of bad news. Profits were down. Unemployment was up. The price of residential real estate was in free-fall, and the price of everything else was skyrocketing.

In October, the county commissioners did the unthinkably stupid and approved the property tax increase that my mother's boyfriend Frank had been demanding for the school system. Frank was uncharacteristically gracious in victory, somberly telling reporters that he and his fellow bureaucrats "understand the additional burden this will place on some residents during the current economic crisis, but we know the people of Walton will always unselfishly put the needs of the children first."

What Frank didn't know was that the children of Walton were taking care of their own needs quite nicely, thank you, and his precious school system did little more for them than get in the way of business.

About two weeks before Halloween, as Sam and I rode home on the school bus together, we held an impromptu meeting about the state of Desserts Express. Sam was particularly annoyed that our growth was starting to level off.

"It stinks," Sam exclaimed. "I had to turn down sixty kids today who want to buy our desserts. We could be pulling in another five hundred dollars a week without even trying, if Celeste could just bake faster."

"I know," I said. This was not the first time we had had this conversation. "But Celeste is going as fast as she can. When I tried going over her house to help her last week, I only got in the way. Both racks in her oven are full constantly, from the time she gets home from school until we pick up the goods at night. The second that one baking tray comes out, the next one goes in."

Sam fiddled with the knobs of his new handheld video game, which he treated himself to from our business profits. I had wanted him to keep plowing our profits back into business growth, but until we figured out what to about our production capacity, there was nothing to do with the excess cash but spend it.

"Maybe we can buy Celeste a second oven," Sam suggested.

"Yeah, right. You don't think her parents would notice a second oven in their home?"

Sam shrugged. "Beats me. I don't know how they don't notice her baking for six or seven hours straight every night."

"I asked her about that once," I said. "Celeste's mom is a drunk who's passed out by mid-afternoon, and her father is never around. That's why she got so good at baking. She's pretty much been cooking for herself since she was eight. Unfortunately, nobody was ever there to tell her to make something else for dinner besides pies, cakes and cookies."

Sam looked like he felt bad for Celeste, and I did too. "Lucky for us," he said.

"Yeah. Lucky for us."

As we stepped off the bus at our stop, Sam announced, "I don't care. We have to get more desserts to sell. We'll just have to hire more bakers."

"I'd love to Sam, but talented chefs don't grow on trees, ya know. Remember the problems we had just finding one supplier."

"I know," Sam said. "Don't remind me. And that's another thing. We have all our eggs in one biscuit."

"One basket," I corrected him.

"Whatever. Mark, if anything happens to Celeste, we're out of business. It's too risky."

There was nothing I could say. The little brat was right.

Wanting a diversion from the pressures of business, we decided to take a detour through our mom's dessert shop for a quick break and some cheering up. It turned out, however, that we weren't the ones who needed cheering up.

When we got to the front of Ellen's Pastry Place, we found our mom sitting on the front step, her eyes bloodshot. Sam and I looked at each other. We could both tell that she had been crying.

"Now is not a good time to bother me," she wheezed between sniffles. "Go away."

"Mom, what's the matter?" I asked in my softest voice.

"They're going to shut me down. I know it!" More sobs ensued.

"Who's going to shut you down?" asked Sam.

Our mother let out a deep sigh. I noticed that she was staring at an official-looking document in her lap. "The Walton Board of Health. They're hitting me with a dozen different violations."

Sam and I looked at each other in bewilderment. What could the Board of Health possibly have on our mother's shop? Whatever else may be wrong with her business, it was not unsanitary. If anything, our mother was a neat freak. You couldn't find a speck of dirt anywhere in the place.

"That's crazy, Mom," was all I could think of to say.

She nodded and stood up. "I know. I've always had glowing health inspections. Now the fines will cost me thousands of dollars, and fixing the 'violations' will cost me tens of thousands of dollars. I'm not making enough money to keep the lights on these days as it is. Worst of all, word is going to spread fast through this gossipy town that Ellen's Pastry Place is a health hazard, and no one will come here anymore. I might as well close up for good right now."

As no one had visited the shop all day anyway—except for the health inspector, apparently—and she was so bummed over her failed inspection, our mom closed the store early and walked back to the house with Sam and me. Part of me wanted to respect her privacy, since she obviously didn't want to talk about it, but mostly I was dying to get to the bottom of the story. Sam couldn't contain his curiosity either, and probably for no other reason than to shut us up, our mom opened up to us while she prepared our dinner.

"There is absolutely nothing unhealthy or unsanitary about my shop," our mother said. "I want you boys to understand that and believe me."

"We believe you," we both said in unison. It was true. Neither of could even momentarily believe that our mother the neat freak was a health risk.

Mom continued, "They caught me on completely petty, ridiculous violations. My kitchen sink has one big basin, when it's supposed be divided into two sections."

"Why is that a problem?" I asked.

She shrugged. "Who knows? The refrigerator doesn't have a thermometer. The light fixtures are the wrong kind."

"The light fixtures?" my brother Sam asked. "Why does the health inspector care about that?"

"I don't know, sweetie. I wish I knew. They're all crazy violations like that. They even fined me for not having a sign that says 'All Employees Must Wash Hands Before Returning to Work.' I don't need a sign like that. I'm the only employee, except for Mrs. Whitney, my part-time helper, and we both already *know* to wash our hands before returning to work. A sign wouldn't make us any cleaner."

I was stumped. None of this made any sense. Not that government bureaucrats ever made sense, as far as I could tell, but this was worse than usual. "Are these new regulations, Mom? Why didn't they ever bust you for these before?"

She let out a deep sigh. "Most of them have been on the books awhile, but they're usually not enforced. Sometimes I get a warning on a single violation or other, and once in a blue moon I get a small fine, especially when I refuse to pay them the bribes that they get from all the other businesses around here. But this is the first time they ever hit me with a string of violations at once."

"What changed?" I asked.

"The economy, for one thing," my mom said. "Even with that property tax increase they just pushed through, the township of Walton is having its biggest budget crisis ever. The inspector told me, off the record, that everyone in his department has been given strict orders to increase the violations they issue. The township needs the money from the fines to balance the budget, so they're taking it out on all the business owners. They gave me seven days to fix everything and pay the fines. There is no way I can afford to do that with the way business has been."

The three of us stood there in the kitchen in silence for several minutes. Our mom tried to concentrate on preparing dinner, but she dropped the chicken on the floor while she was plucking some stray quills from the skin. She was completely frazzled.

Sam and I went up to our rooms until dinner was ready. We wanted to say something to console our mother, but there wasn't much to say. She was a single parent with two delinquent sons, a husband in jail, a total jerk of a live-in boyfriend who was pushing her to divorce her jailed husband, and the government was doing everything it could to put her out of business.

Maybe she'd qualify for welfare once her shop closed. That would be ironic, I thought. Some of the same money the government took from her in fines might make it back to her in a welfare check.

Meanwhile, Sam and I had been depressed because our business wasn't growing as fast as we thought it should. Our mom's problems put our own petty concerns in perspective. For a twelve-year-old and an eight-year-old, we were making good money, probably better than a lot of the adults in Walton these days.

Soon enough, however, we had real problems of our own.

Shortly after the light went out in our mom's bedroom, Sam and I sneaked down the stairs for our nightly bike ride to Celeste's house to pick up our pastries. Weeks ago, I had given up trying to carry everything on my bike by myself. Sam couldn't carry many bags on his handlebars without losing balance, so we always wound up making at least two trips anyway, but he was able to take some of the load off me.

To save time, Sam and I discovered a narrow dirt path that cut through the woods between Celeste's neighborhood and Walton Street where we lived. It was always dark out when we made our nightly rides, and the trees blocked much of the moonlight from shining through, but we could see well enough to ride without lights on our bicycles.

As we made our second and final ride of the night, Sam and I entered the dirt path with me riding in the lead. Approaching the wooded area, I noticed a tiny orange light a few yards ahead of me. It was the flame of a cigarette lighter.

Wham! Something caught my front tire, and my bike flipped over, hurling me headfirst into the underbrush. Sam, who liked to tailgate, crashed into my bike and landed on the cherry pies he was carrying.

"Ha ha!" somebody's voice cackled.

I sat up and looked around. We were surrounded by six kids. Six big kids.

Eighth graders!

And not just any eighth graders, but the worst troublemakers at Dewey Middle School. They had been hanging out in the woods and smoking cigarettes. One of them had what looked like a large bottle of beer in a brown paper bag.

"Did you see me stick that branch in that kid's spoke?" the kid nearest me asked his friends with a chuckle. I recognized him. His name was Johnny Schmidt. We had spent a lot of time together in the same detention hall. "He must have gone ten feet in the air." The rest of his gang joined in the laughter.

I stood up. "Yeah, real funny, you big ape!" I yelled as I whipped a handful of smashed chocolate cake in Johnny Schmidt's face.

Oops, bad move. Cake dropped from the single eyebrow that spanned Johnny's sloping forehead, and rage contorted his already-brutish face. "Are you nuts?" he bellowed. "I'll kill you!"

Now I was one of the biggest kids in my class, but Johnny was at least a full year older than me, maybe more. He was in the eighth grade, and I'd be surprised if he wasn't held back at some point. As he stepped menacingly in my direction, he towered over me. Johnny's big chest and bulging biceps would have looked impressive on a grown man, to say nothing of an adolescent boy.

Sam just lay there on the ground, paralyzed with fear. I should have been terrified too, and I probably was, deep down. But closer to the surface, I was angry. We had just lost half our inventory.

"Yeah, you're a real tough guy, hurting an eight-year-old kid," I said as I pulled my little brother to his feet. "Why don't you just get out of here before the zookeeper finds out you're missing from your cage?"

Johnny glowered at me, and then he lunged forward and shoved me in the chest. The next thing I knew, I was flat on my back, and my head smacked against the frame of my bicycle. One of Johnny's fellow thugs had sneaked into a crouch behind me to make it easy for him to knock me off balance—one of the oldest playground dirty tricks in the book. The gang of eighth graders burst into laughter again.

Before the kid who helped Johnny could get to his feet, I brought my foot down on his ear and then snapped it up quickly, smashing it into his nose. As the kid grabbed his broken nose and shrieked in pain, Johnny and three of the other delinquents pounced on me. One sat on my legs, and the other two each held back one of my arms, while Johnny pummeled my stomach. I didn't want to give them the satisfaction of showing my pain, but an involuntary scream of agony escaped my mouth.

"What's that?" Johnny sneered as he continued to punch me. "You say you're hungry? Here, have a cupcake!" He grabbed one of the cupcakes from the spilled bag and shoved it in my mouth, paper and all. I tried to spit it out, but I was having a hard time with the air being knocked out of me with every blow.

Out of the corner of my eye, I could see that two of the other kids were holding down Sam. They weren't really beating him up, but they we were tormenting him by poking him with sticks, shoving leaves down his pants and shirt, and smearing desserts on his face. Seeing my little brother abused jolted me into another rage, and I struggled to get up, but the big kids had me pinned down hard.

After what seemed like an eternity, but was in reality a few minutes at the most, Johnny and his gang of delinquents finally let go of us. I was in too much pain to get off the ground, much less attempt to retaliate. Sam laid next to his bicycle and sobbed.

"Aw, does the baby want his bottle?" Johnny mocked. He leaned over Sam menacingly, his smelly breath right in Sam's face. "Does the baby need his diaper changed?"

"Come on, Johnny. Let's get out here," one of the other thugs suggested.

They each helped themselves to a dessert as they left. "Thanks for the treats, jerks," Johnny said through a mouthful of oatmeal-raisin cookies. Sam and I laid there and listened to their giggles and guffaws drift down the path through the woods.

Slowly I sat up and looked around. It was dark out, our desserts were ruined, and my brother and I were a mess. I picked out a few of the items that seemed to still be intact, and I found one bag that wasn't ripped, so that I could carry the remaining desserts home.

Sam was still crying and not making any attempt to get up. "Are you all right, buddy?" I asked. More sobs were his response. I walked over to him and gently wiped the tears and dessert smears from his face. Then I sat him up and helped him pull the leaves out of his shirt.

"Come on," I said. "Let's get out of here. We'll have a better day tomorrow."

"No," Sam whimpered. "I can't."

"Yes, you can," I said. "You can't spend the night lying here in the woods and getting frostbite. Let's go home and get cleaned up. You won't even have to package desserts tonight. I could only save five of them. We'll just get you a nice hot bath, get you into bed, and you'll feel better in the morning. I promise."

A few minutes of coaxing later, we were both on our bikes and pedaling as fast as we could out of the dark woods and towards our house. Our one bit of luck that night was that neither our mom nor Frank woke up when I ran the bath water for Sam. By the time I got him cleaned up and dried off, he was practically sleepwalking, so I just dragged him to his room and dumped him in bed naked. Less than a minute later, I passed out in my own bed.

We spent the next morning apologizing to our customers, most of whom didn't get the desserts they ordered, and retelling the previous night's misadventures. I was talking with Vic and Neil at the bus stop when Vic's eyes bugged out of his head.

"Hey, Mark, look behind you," he said with clear panic in his voice.

I looked over my shoulder and saw Johnny Schmidt smoking a cigarette with his friends at the other end of the bus stop. He saw me looking at him and gave me an evil grin as he rubbed his belly in satisfaction before returning to whatever passed for conversation between him and his fellow baboons.

"What are you going to do?" Neil asked.

I shrugged. "I don't know, but he'll be sorry."

Neil and Vic both gave me a suspicious look that showed their skepticism at the likelihood of my making Johnny repent. I was skeptical myself.

When Sam and I made the ride to Celeste's house that night, we prudently took the long route under the relatively bright streetlights of Walton, rather than chance another run-in with Johnny in the dark woods. We made it home with our merchandise and ourselves intact. The next morning, however, as we lugged our bags of desserts to the bus stop, Johnny and the other eighth-grade bullies pounced on us.

"Hey, Hoffman," Johnny called out, "got any more treats for me?"

I didn't flinch. "Sure. How about a knuckle sandwich?"

Two of Johnny's goons grabbed me, and a third one grabbed Sam. As I struggled to break free, Johnny walked up to me and punched me in the gut. Why did he always go for my stomach? It was really starting to hurt, but I suppose it was better than a broken nose or missing teeth.

As I doubled over and gasped for air, Johnny reached into one of my bags and helped himself to the goodies. "Hey, look everybody. Hoffman brought snacks for all of us. Who wants some brownies? Steve, you like brownies?"

The goon holding my left arm laughed. "Sure, who doesn't? Thanks, Johnny."

"Yeah, give me some too," the goon on my right added.

I kept looking over at my friends Vic and Neil in the hope that they might help defend me, but they wisely protected themselves and watched from a distance.

Johnny grabbed me under my chin and pulled my face toward him. "Now look, punk. You're gonna bring dessert for my buddies and me to this bus stop every morning, or you're gonna get beat up every morning. Got it?"

"Go to hell," I answered.

Johnny's fist slammed into my nose, snapping my head back and triggering a stream of blood down my face. Yes, a punch in the stomach was definitely preferable to a broken nose, but I had to find out the hard way.

"Stop it!" Sam screamed. "We'll bring you your stupid brownies! Just stop it!"

Johnny walked over to Sam and gave him a soft slap on the cheek. "Smart kid. You must be the brains of the business."

"That's what I keep telling him," Sam replied.

All the goons got a big laugh out of my smart, funny little brother, and they let us go just before the bus pulled up.

Vic and Neil did help me after the fact by carrying my remaining bag of desserts onto the bus. With Sam's help, they even handed out the desserts and collected money for me from some of my customers on the ride to school. Meanwhile, I tried to stop the bleeding from my nose. Every time I touched it, pain shot through my head.

To my surprise, Karen Thomas sat down next to me and pulled a package of tissues from her backpack. "Let me help you clean that up," she offered.

"How much are you charging?"

Karen giggled. "I should charge you, just because you're so mean. But I figured I owe you. The last time you stood up to the big kids, we were in the first grade. Remember?"

"I remember. They took your Powerpuff Girls lunchbox, and I had to get it back for you. I guess I haven't gotten any smarter over the past six years."

"Nope," Karen agreed. "You're still just as brave and stupid and cute."

Cute?

Vic walked back to where Karen and I were sitting and handed me the money he collected for me. "So what are you going to do tomorrow?" he asked.

"I don't know," I said, "but I know for sure that I'm not giving that jerk Johnny Schmidt any brownies."

"You have a gun," Neil said matter-of-factly. "Just shoot the creep the next time he threatens you.

Neil was definitely born in the wrong century. As I've mentioned, he's a gun aficionado, just like his father. (All right, they're both gun nuts, but aficionado sounds classier.) And if it was Neil who was being bullied, he probably would have settled it the way they did in the Old West. I think the whole school suspected that as well, which probably had a lot to do with why no one ever bullied Neil. But for me, there were two big flaws in Neil's suggestion. First, it was true that I did own a gun, but it was a small-caliber rifle—a .22 Remington—that I used for target practice whenever Neil's dad and my dad would take us kids to the town shooting range. The weapon was almost as long as I was, so it wasn't exactly concealable. Second, if I brought the rifle anywhere near the school bus stop, which was a "gun-free zone," the school administrators would have me in round-the-clock therapy and a diet of Ritalin and Prozac until I was thirty. Kids weren't even allowed to say the G-word at school, and if you so much as drew a picture of gun it was likely to earn you a few trips to the school psychiatrist for evaluation. That's the way it was: Some bullies beat you up, and the kid who wants to defend himself ends up in therapy, or juvenile detention center.

"You just shouldn't take the bus," Karen suggested. "Get your mom to drive you."

I shook my head, which sent another shot of pain through my skull. "No, Johnny would find me eventually, and the beating would be even worse. Anyway, a lot of our customers expect us here first thing in the morning to get their desserts."

Sam smiled at me. "I already said we're going to give Johnny his brownies."

"And I already said we weren't. I won't be bullied. End of story."

"Tsk-tsk," Sam said. "You really aren't very smart at all, are you?"

"Look, Sam, I'm not in any mood for your stupid games. If you have something you want to say, just say it."

Sam looked uneasily at Karen, Vic and Neil, then back at me.

"Don't worry about them," I said. "Just say whatever's on your mind."

"Well," my brother reluctantly asked, "remember that time last summer when you couldn't poop for a whole week?"

Vic and Neil snickered uncontrollably. Even Karen, who wasn't much for gross-out humor, couldn't suppress a grin.

"Not really," I lied.

"Sure you do, Mark. Remember, you walked around for a week moaning and groaning, holding your belly and whining about how nothing happened no matter how long you sat on the toilet."

This was really embarrassing. "What's your point, Sam?"

"Well, Mom finally dragged you to the Rite Aid, and the pharmacist gave you that medicine that looked and tasted like little chocolate bars. You got a whole bunch of them. Do you still have any left?"

I had to smile myself as I realized where Sam was going. "Oh yeah. The chocolate-flavored maximum-strength Ex-Lax. Yeah, I've got about fifty of those things left, in case I ever get constipated." I saw Karen looking at me kind of strangely. "It's nothing, really. I don't even take them anymore. I just needed to get more fiber in my diet. That's why I have so many of the Ex-Lax left over."

"So," my fiendishly brilliant little brother concluded, "when you give Celeste today's orders, let her know we have a request for an extra-special recipe. We'll rush the secret ingredient over right after school."

The next morning, Sam and I were at the bus stop bright and early. So were Johnny Schmidt and his gang.

"Well, Hoffman. You got something for me?" he sneered.

Sam stepped forward to hand Johnny a small bag containing chocolate brownies, prepared especially for him. I put a hand on Sam's shoulder, pretending to try to stop him.

Johnny snatched the bag from Sam's hand and shoved me backward. Glaring at me, Johnny stuffed one brownie in his mouth, followed quickly by a second. I stared back at him. "What are you looking at, Hoffman? Did you think I was full of crap?"

As a matter of fact, yes, I thought to myself. But you won't be for much longer.

Sometimes you just get lucky. The bus was ten minutes late picking us up, and by the third brownie, I could see a look of mild panic passing over Johnny's face. When the bus finally arrived, it only took us about two blocks before coming to a stop at a railroad crossing.

Sam, Neil, Vic and I slouched down in our seats, hoping Johnny wouldn't see us giggling as we watched him squirm. There wasn't much chance of him noticing us, however, as Johnny had more urgent matters on his puny mind.

The train kept coming, and finally Johnny got up to ask the driver if he could get off the bus. The driver told him to get back in his seat. As Johnny hesitantly sat down, I noticed his feet shuffling nervously and his hands squeezing each other.

"What's up, Johnny?" one of the other eighth-graders asked him. "You're acting kind of funny."

"Shut up!" Johnny snapped as he began to exhale rapidly.

About twenty minutes later, the bus pulled into the parking lot in front of Dewey Middle School, and Johnny bolted to the front to be the first one off. It was probably the first time in his long juvenile delinquency that Johnny Schmidt was in a hurry to get inside the school building. My friends and I laughed as we watched his tight, awkward stride as he tried to squeeze his butt cheeks together while he ran for the front entrance.

Unfortunately for Johnny, the bus was so late that the second bell had already rung and class was under way. Johnny ran for the boys' room, but Vice Principal Atkins was standing in the doorway.

"You're late for class, young man."

"But," Johnny gasped, "I need to use the lavatory, sir."

"I see. Just like you had to use the lavatory when I found you and those other hoodlums smoking cigarettes during sixth period last week?"

"Yes… I mean, no. Just let me through." Johnny actually tried to push his way past Atkins, but the old man was sturdier than he looked.

"You're not going anywhere, mister, except to your homeroom. Now go."

"But…"

Atkins pointed down the hall. Johnny glanced around in a panic and ran. I wanted to follow him to see what happened next, but Atkins saw us and sent us on our way.

At lunch, the rumor in the cafeteria was that Johnny Schmidt was sent to the principal's office sometime that morning. His mother met him there a short time later with a clean pair of jeans and underwear. I don't know if Johnny ever figured out exactly what happened to him, but even if he did, he wasn't about to tell anyone.

He wasn't on the bus home that afternoon, or the next day. I guess he decided to walk from now on.

A few days later, we started noticing some new graffiti on the stalls in the boys' room: "Johnny Schmidt was (ALMOST) here!"

Chapter Ten

Halloween

Once we took care of Johnny Schmidt, Sam and I were able to focus on growing Desserts Express. The next brilliant idea came from me instead of my little brother. It was about time.

The health department carried out its threats and closed Ellen's Pastry Place. For the next several weeks, our mom moped around the house. Having her constantly under foot and in a foul mood made it all the more difficult for Sam and I to go about our business in secrecy.

Late one evening, as we were returning from Celeste's house, each of us weighed down with desserts, our mother appeared out of nowhere to stand in our way at the top of the stairs.

"Halloween's not until next week, boys. It's a little early to be walking around at night with bags of treats."

"Ha ha. That's a good one, Mom," I chuckled feebly. Our mother wasn't laughing though.

"Open those bags at once," she demanded. "What on earth! Where did you get all those desserts?"

"What's going on out there?" we heard Frank yell from their bedroom.

Sam and I both looked desperately at our mother, our eyes saying we would tell her everything if she would just leave that jerk Frank out of it.

"Nothing, sweetheart," our mom answered. We hated it when she called him sweetheart. She used to call our dad sweetheart. "I'm just putting the boys to bed."

Our mom followed Sam and me into my bedroom. She leaned wearily against my computer station while my brother and I sat on the foot of my bed. "All right, boys, let's have it. What are you up to this time?"

I took a deep breath and began. "Remember when we accidentally caused that fire in your shop's kitchen?"

She furrowed her eyebrows in anger. "You mean the shop that was my lifelong dream, that you two almost burnt to the ground just before the board of health finished the job for you? Yes, I think I recall something like that."

I stared down at the bag of desserts at my feet, not wanting to deal with the fury in our mother's eyes. "Yeah, well anyway, remember we told you how Sam and I wanted to start our own dessert business, which was why we were in the kitchen in the first place?"

"Oh no!" our mother exclaimed. She shot up and darted for my bedroom window, straining to see through the darkness. "You've been using my kitchen again! How could you?"

"No, nothing like that," I assured her. "Honest. We haven't been near your shop."

"But... then where—"

"We tried to negotiate with you," Sam interrupted. "But you wouldn't listen. So we found another supplier."

"Oh," she said quietly. As she walked slowly back to my computer station, she kept her back to us. "Your new supplier... Are her desserts better than mine?" I noticed a distinct tone of jealousy in her voice.

"Of course not, Mommy," Sam consoled her as he stood up to give her a big hug. "Everybody knows your desserts are the best. But Celeste's are really good, and her price was good."

She lifted Sam into her arms and held him tightly. "Thank you, sweetie. Who is Celeste?"

"Celeste Szuck," I said. "She's in my class."

"Oh, yes. I think I remember her. The ... uh ... heavyset girl with the pretty smile and sweet personality."

"You mean the fat girl," I corrected her. "And the only thing sweet about Celeste is her pastries."

"That's not nice, young man. You know better than that."

The three of us sat there and looked at each other. Finally, I stood up and said, "Well, if there's nothing else, Sam and I have a lot of work to do yet tonight, slicing and packaging these desserts for our customers."

"One more thing I just have to know," our mom whispered. "I promise I won't tell Frank. How much are you boys making from this little venture of yours?"

Sam and I looked at each other and shrugged. "That's sort of private," I mumbled.

"I'm your mother!" she cried. "I gave birth to you, and you live in my house."

I wasn't really sure what that had to do with anything, but the old gal seemed to be really stressed out, and I just wanted to end the conversation and return to our work. "If you must know, I think we've been clearing about three hundred a week each, after expenses."

"Three hundred!" she yelled. "Dollars?"

"Shhh." I put a finger to my lips. The last thing I wanted was for Frank to know how much money we were bringing in.

"Actually, I think it was closer to three forty last week," Sam corrected me. I walked over to my closet and removed a stack from our dwindling supply of individual dessert containers. Maybe if we just got down to work, our mom would take the hint and leave us alone.

No such luck, however. Our mom held onto my computer monitor to steady herself. Her eyes looked vacant and her mouth hung open. "Three hundred forty dollars a week each," she marveled. "A twelve-year-old and an eight-year-old. In business for less than two months. And here I am out of business and going broke. What in the world is going on?"

"Mommy, you're babbling," Sam noted helpfully.

That's when I got my brilliant idea. Okay, it was an obvious idea, and an idea we already had six weeks ago, but it was still brilliant. At least that's my story, and I'm sticking to it.

"Look, Mom," I said, "this is crazy. Our business should be growing even faster, but we're stuck with one supplier who's already at capacity. You have the talent and the professional kitchen, but nowhere to sell your product. Why don't you reconsider and come to work for Sam and me?"

Our mother drifted back from wherever her mind had wandered. "What? Oh, I don't know. I mean, you're my children. I'm supposed to take care of you."

"And you do," I assured her. "You're a great mother. Well, a good one anyway. But this isn't about motherhood. It's about business."

"Really, Mom," Sam added. "Swallow your pride and take the job."

"Gee, thanks, I didn't really have much use for my pride anyway," she said with a roll of her eyes. "But there's also my problem with the health department to consider. If they catch me in that kitchen, they'll hit me with another penalty."

"Don't worry about that," I said. "Ellen's Pastry Place will stay closed. Keep your storefront locked up. That will keep the health inspectors away, and you can use the store's kitchen to work for us."

For the first time in weeks, our mom smiled, and that made Sam and me smile too. "So you boys really have this all figured out, huh? Well, why not?"

"Yeah!" Sam exclaimed.

We showed our mom how much we were paying Celeste, and she agreed to match those same prices. Sam and I compared notes to figure out how many additional desserts we could order from her and be confident of selling. Our mom thought the number sounded overly ambitious, but we assured her that we were good for it. Then we sent her off to her room so that we could finish packaging the next day's orders.

Putting our mother on the payroll more than doubled our production capacity, and our business mushroomed in size, but Sam and I soon realized there was no way we could deliver all of our orders by ourselves. Within a week, we hired two more employees—a pair of ambitious sixth-graders who met us at our house each morning before school. For twenty-five cents an order, our new couriers rushed their sweet cargo to our hungry customers, collected the payment, and delivered the money to Sam or me before the school day was out.

Finding ambitious kids who were willing to work was easy; the hard part was getting to them before they went into business for themselves. The entrepreneurial bug had swept Dewey Middle and Elementary Schools worse than an epidemic of chicken pox. Just about every day I received an email from some kid striking out on his or her own. Some of them were as old as fourteen, but others were as young as seven. The ones who weren't in business for themselves soon found themselves working for their classmates.

I knew things were really getting strange when my mom caught me off guard with an unusual question.

"What are you going to be for Halloween this year, Mark?" she asked a few days before the end of October.

The reason that question was strange was that most years it would have been completely unnecessary to ask. I usually announced my choice of Halloween costume sometime in August and feverishly anticipated the big night with unbridled greed. I would pester my mom to either make the costume for me or take me shopping for it weeks ahead of time, and then I would parade around the house in costume, getting into character. I was a method trick-or-treater.

"I don't know," was my answer this year. "I haven't really had much time to think about it."

"What about you, Sam? Do you have a special costume in mind?"

Sam shrugged. "Not really. Maybe one of Mark's old costumes will fit."

Her face showed disappointment. "Now, boys. I know how busy you are, but you can still take time out for something as special as Halloween. Even Bill Gates takes a vacation every now and then. You need to get away from work once in awhile, or you'll burn yourselves out."

Maybe she was right, but I still couldn't get excited about Halloween, or even force myself to think about it for very long. Of course, I was getting older, so my losing interest was probably inevitable, but Sam was a third-grader, for goodness sake. That was prime trick-or-treating age, and my little brother seemed as disinterested as me.

We decided to give our mom the benefit of the doubt on this one, however. She couldn't be wrong about everything after all, and Halloween had always been loads of fun in the past. Perhaps we did need to get away from work for a breather.

So Sam and I had our mom drive us down to the Wal-Mart the day before Halloween, and we quickly picked out some costumes. The next day, we realized that we wouldn't be very busy on Halloween anyway. Most of our usual customers didn't order anything, as they knew they would be filling their bags with free candy in a few hours. I met Sam on the playground at lunchtime for a quick meeting, and we decided that under the circumstances we might as well just close Desserts Express in honor of the holiday. We gave our mom and Celeste the night off.

After school, we did our duty as kids and walked up and down Walton Street knocking on doors and asking for handouts. It was fun, to be honest. But it wasn't great, the way Halloween had been in years past. I could tell that a lot of the other kids on the trick-or-treat circuit felt the same way by the way they shuffled half-heartedly from house to house. The "official" trick-or-treat hours for the township of Walton were from six to eight p.m., but Sam and I and a lot of our friends were all home fifteen minutes early. The police must have been stunned by the lack of pranks reported that night. No houses were rolled in toilet paper, and no eggs were tossed at windows. The kids of Walton had better things to do now.

Well, most of the kids had better things to do. For a stubborn few who lacked both imagination and ability, a night of panhandling in costume was still the best deal around.

The resentment of the haves by the have-nots—or to be precise, the achieves and the achieve-nots—had been simmering for weeks, ever since our little underground economy took off. It was an open secret that many of us were raking in a lot of money, and as a result, other kids were building up a lot of envy.

A few days after Halloween, I was late for the start of the school day, as usual. As I quietly opened the door to my classroom, I saw Susie Kendall, the class snitch, standing in front of the class. No doubt she was handing Miss Farkas a list of kids who had talked in class, passed notes, thrown spitballs or otherwise misbehaved recently. My name was sure to be on the list. Susie had a great career ahead of her as a stool pigeon, I thought.

Miss Farkas looked down at me through the eyeglasses perched on the tip of her nose. "You're late again, Mr. Hoffman. I'll give you your detention slip later. Take your seat so Miss Kendall can finish telling us about the Sharing is Caring program."

The what program?

"Thank you, Miss Farkas," Susie said as she forced a tight little smile through her mouthful of braces. Susie Kendall never smiled. There was too much evil in the world for her to be happy. She had long taken it as her personal calling in life to tell the teacher whenever someone misbehaved, to remind the teacher to assign homework, and generally to stick her nose in everyone else's business.

"The Sharing is Caring program will allow all of us to share the joy of Christmas…"

Miss Farkas cleared her throat.

"Oh, excuse me, Miss Farkas," Susie apologized. "I meant the joy of the holiday season."

God forbid anybody should refer to Christmas as Christmas in a public school. It was a miracle we were still allowed to use the C-word at home.

"Each class in Dewey Middle School will compete in a charity drive to help the less fortunate children in our special-education classes. We'll raise money from now until the week before Chris, I mean, winter break. We all know that some of our classmates have been especially, um, fortunate lately. Naturally, those of you who are lucky enough to have the most money will be expected to give the most."

Vic raised his hand. "By fortunate and lucky, do you mean hard-working and risk-taking?"

Susie frowned. "I'm sure most everyone who has been earning money in this terrible economy deserves it, but others deserve money too. Not everybody has the same opportunities. Some of our schoolmates are busy playing on our sports teams, or need more time to study, or just haven't been blessed with the same advantages. We don't want to penalize them as we help the special-ed students."

"No, you want to penalize success," I mumbled.

"Raise your hand if you have something to say, Mr. Hoffman," Miss Farkas commanded.

Rolling her eyes, Susie said, "I know that all of you will get into the spirit once we get going. We're going to hang a big red paper thermometer outside the cafeteria that will measure our progress and encourage you to give more. Volunteers will walk around the cafeteria at lunchtime today so that you can make your pledges."

Vic, Neil and I had a good laugh about the Sharing is Caring nonsense at lunchtime.

"So we're supposed to bust our butts and stay up late working just to give our money to the 'tards?" Neil scoffed. "I don't think so."

"I know," I agreed through a mouthful of tuna sandwich. "Susie and the rest of the do-gooders are going to be in for quite a surprise. I hope their paper thermometer can measure zero."

Karen Thomas and Wendy Siegel walked up wearing big smiles. "Hey, Karen. Hey, Wendy," I greeted them. "We were just talking about that Sharing is Caring business."

"I know," Karen said. "We're here to take your pledges."

Chapter Eleven

Sharing and Caring

"You can't be serious!" Neil snorted.

"And why not, Neil?" Wendy retorted. "Just because you're a selfish creep doesn't mean everybody else is."

Neil shrugged and returned to his sandwich. "Whatever. Just leave me out of it."

"Me too," Vic concurred.

Karen shook her head. "That's too bad, but I guess I shouldn't be surprised. At least there's one gentleman at this table."

There was? Where? Oh wait, she was talking about me. I saw Karen and Wendy look at me hopefully.

"Well, Mark?" Wendy asked with a smile. "How much can we put you down for?"

"Oh, I don't need any charity," I smiled back. "There are other kids much less fortunate than me." Vic and Neil cackled while the girls glared at me.

"Very funny, mister," Karen said. "Are you going to contribute, or are you going to be a selfish creep like your friends?"

"Well, when you put it that way… I'll be a selfish creep like my friends."

My selfish friends and I had a good chuckle at that one. Karen's face reddened, and I thought she was going to cry, but before any tears flowed she turned her back and stormed off. Wendy made a crude hand gesture that I had never seen a girl use, before running over to comfort her best friend.

The boys congratulated me on my quick wit, and we continued to wisecrack about the do-gooders and their Sharing is Caring program throughout lunch. Deep down, however, I felt bad about laughing at Karen. Her heart was in the right place, even if her head wasn't.

On the bus ride home, I tried to patch things up with Karen. She was in the seat in front of me, so I leaned over and asked, "How's business?"

"Go away," she replied without looking at me.

I gave it another try. "I hear you're hosting a Thanksgiving party. I was thinking about buying a ticket."

Wendy, who was sitting next to Karen, turned toward me and scowled. "Can't you take a hint, creep? Leave us alone."

"Nobody was talking to you, Wendy the Witch," I replied.

I walked home with Sam, trying to put Karen out of my mind. Sam suggested we stop by our mom's kitchen to check on the day's production. Like all of our employees, we used the rear entrance facing our house. Any nosy health inspectors driving by might get suspicious if they saw people coming and going through the old storefront.

There was a buzz of activity in the kitchen, as there usually was these days. Our mom flitted from refrigerator to mixing bowl to oven, working on several batches of desserts at once. Mrs. Whitney, the old lady who used to help out our mom a few hours a week in the morning, was now there eight, ten hours a day in a futile effort to keep up with demand. In another hour or so, our young employees would begin filing in, using every available inch of space in the large professional kitchen to cut desserts and package them for delivery.

"Oh hi, boys," our mom said as she rushed past us with a tray of blondies. "That shipment of plastic containers you ordered came today. I signed for it and had them put the cartons in our garage. You'll have to get them up into the attic fast if you don't want Frank to see them when he gets home. But you may be wasting your time trying to hide all this from him much longer. Contrary to what you boys may think, Frank isn't stupid."

"Yes, Mother," Sam sighed.

I turned to Sam. "As soon as our employees get here, send a team of them to the garage to deal with that. Give me the orders you took today, and I'll go upstairs and get started on the delivery labels."

"Okay," Sam answered. "How did you get those containers delivered? I know we don't have any credit cards."

"I know," I said. "I paid up-front in cash at another close-out store. I asked them to deliver since we were cleaning out their entire stock, and they agreed."

"Cool."

I went up to my bedroom and powered on the computer. Before I could reach for the delivery labels, the instant messenger window popped up, and I noticed I had a message. It was from Karen.

Karent32: R U there?

Against my better judgment, I replied.

Burpmaster7: yeah I'm here

Karent32: I want to talk.

Burpmaster7: ok so talk

Karent32: I want to know what got into u at lunch 2day...

Burpmaster7: meatloaf mostly, and some peas and mashed potatoes ☺

Karent32: ☹

Burpmaster7: sorry

Karent32: This isn't like u. U used to be so nice. What happened?

Burpmaster7: I'm still nice...

Burpmaster7: ...I'm just not a sucker.

Karent32: Don't u think u owe something to the less fortunate?

Burpmaster7: no. did the less fortunate lend me money or something, and I forgot about it?

Karent32: Be serious!

Burpmaster7: I am serious. I owe something to my customers and to myself. Nobody else.

Karent32: But that's so selfish!

Burpmaster7: maybe, but what u call selfishness seems to be making A LOT more people happier than any do-gooders ever did.

Karent32: ?

Burpmaster7: look what we've accomplished in just a few months of everybody forgetting about the old rules and looking out for themselves. Sam and I didn't build desserts express to make other kids happy. We did it to make money and make ourselves happy. But the only way we could do that, without stealing or lying or beating someone up and taking what we wanted, was to come up with something that made lots of other kids happy. Our customers win, our employees win, and we win.

Karent32: Well, maybe...

Burpmaster7: and u did the same thing, and so did neil and vic and all the other productive kids.

Karent32: Yes, but not all the kids...

Burpmaster7: no, not all the kids. But u can't create happiness by trading my something for their nothing. Your sharing is caring nonsense just makes them happy at my expense. Only what u call selfishness—but what I call smart business—can make both sides happier!

Karen had to think about that one for a minute. Finally, she replied:

Karent32: So u don't ever do something for someone else, just because it's the right thing to do, even if there's nothing in it for u?

Burpmaster7: there's always something in it for me, or for you, or neither of us would do it. There's just no other way. If I do something nice for my dumb little brother, it's because his happiness is important to me. If u do something nice for the tards, then their happiness must be important to u, tho I can't figure out why

Karent32: Well, that's your problem. I still say we have a responsibility to help the less fortunate.

Burpmaster7: No, that's your problem. But just to show I'm not a total creep, I'll give any of the tards who wants one a job tomorrow packing desserts. Think any of the tards can handle that?

Karent32: ☹ I'm not answering you until you stop calling them that horrible word.

Burpmaster32: fine. Think any of the special education students are special enough to put a piece of cake in a plastic clamshell?

Karent32: I don't know. Probably. Will you pay them as much as your other employees?

Burpmaster32: heck no!

Karent32: But that's not fair!

Burpmaster32: and it's not fair that I can't hit a 100 mph fastball 450 feet in the opposite direction. Should the yankees give me a spot in their lineup anyway, and pay me as much as their other players?

Karent32: That's different.

Burpmaster32: how?

Karent32: It just is, and you know it.

Burpmaster32: whatever u say. I have work to do. C ya.

I closed the instant messenger window and opened my label maker program, but the instant messenger popped back up.

Karent32: Wait, I have one more question...

Burpmaster32: ?

Karent32: U said u only help people when their happiness is important to u...

Burpmaster32: Yeah...

Karent32: Well, u defended me from those bullies when we were little. Does that mean my happiness is important to u? ☺

Burpmaster32: Within reason. ☺

Two weeks went by, and Karen seemed to have mostly gotten over her anger at me for being a selfish creep. Nevertheless, she, Wendy Siegel and Susie Kendall were getting really bummed at the lousy performance of their Sharing is Caring program. They posted their paper thermometer by the entrance to the cafeteria, but the red part barely reached above the base.

Susie Kendall decided to do what she does best, which is to write lists of kids' names. Only this time, instead of writing a list of everyone who talked while the teacher was out of the classroom, Susie created a giant round poster displaying the names of everyone who had contributed to the Sharing is Caring program. There were several blank spaces at the bottom with "Your Name Here" placeholders. Along the top of the round poster was the title "Circle of Sharers." The whole thing was done up with bright paint, glitter and foil. It was quite impressive, in a stupid sort of way.

I guess the idea was that everyone whose name was on the poster would be the envy of the school, and Susie hung the "Circle of Sharers" next to the big thermometer at the entrance to the cafeteria. The idea backfired on Susie, however, when someone changed the lettering on the poster to read "Circle of Suckers." Susie's face turned bright red as she stood outside the entrance with her signup forms for the Sharing is Caring program, and instead of pledges, she collected a lot of ridicule, as did the suckers whose names were now on display for the entire student body to see.

By early December, it became clear to the Sharing is Caring organizers that many of the most productive students at John Dewey Middle School did not care to share. Susie got permission from the school principal to call a mandatory student assembly on Friday afternoon to discuss the situation.

"Can you believe this?" Neil shouted to me as we made our way into the noisy gymnasium on Friday afternoon.

I shrugged. "Whatever. If they insist on looking dopey in front of the whole school, I won't stand in their way. This couldn't be any more boring than the science class I'm missing."

Vic looked worried. "I don't think you'll be bored, Mark. They may be up to something."

"They're too dumb to be up to something," I scoffed.

I was mistaken.

"Okay everybody, quiet down!" Susie Kendall shouted from the podium on the stage. "I said quiet! Now!" In response, a spitball bounced off her forehead, and the resulting laughter made the room even louder. "Vice Principal Atkins, that student in the front row, Jackson Jelenic, hit me with a spitball. Yes, him." As Mr. Atkins pulled a pad of detention slips from his pocket and walked to the front row, he was greeted by a chorus of boos.

Eventually the students quieted to a dull murmur (accented by Neil's snoring), and Susie continued. "As most of you should know, we're more than halfway through the fundraising period for the Sharing is Caring program, and we are well below our goal. We've moved the thermometer from the cafeteria entrance to the stage behind me. As you can see, we're still way down here, and we should be way up there by this date."

"Many of you have been very generous," Susie went on, "and your names have been publicly posted in the Circle of Sharers. Unfortunately, many others—who shall remain nameless—have not been so generous, despite the fact that they are known to be the most fortunate among us, financially speaking. Because of their selfish attitude, we are in danger of not achieving our goal. That would be a huge disappointment to all the special-ed students who are so deserving."

"We had hoped that everyone would get into the spirit of giving on their own. When that didn't work, we hoped peer pressure and public shame would do the trick. But that didn't work either. Therefore, I think we have to consider establishing mandatory minimum contribution guidelines."

The steady murmur of the audience burst into a deafening roar.

"What!" I exclaimed. "Did she just say she's taxing us? Who gave her the right to do that?"

"Apparently Susie knows better what we should do with our money than we do," Vic replied. Neil continued to snore with his head bent back and his mouth hanging open. I nudged Neil with an elbow.

"Knock it off," Neil muttered with his eyes closed.

"Quiet, please," Susie continued from the podium. "Now I know what some of you are thinking. This isn't a dictatorship, and I can't just impose a minimum contribution on everybody."

"Even though you'd like nothing better," I added for the benefit of the students sitting near me.

"We're going to do this democratically, so no one can complain. Wendy Siegel is coming down the center aisle right now with a stack of ballots. I'd like the student at the end of each row to take some from Wendy, keep a ballot for yourself, and pass the rest down."

Sure enough, a stack of small squares of paper made its way down our row. Against my better judgment, I took one and read it:

JOHN DEWEY MIDDLE SCHOOL
STUDENT RESOLUTION

On December 4, we the students of John Dewey Middle School voluntarily establish a mandatory minimum contribution to the Sharing is Caring program. The mandatory minimum contribution shall be the greater of $20 or 5 percent of the student's gross revenues for the month of November from any source at the student's disposal, including student-owned and operated businesses. The mandatory minimum contribution shall be payable no later than December 15. Exceptions shall be made for hardship, students involved in approved extracurricular activities, etc.

Please circle one: YES NO

"As you can see, the issue is very straightforward," Susie explained. "We'll have one student speak in favor of the resolution and, just to be fair, we'll ask for a volunteer to speak against the resolution. Then we'll vote, and we'll all go along with the outcome. Majority rules. Nothing could be fairer, right?"

"Well yes, actually, it would be fairer to leave everybody the heck alone," Vic observed.

I noticed that Neil was still snoring away, so I rolled up one of the ballots and stuck it in his open mouth. Neil sputtered and gagged before yanking the ballot out. "Cut it out, jerk!" His eyes were finally open, and he was sitting up.

"Why don't you read that little slip of paper and pay attention?" I suggested. "Susie Kendall and her gang are about to do to you what Johnny Schmidt and his gang did to me."

"Huh?" Neil asked, still half-awake.

"If it's okay with everyone, as long as I have the microphone, I'll speak in favor of the resolution," Susie announced. She went on to rehash the announcement she made in homeroom a month ago—the spirit of the "holiday season," whatever that was, the lack of opportunity available to many students, the unfair success of others, blah blah blah.

When she finished her pitch for junior socialism, Susie asked for a volunteer to make the rebuttal. She stood back and smiled smugly, as if she expected that no one would dare challenge the obvious righteousness and goodhearted truthfulness of the nonsense she had just spewed. Neil jumped up and raised his hand. I sat up in my seat. It should be fun to hear Neil shut the do-gooders up once and for all, I thought.

"Mark Hoffman will give the rebuttal!" Neil shouted as he pointed to me. Not exactly what I had mind. I shook my head to decline. Not that I couldn't have completely destroyed Susie's pathetic gibberish—her blather wasn't even logical enough to be fairly called an argument—but I was in no mood to give credibility to this whole sham by playing along.

"Mark! Mark! Mark!" Neil started chanting. Vic joined in, and soon most of the assembly was chanting my name. Sheesh.

"I'll get you for this, Jones," I warned a grinning Neil. I knew they weren't going to shut up until I relented, so I stood up and made my way down my row to the aisle. Applause broke out, and I waved to my adoring fans. As I approached the stage, I threw air-kisses to the audience.

I bounded up the stage steps, thrusting my palms toward the ceiling to encourage my fans to pump up the volume. Susie Kendall eyed me with icy contempt as she warily handed me the microphone. Taking a deep, majestic bow, I held a cupped hand to my ear, pretending that I couldn't hear the applause. I then placed the microphone under my lips and waited patiently for the audience to quiet.

When the gymnasium fell silent moments later, I let out a huge belch I had been saving. That got them all fired up again, and over the laughter I yelled into the microphone, "Don't worry, I'm not as full of hot air as Susie."

The crowd was howling with laughter when Mr. Atkins stomped up the stairs of the stage and grabbed the microphone from my hands. "If the audience and the speaker cannot conduct themselves in a mature manner, we'll skip this speaker and go straight to the vote." He was answered with jeers, of course, and he reluctantly handed the microphone back to me.

"Okay, everybody, calm down," I said. "Let's get this charade over with. I know most of you are expecting me to tell you to vote no, but I'm not going to do that." A murmur of confusion swept through the crowd. "Don't get me wrong. This whole thing is an idiotic idea, and it deserves to be defeated for the mindless, guilt-driven sham that it is. Taxing the productive to reward the unproductive is about as stupid an idea as there ever was, but that doesn't keep the Susie Kendalls of the world from forcing it on us, whether it's in this school, in the state capital in Albany, or in Washington, DC."

"But there is another idea that keeps coming up," I continued, "and it's nearly as dumb as taxation, or theft, or 'mandatory minimum contributions,' or whatever they're calling it this week. And that dumb idea is voting." Now everyone, students and teachers alike, were murmuring in confusion. Even my friends sitting in back looked like they thought I had lost my mind.

"Let me ask you something," I said to my audience. "Suppose a scary motorcycle gang breaks into your home tonight. There are about twenty of these thugs circling around you and your parents, and they take everything. All of your parents' money, your money, your baby sister's money, the TV, the DVD player, your computer, everything. Would that be right or wrong?"

Nobody said anything.

"Come on. That was an easy question," I insisted. "You, the girl in the front row. Karen Thomas, is it? Motorcycle gang takes everything in your house. Good thing or bad thing?"

Karen blushed. "That would be a bad thing, but if you're trying to equate this—"

"Uh-uh, not me," I said. "Karen Thomas says that would be a bad thing. That is the correct answer. Now the questions are going to get a little harder. Okay, suppose a scary motorcycle gang breaks into your home tonight. There are about twenty of these thugs circling around you and your parents. But they don't take everything. This time, they only take the DVD player. Would that be right or wrong? Yes, the young lady sitting next to Karen. Wendy Siegel, do you have an answer?"

"This is absurd," Wendy scoffed.

"Yes, it is, but it wasn't my idea," I replied. "Somebody else, perhaps? Let's try in back. Yes, the gentleman with his hand raised back there. Would taking your parent's DVD player—but leaving everything else—be right or wrong?"

"That would be wrong," the kid answered.

"And why is that?" I asked.

"Because theft is still theft, whether they steal a lot or a little," he explained. "The amount doesn't matter."

I nodded in agreement. "Did everybody hear that? Theft is theft, no matter what the amount stolen. Does anybody disagree with that?" Susie Kendall started to raise her hand, but quickly thought better of it.

"All right, this one will be harder. I promise. Ready? A scary motorcycle gang breaks into your home tonight. There are about twenty of these thugs circling around you and your parents. One of the thugs says, 'We're gonna have us a little vote to decide whether we should take all of your stuff. You people get to vote too.' They count the votes and there are twenty votes in favor of the gang taking all your stuff, and three votes—you and your parents—opposed. The gang takes everything. Your father tries to protest, but the gang just laughs and says it was majority rule. Democracy in action. Is that right or wrong?"

"Wrong!" a bunch of kids yelled.

"Wow, I'm impressed," I said. "I thought that question was going to stump you. Who can tell me why it would be wrong? Isn't majority rule the American way? No? What went wrong?" A girl in the third row raised her hand. "Yes?"

The girl stood up and said, "It's wrong because the motorcycle gang had no right to put my parents' property up for a vote. They were still using the their strength in numbers and physical size to take what they wanted. The vote just gave them a phony way to make the robbery look fair, but my family didn't freely agree to the vote. Otherwise, any large group of people could take anything they wanted from any smaller group of people and call it democracy."

Now it was my turn to applaud. "Excellent. That was a perfect answer. Now, what if they voted just to take the DVD player?"

"Duh!" the girl exclaimed. "It would still be wrong for the same reasons."

"What if the motorcycle gang promised to give the DVD player to some poor kids who didn't have a DVD player of their own?"

"Duh!" she repeated with more emphasis.

Many of the other kids in the audience were now nodding in agreement. Time to reel this fish in, I decided. "One last question. Instead of a motorcycle gang, what if it's a gang of do-gooder students, teachers and school administrators? This gang is still bigger and stronger than you. What if, instead of your DVD player, they just wanted a cut of your money? And they tell you that you're going to vote on this and have to go along with whatever the majority decides. Would that be right or wrong?"

"Wrong!" almost everybody in the gymnasium yelled.

"What was that?" I asked in jest, cupping a hand to my ear. "I can't hear you!"

"WRONG!" they yelled again.

I smiled and walked to the front of the stage. "It's wrong. Theft is theft, even if the thieves put it to a vote and call it a "mandatory minimum contribution" and even if the thieves want to do something really nice with the money once they've robbed you. Your money that you earned is yours. Do whatever you want with it. Save it, spend it, or give it away voluntarily. If a gang of thieves is going to take some of your money, try to stop them if you can. If you can't, then you may have to give up some of your money to survive. But whatever you do, don't think you can beat them at their own game. You can't. The game is fixed, just like the vote with the motorcycle gang and your family. Your dad isn't going to convince a majority of the motorcycle gang to vote against the theft, and you're not going to convince a majority here to vote to do the right thing. Even if you could, you shouldn't have to, because as we just proved, the thieves have no right to call a vote in the first place. Voting will only let them sleep better at night. Don't give them the satisfaction. Refuse to play along in this sham."

Cheers and applause erupted. A standing ovation started in the back of the gymnasium and spread to the front. Most of the do-gooders stayed seated. I looked at Karen Thomas, and I noticed that Wendy Siegel was watching her too. Karen hesitated, but after a few seconds she stood and joined the applause. She was smiling at me.

What a pretty smile, I thought.

Mr. Atkins walked back onto the stage to take the microphone from me. Before he could, I decided to say one more thing. "Oh yeah, here's a bonus question. Don't answer it now. Save it for the dinner table tonight with your parents. What if the gang calls itself "the government," and they call the theft "taxes?" Thanks again. You've been a beautiful audience! And don't forget to order from Desserts Express!"

A red-faced Mr. Atkins shook visibly as he seized the microphone and tried to speak. "Th-that was outrageous. Disgraceful. You all should be ashamed of yourselves for applauding such boorishness." He looked around the gym, probably hoping that someone would tell him what to do next.

Raising her hand, Susie Kendall asked on cue, "Are we going to have the vote now?"

"Uh, vote?" Mr. Atkins mumbled. "Yes, of course. I know all of you—or at least most of you—will search your consciences and vote accordingly. When you have marked your ballot, please pass it to the end of your row, and then pass them forward to the center."

Neil crumpled his ballot into a ball and tossed it toward the stage, but it fell short and landed on the gymnasium floor around center court.

"Who threw that?" Mr. Atkins shouted as he glanced around the audience. Two more balled-up ballots joined Neil's. Then another one. Vic and I both threw ours. "Stop it! I'm getting all of your names down. Everyone who throws a paper ball is looking at a detention. Just stop it this instant!"

Dozens of balled-up ballots dropped onto the court, and in less than a minute there were hundreds. The Sharing is Caring vote was over. The tyranny of the majority had been overthrown before it could even start.

As we made our way out of the gym back to our classrooms, I spotted Susie Kendall standing by herself near the stage. Her eyes looked red and puffy even from a distance. I don't know if she was crying for the poor special-ed students, or for herself.

Chapter Twelve

Christmas

As far as I know, nothing more was ever said about the mandatory contributions to the Sharing is Caring program after that student assembly. The sympathy that once existed for Susie's scheme dried up. I think she and a handful of other nerds quietly gave the little money that was raised to the special-education teachers, who used it for a pizza party for their students the day before the "holiday break."

Speaking of the holidays, it was a merry Christmas indeed for Desserts Express. We processed hundreds of orders for Christmas cookies and quite a few Hanukkah treats as well, like jelly donuts and latkes. I felt a little like Ebenezer Scrooge, keeping all our employees working their butts off right up through Christmas Eve. Sam and I agreed to close up for Christmas itself and the day after, however. Unlike Halloween, when we failed to get into the spirit of things, we were both hardcore Christmas junkies. Only the incredible amount of money we were bringing in kept our minds focused on business leading up to the big day.

When our employees left our mom's kitchen on Christmas Eve, Sam and I handed each of them an envelope with a card and a large holiday bonus—the size varying according to the employee's recent performance. None was for less than one hundred dollars.

That was Sam's idea, and it was another great one. Our employees had earned our gratitude, and we had earned their loyalty.

"Two thousand dollars!" our mom screamed when she opened her envelope and looked inside after everyone but Sam and I had gone. "Have you boys lost your minds?"

"Probably," I grinned, "but Sam insisted on doing something good before Santa visits."

Our mom stuffed the bills back in the envelope and held it out toward us. "This is crazy. Here, take it back. I can't accept this."

"Sure you can, Mom," Sam said. "Just keep it somewhere Frank won't find it."

"Like the snow blower," I added helpfully. "He never touches that." We already had a couple of early winter blizzards, and I was the only one who had bothered to clear the driveway. I would have ignored it and let Frank get snowed in, but we needed to keep the driveway clear for our employees and suppliers.

"That's not what I meant. You boys may be the bosses, but you're still my children, and I can't take this much money from you."

I shook my head. "You're not taking money from us. You earned every cent. You're our best employee. Keep up the good work, and it may be even bigger next year."

"You're not just doing this because I'm your mother?"

Sam shrugged. "What if we were? It's our money, and we can do what we want with it. But no, we're giving you that money because it's the smart thing to do. If you're happy, our customers are happy. And it's a lot less expensive than giving you a raise."

I elbowed Sam jokingly. "I told you not to use the R word."

Our mom laughed and placed the envelope in her purse. "Well if you put that way," she said. "Let's go. Santa's going to pass by our house if he sees you two up this late."

Or he might pass out on our couch, I thought, as the three of us trudged through the back door of our home and saw Frank slumped on the living room sofa, holding a glass of red wine as he stared through bloodshot eyes at the Christmas tree. The Beach Boys Christmas CD was playing quietly on the stereo.

"Merry Christmas, dear," our mother called out cheerfully as she kicked off her slushy boots before walking over to give Frank a peck on the cheek.

"Merry Christmas," he replied coldly without looking at her.

I decided I would make an effort to be nice to the big creep in the spirit of the season. Big mistake. "Merry Christmas, Frank," I said.

Frank slowly turned his head and looked at me with barely concealed contempt. "Merry Christmas, Mark. You too, Sam," he slurred before turning around and pouring the remainder of his bottle of wine into his glass.

"I think I'll have a cup of coffee," Mom said. "Would you like one, Frank?"

"No."

Mom looked oddly at Frank for a moment and went to the kitchen. As much as we didn't enjoy Frank's company, Sam and I both liked sitting around the Christmas tree when it was all lit up, so we were still there when our mom returned with a steaming mug in her hands.

"I thought I told you boys to hit the hay," our mom chastised us. "Santa's probably passing by our house right now." I hoped she was spouting all this Santa stuff for Sam's benefit. I would have felt insulted if she thought I still bought into it. Even Sam was probably at the age where he knew better, or at least suspected.

"Aw, Mom," Sam whined.

"Santa came while you were out," Frank mumbled with a jabbing gesture toward the bottom of the tree.

"Oh look, Frank's right!" our mother exclaimed. "All the presents are here."

"Can we open them now?" my brother and I asked in unison.

"Well, I don't know," our mother said. "What do you think, dear?" Frank grunted and drained his glass. Our mother smiled at us and nodded. Sam and I tore into the gifts like starving dogs.

We unwrapped an impressive pile of video games, board games, CDs, books and assorted clothing. (Clothes couldn't be avoided. They're the green vegetables of Christmas presents.) The loot was especially impressive, considering our mother's recent business problems. She probably would have bought us even more if she'd known she was getting a bonus from Desserts Express, which was one of the reasons we waited until the last minute to give it to her.

Midway through our gift-opening frenzy, Sam and I remembered our mom's present. Excusing ourselves, we ran upstairs to Sam's bedroom and returned lugging a large gift box. We gently laid it on the coffee table in front of our surprised mother.

"But you already gave me such a generous gift," she protested, referring to the bonus.

"What was that?" Frank asked. Great, now he decides to pay attention.

"Huh? Oh, I just meant that having two sweet sons was the best gift a mother could ask for." Nice recovery, Mom. Frank stood up and stumbled to the wine rack to retrieve another bottle.

As our mother carefully unwrapped the present before her, her mouth hung open. "I don't believe it," she gasped.

"Do you really like it, Mom?" Sam asked as he jumped onto the spot on the couch where Frank had been sitting.

Wrapping one arm around my little brother and lifting the gift with her other hand, she exclaimed, "It's exquisite. How in the world did you know?"

The gift was an antique spice cabinet that our mother had noticed in a local shop more than a year ago. It was made of green-stained wood with a leafy design on its two doors. If it were up to me, I would have dismissed it as someone's old junk that belonged in a yard sale, but our mother thought it had tremendous value. The seller agreed and priced it sky-high, which was why our mother had never purchased it for herself.

"We have reliable sources," I answered with a grin.

"Where did you kids get money for something like that?" Frank asked accusingly as he poured another glass of merlot.

Ignoring his question, I cheerfully tossed a small package in Frank's lap. "Here, we didn't forget you either."

Frank unwrapped it and held up the gift. It was a red and black necktie that Sam and I took about all of thirty seconds to pick out at Wal-Mart.

"Oh, it's lovely," our mother bluffed.

"Thanks," Frank said quietly. He pointed to our pile of loot. "Some of those gifts are from me."

"Thanks, Frank," Sam said for both of us, or so I assumed.

Our mother sat on the couch admiring the antique spice rack in her hands. "I just don't believe it," she repeated.

"Me neither," Frank mumbled sarcastically. Then in entirely too loud a voice, he said, "You kids must think I'm stupid."

With my back turned as I ejected the Beach Boys Christmas CD from the stereo and replaced it with one of the new disks I just received, I said, "If we thought you were stupid, we would have bought you a clip-on tie." Sam giggled.

Frank finished his glass and, in a drunken slur, bellowed, "You kids think I'm *really stupid*. You think I don't see what's going on around here! I know all about this little underground cookie business of yours."

Sam and I looked at him in genuine surprise. We knew he would figure it out some day, but we had hoped to delay it for as long as possible.

"Please, Frank," our mother pleaded gently. "Let's just all enjoy ourselves and be kind to each other, tonight of all nights. Let me pour you another glass."

Frank ignored her and glared at me. "I also heard about that stunt you pulled down at the middle school, ruining the holiday charity drive. That's right. I'm the superintendent, you know. You think this stuff gets past me?"

"I think I don't care," I answered.

"You'd better care, mister," he said with a menacing smile. "Because it's all coming to an end. I won't be made a fool of in my own home."

"This isn't your home," Sam observed.

"Shut up, you little brat."

"Frank!" our mom shouted. "Stop it this instant. You're behaving like a drunken fool!"

"You think you're so smart, Mark, with your little junior achievement enterprise and your heartless libertarian rhetoric. You even have your little brother Sam brainwashed. It's easy to be smug while you're sitting in this nice warm house in front of a Christmas tree, and you can sit back and have your minions sell your little desserts. Meanwhile, the *real* economy in this town and in this entire country is going to the dogs. Well, enjoy it while it lasts, because it's all coming to an end." Frank was smiling for the first time in months.

"What kind of nonsense are you yapping about?" I asked. I didn't want to let on, but his drunken threats had me a little concerned.

Frank smirked and nodded. "You'll find out, smart guy. You won't be buying anymore expensive antiques, that's for darn sure." Standing up on wobbly legs, he loomed over our mother's spice cabinet and pointed at it with his wine glass. "Look at that thing. Why I—"

The dark red wine slopped over the brim of Frank's glass onto the face of the cabinet. "Frank!" our mother screamed.

"You unbelievable jerk!" Sam yelled.

"It was, uh, an accident," Frank said sheepishly as he clumsily blotted at the wine stain with the edge of his bathrobe.

Our mother pushed his hand away. "Leave it alone! You're making it worse!" she cried as she struggled to hold back tears.

"You've done more than enough already. Just go to bed!" Frank tried to put a reassuring hand on her shoulder, but our mother shrugged it away and ran with her spice cabinet to the kitchen to try to remove the wine stain.

Frank and I scowled at each other. "You have something to say?" he barked.

Actually, there was a lot I wanted to say, but just as I was about to lay into this rotten excuse for a man, I noticed Sam, who was still sitting on the couch right behind Frank. The horrible look on my little brother's face startled me. It wasn't the timid look I had come to expect from him. It was more of a white-hot anger. All the color had washed out his face, and he peered at Frank through squinted eyes that reminded me of a midget-size Clint Eastwood. Although I was four years older and ten inches taller than him, at that moment my little brother frightened me.

Noticing that my eyes were focused behind him, Frank turned his head and looked down. "What about you then, Sam? Do you have something you want to say to me? Huh? You better not, if you know what's good for you."

No, Sam didn't have anything to say to Frank, at least not verbally. But he did have a message for Frank. Without even getting off the couch, Sam lunged forward and sank his teeth into Frank's arm, just below the wrist. Frank howled in pain and dropped his wine glass, which shattered on the coffee table.

The bite probably only lasted a second or two, but it seemed frozen in time. When Sam finally released his teeth from Frank's wrist and stood up, Frank tried to smack Sam with his other hand. Luckily, Frank was too old and drunk, and Sam was too small and quick, and the old guy's open palm breezed harmlessly above Sam's head. The color returned to my little brother's face, and I watched in amazement as he calmly picked up a few of his Christmas gifts and walked upstairs to his bedroom. Frank sat back on the couch, clutching his injured arm and whimpering pathetically.

I decided that would be a good time to follow Sam upstairs with my presents. It was a good thing we opened the gifts early this year, I thought.

Chapter Thirteen

New Money

Business slowed down a little at the start of the New Year, but that was understandable considering the boom we had leading up to Christmas. Desserts Express was still pulling in serious money, and so were the businesses run by Neil, Vic, Karen and the other kids of Walton. Almost every day we lost a good employee when some kid quit to start his own enterprise. Sam and I didn't mind, because we already had a list of other kids who wanted to work for us, and because the new businesses were usually brilliant ideas that quickly made all of us better off.

One employee we knew we couldn't afford to lose was Celeste Szuck. Ever since we brought our mom on as a second supplier, Sam and I noticed a hint of jealousy from Celeste, even though we kept her just as busy as ever. If she ever decided to go into competition against us, our business would take a beating. We decided the best way to buy her loyalty was with an equity stake in the business, so we offered Celeste one-third ownership of Desserts Express. She accepted immediately. That would prove to be one of the smartest business decisions we could make, as Celeste threw herself into her new role as our business partner.

While the children's underground economy was booming, nobody could say the same about the grown-up version. Every morning at the breakfast table, Frank made us listen to that stupid NPR radio show he liked. The business news was grim. Retailers had their worst Christmas season that anyone could remember, which capped off the worst overall year for sales in decades. More layoffs were inevitable.

Locally, the economy was even worse than the national slump. The property tax hike that Frank had helped to push through had the predictable effect, which is to say the opposite effect of what Frank and the other bureaucrats intended. Instead of increasing revenue for the township, the new taxes were the straw that broke the camel's back for many families in Walton, and a lot of them moved out. Fewer families in town meant even fewer people spending money at the grown-up businesses. That meant fewer sales taxes for the town. With so many families fleeing Walton at once, there were suddenly more homes for sale than there were buyers. Desperate families cut the asking prices on their homes. Since property taxes are based on property values, the bottom line was that Walton was now taking in less money in property taxes than before the hike.

All of this was even having a small effect on our kid-run businesses. Sure, we were growing fast, but we'd be growing even faster if we didn't keep losing employees and customers whenever their parents fled town. What really started to hurt us was the inflation that was spinning out of control around the country. That stupid NPR show called it "stagflation," since it combined inflation with a stagnating economy. Usually you get inflation when the economy is overheating and prices rise too fast, NPR explained, not when it's grinding to a halt. But with the government taking in fewer taxes, the feds decided to print more money so they could keep up their spending.

"I don't get it," Sam told me one evening while we packed deliveries. "More money is a good thing, right? If they print more money, then we can all be rich."

"More money is a good thing when you earn it, but not when the government just prints more of it," I explained. "Money is just like anything else. The more there is, the less it's worth."

"I still don't get it."

I tried to be patient with my little brother. "Okay, look at it this way. You know that Derek Jeter rookie card you have on your desk? Dad spent a lot of money on that when he bought it for you. Do you know why it cost so much?"

"Well, sure," Sam said. "Because they're hard to find. Nobody knew how good Jeter would be when he was a rookie, and a lot of the cards probably got lost or damaged. Now everybody wants a Jeter rookie card, but there are only a few of them around, so they're worth a lot of money."

"That's right," I said. "Now imagine if Topps decided to go back and print a whole bunch of new rookie cards for Derek Jeter, so they could sell them and clean up."

"They can't do that," Sam objected. "Jeter isn't a rookie anymore. They're only allowed to print new cards with the current year on them, and the new ones aren't worth as much."

"I know that, Sam, but suppose they did it anyway. Suppose tomorrow they started printing more of the rookie cards, thousands of them, and the new cards were identical to the old ones. What would that do to the price of your card?"

Sam thought about that for a moment. "If it's not so rare anymore, I guess the price of my Jeter rookie card would go down."

I nodded. "That's right. It's the same thing with money. We thought our dollars were worth a certain amount, because there were only so many of them. Then the government tricked us and started printing a whole bunch more of them because the politicians were greedy, and now there are so many dollars around that the money in that little safe under your bed isn't worth as much as it used to be."

"Holy cow," Sam exclaimed. It took him a moment to understand what I'd told him, but then he got it. "It's like they stole money right out of my bank to spend on themselves, and they didn't even have to go into my room to do it."

"That's about the size of it," I agreed.

While Sam and I talked, one of our best employees, a pretty little girl about Sam's age named Alana Poponna, was listening while she worked. She always struck me as being not only cute but incredibly bright, and we knew it was only a matter of time before she would move on to bigger and better things. As it turned out, that time would come sooner than we thought.

Alana finished her job even faster than usual and rushed home that night. But instead of going directly home, she went the opposite direction on Walton Street to the home of David and Harrison Wolfe, a couple of kids who had turned their interest in baseball cards into a thriving trading card, comic book and collectibles store. After casually looking at the prices of various cards, pretending she was buying a gift for her father, Alana asked about the Derek Jeter rookie card. The Wolfe brothers had three in stock, which they were selling for twelve dollars each. Alana shrewdly negotiated a deal to take all three cards for thirty bucks. That seemed like a rather strange gift, Harrison Wolfe told her, and he suggested some other players for variety. The customer was always right, however. Alana took her three cards, and she told them to email her when they came across more that could be had for a good price.

We all soon learned just what Alana had in mind, and it turned out to be sheer genius. The next day, all the kids in Walton received an email announcing the grand opening of Alana's Bank. Like most banks, this one would offer deposit accounts and loans. However, unlike any other bank in the United States since the end of the Civil War, Alana's Bank would issue its own currency.

Specifically, it printed jeters.

While the dollar was backed by the full faith and credit of the United States, the jeter was paper currency backed by something of real value. Each jeter note was marked "redeemable for one mint condition Derek Jeter 1993 Upper Deck rookie card." Alana's Bank also issued two-jeter, half-jeter, and quarter-jeter notes. Businesses and consumers alike were encouraged to open accounts with Alana's Bank and to buy and sell exclusively with jeters, which were virtually inflation-proof. The jeter notes were also much more practical for carrying around in one's wallet or pocket than actual baseball cards or other things of value that could be exchanged for good and services.

The wild inflation of the U.S. dollar made the jeter the currency of choice among the children of Walton. Within a few days, we converted the price list for Desserts Express from dollars to jeters, and most of the other kids' businesses followed suit. Before long, kids were turning up their noses at traditional greenbacks or insisting on a premium price from anyone who could only pay in dollars.

In addition to curing much of our inflation problem overnight, Alana's Bank made business easier for us in many other ways. For the first time, we could conduct purely electronic transactions. None of us kids could get traditional checking accounts or credit cards, which we needed for online business. Now, however, somebody ordering cookies from Desserts Express could just email their order to us and copy Alana Poponna, and Alana's Bank would automatically transfer the right amount of jeters from the customer's account to ours.

Of course, we weren't completely insulated from inflation. All of us, to some degree, had to buy things in the adult economy, and those businesses weren't yet taking payment in jeters. Desserts Express needed to buy eggs, flour and other raw ingredients every day, and our suppliers demanded old-fashioned government currency for those purchases.

For better or worse, we couldn't completely protect ourselves from the harmful side effects of dealing with the miserable adult economy. Little did we know, however, that the adults would soon go from nuisance to menace.

While we were all spending lots of time working and making money, none of us was spending much time in the classroom. This didn't bother me much, since I had long ago decided that John Dewey Middle School was a huge waste of my time. But I felt a slight pang of guilt that Sam was starting to miss school more often, since I vaguely recalled third grade being the last time I learned anything useful—multiplication and division, I think. On the other hand, I could teach him that stuff, and he would get lots of chances to practice his math skills on the job.

To be honest, though, I was also growing a little worried about my own education. If we were going to continue to grow Desserts Express, there were things I needed to know. Common sense and good instincts can take you a long way in business, especially when you're able to avoid taxes and stupid regulations, but even I had to admit there were a few areas where some formal business education would be helpful. My bookkeeping skills, for example, sucked. Tracking inventory was another problem. We had to shut down our kitchen for an hour one afternoon when we ran out of sugar and butter.

The other kids were going through similar growing pains. Neil finally decided to do something about it. One Friday afternoon in late January on the bus ride home from school, we noticed that Neil's book bag was overstuffed.

"What's with you?" I asked. "You think you can catch up on everything you missed over the past five months?"

"The heck with that," Neil replied. "I'm bringing home all the stuff that was in my locker. Today was my last day at Dewey."

Vic and I glanced at each other. "I think he might be serious," Vic said.

"You bet I am," Neil said with a big grin.

I shook my head. Neil was obviously cracking up under the stress of running his many enterprises. "Um, you see, the thing of it is, Neil, the government owns you for the next few years. You're a political prisoner, held against your will by the state without being convicted of any crime. You try to leave school before you're sixteen, and New York State sends the truant officer to come get you."

"That's what you think, Mark. I'm not completely free, but it's pretty darn close. I guess you might say I'm under house arrest."

Now Vic thought Neil was losing it. "What in the world are you talking about?"

Neil's grin widened. "My parents have agreed to homeschool me."

"Homeschool you?" I exclaimed. "You mean like one of those wacko religious families upstate?"

"Or like those racist militias out west?" Vic asked suspiciously. "How come you haven't shaved your head?"

"Yuk-yuk," Neil said. "Very funny. That just shows how narrow-minded you two buttheads are to think of homeschoolers in those stereotypes."

"Okay. Enlighten us, Cletus, I mean Neil," I said with a smirk.

Neil ignored the jab at his newfound white-trashiness. "All kinds of kids are homeschooled for all kinds of reasons. It isn't just for Jesus freaks and militias anymore. Then again, my dad did say I could study ballistics for the math component of my curriculum."

"What curriculum?" Vic asked. "You mean, whatever you feel like doing that day."

"I wish. It's not that loose, but my parents are giving me a lot of leeway. The state makes all homeschoolers submit a formal lesson plan for the year that includes 900 hours of home classroom time. Also, there are certain subjects that have to be covered, and I'll still have to take all those stupid standardized tests every couple years."

I shook my head. "Some things you just can't escape, I guess."

"Yup. But other than that, I can pretty much study whatever interests me, at whatever time of day suits me. And right now, the subjects that interest me are running a small but growing business, and of course, guns and fishing."

Wow. I must admit I was envious. Sam and I wondered if our mother could be persuaded to homeschool us. There wasn't a chance, we both knew deep down, but we could always hope. Her dopey boyfriend Frank was the superintendent of the Walton public school system, after all, and he would take it as a slap in the face. Not that Sam and I wouldn't have loved to slap him, of course. Our mother was still a big believer in the public schools herself, for that matter. She was always talking about how the public schools made our country great and gave everyone an equal opportunity. They gave everyone an equal waste of time, if you ask me. And time was something that was getting more valuable to us every day we were in business.

The more Neil told us about his custom-made curriculum, the more jealous I got. For starters, the whole thing would only take about three to four hours a day, and he could schedule it any time of day or night. So if his businesses demanded his undivided attention all afternoon, Neil could spend an hour in the morning in class and another three hours after dinner. While the rest of us were rotting in Dewey Middle School, Neil would be making money.

In fact, he told us that some of his work would actually count toward "educational credit." His businesses were just one big field trip. The little time he did spend listening to actual lessons from his mother or reading textbooks almost entirely related directly to his businesses.

Because of Neil's peculiar academic interests, his father hired some tutors who were doctoral students at Columbia University's School of Business. The tutors worked with Neil on stuff that the rest of us couldn't hope to see until high school or college—accounting, microeconomics, marketing and management. Neil was getting the middle school version of an executive MBA.

After a few weeks of hearing about the joys of educational freedom from Neil, I had enough. As I suspected, my mom wouldn't even consider homeschooling for me, but I decided there was no reason I couldn't supplement public school with some actual education. It would put even more demands on my time, but after talking it over with Sam, I decided it was a good investment. I talked to a few of Neil's tutors, and they agreed to take me on as an additional client. Vic signed up too, as did Karen Thomas. Twice a week, we all headed over to Neil's house after school for our customized business studies seminar.

If Miss Farkas or any of our other teachers had seen us, they wouldn't have believed their eyes. Three of the worst troublemakers in the history of John Dewey Middle School were voluntarily sitting in a classroom, listening to a teacher they had hired using their own money. There were no spitballs, wisecracks or crude bodily noises. The only sounds were pencils scribbling furiously, calculator buttons clicking, and serious, thoughtful questions being asked.

For the first time in years, I felt challenged by class work.

"What are you guys up to anyway?" Karen asked one evening as we were leaving Neil's house, our brains fried from a lecture on Nash Equilibrium pricing theory.

"The same thing you're up to, Karen," I replied with a smile. "We're just trying to get a good education."

"Give me a break," she said as she rolled her eyes. "You haven't cared about getting a good education in the eight years I've known you."

I shrugged. "I never had the opportunity for a good education until now. You know that. You're a model student. I'll bet you learned more tonight than you've learned all year at Dewey."

Karen giggled. "I'm not saying. That reminds me... I have to get home and work on my diorama for social studies class. It's going to show Sacagawea guiding the Lewis and Clark expedition. I'll probably be up all night."

"And that busy-work will give you a good education how?"

She thought about it for a moment. "Well, maybe I won't stay up *all* night."

"Give it ten minutes," I suggested.

"I suppose that sounds about right. But I'll have a hard time explaining to my parents that my grades are slipping because my classes were getting in the way of learning."

"They'll get over it," I assured her. "Sooner or later, we all have to stand up to our parents."

Little did I know how much sooner it would be.

Chapter Fourteen

Break-In at Daybreak

"Did you hear that?" Sam asked.

"Hear what?" It was 7:00 a.m. on a weekday morning, and we were already at work in our mom's old bakery, putting in a few hours before school. With Valentine's Day only two days away, we were checking our inventories of raw ingredients against the list of advance orders we had already received for the big day. Our storage room was overstuffed with cartons of baker's chocolate and sugar.

"It sounds like someone's at the front door," Sam answered.

"That's strange," I said. No one had used the front door of the shop area in months, since the health department closed our mother's business. "I'll go take a look."

Before I could move, we both heard the sound of wood splintering and the shop's front door slamming open. Two seconds later, a uniformed police officer and two men in suits and overcoats stormed the kitchen through the rear doorway, which we had left open.

"What's going on?" I demanded.

"This business is operating in violation of a Walton Department of Health order of closure," announced the older of the two plain-clothes men. "We have an order to confiscate the equipment and inventory, and to arrest the owner, Ellen Hoffman. You two children need to follow this officer outside." Two more cops who had broken down the front door now joined us in the kitchen.

Sam jumped down from the counter where he had been sitting. "There must be some mistake!"

"I'll say!" I yelled. "You have it all wrong, mister. Ellen Hoffman doesn't own this business."

The younger guy in the suit looked down at me with a sneer. "Oh really, kid? Then who does?"

I swallowed and tried not to sound nervous as I pointed to Sam and myself and said, "We do."

"And who are you?" the younger guy asked.

"None of your business!" Sam yelled. Everybody in the room gasped at the little kid with the big mouth, but probably nobody was more surprised than Sam himself.

"You know," I added, now that Sam's outburst had boosted my own courage, "my colleague makes a good point. The question isn't who are we, but who the heck are you? We'd like to see some identification, as well as a warrant."

It seemed like a reasonable request to me, but it pushed our intruders over the edge. The older guy turned purple with rage.

"Why you little punks, I told you to follow the officer outside now!" He grabbed Sam and me each by the collar and yanked us toward the door.

"Get your hands off me!" I shouted while dragging my feet. "Let go! Let go!"

The first police officer stepped towards us and set a hand on the older guy's shoulder. "Okay, everybody calm down. Mr. Wilkens, let go of the youths. Boys, you do have to step outside now. See this badge? It's real. My name is Officer Hevia, and my badge number is 0458." Mr. Wilkens let go of us. Sam and I looked at each other and at the cop. "Do this the easy way, and I won't have to put you in handcuffs," Officer Hevia added. With that, we followed him out the door to our backyard.

Just as we stepped outside, our mother and Frank came out the backdoor of the house. Mom looked hysterical, but Frank was suspiciously calm.

"What's going on out here?" our mother demanded. "Has there been another fire?"

"One lousy fire," I muttered, "and we're marked for life!"

"There's no fire, ma'am," Mr. Wilkens said. "Are you Ellen Hoffman?"

"Yes."

"Mrs. Hoffman, the contents of your shop are being confiscated by the Walton Department of Health, and you are under arrest for operating a food business in disregard of an order from the Department of Health."

"But I don't own the store anymore," our mother explained almost tearfully. "I went out of business last fall, after you bastards ruined me with your stupid fines."

Mr. Wilkens glanced from my mother to me, and I shrugged. "Told you so," I said.

"Mrs. Hoffman, these two boys claim that they are the owners of the business that is obviously operating out of your former shop. Is that true?"

My mother hesitated before answering. "I'm not saying anymore without a lawyer, and neither are they." Good answer, Mom, I thought.

"Oh, don't be ridiculous, Ellen," Frank interjected. "Of course these two delinquents run their little black-market racket out of your old shop. They've got you so wrapped around their little fingers that they have you covering for them. Somebody had to put a stop to this nonsense."

With her jaw drooping to her neckline, our mother gasped, "Frank? You know about this?"

Frank nodded with authority and coiled an arm around my mother's shoulders, but she quickly shrugged him off. "You'll thank me for this later, Ellen, I promise. Your boys will too, someday."

"I'll thank you if you have a heart attack, Frank," I said.

Glaring at me for a moment, Frank turned to Mr. Wilkens. "What happens now?"

Mr. Wilkens looked a little confused, as though things weren't going quite according to his plan. "Well, um, Ms. Hoffman, if these children are the ones who have been operating an unlicensed business on these premises, then I'm afraid we are going to have to take them down to the police station and process them."

"You're putting my babies in jail?!" she shrieked, pushing Frank off her again.

"We're not babies!" Sam insisted.

"No, no, of course not," said Mr. Wilkens. "We just have to process them, and then we'll release the youths into your custody, assuming you are their parent or guardian. You can follow us down to the station. The whole thing won't take more than an hour or so."

Officer Hevia set one hand on my shoulder and another on Sam. "Okay, boys. You heard Mr. Wilkens. Let's go."

Sam broke away and ran to our mother, wrapping his arms around her waist and burying his face in her apron. "Mommy, I don't want to go to the police station! Please don't let them take me!" Our mother stroked Sam's hair, as she has always done when comforting one of her children, but she didn't know what to say.

Of course, Frank wasn't short of words at all. "I thought you weren't a baby," he snorted. "You break the rules, you pay the price."

"Frank, haven't you had that heart attack yet?" I asked. "We really would appreciate it."

"You watch your mouth, Mark," he answered as he pointed a finger at me. "Don't dig your hole any deeper."

"Go to hell, you jerk."

Then Frank made his big mistake. He go so mad at me that he took his frustration out on Sam and tried to pry him from my mother's waist. "Come on, kid," he huffed as he pulled at my little brother. "Let go. The officer gave you an order."

Mom slapped Frank across the face, which stunned him like a deer caught in a headlight. "Don't you *ever* touch either of my children again," she said in a low menacing voice. Frank quietly stepped away, as the cops and health department guys looked at our mom and then at each other, hoping someone would tell them what to do.

Stooping down, she took the same hand that seconds ago had struck out so violently and caressed it gently along Sam's face as she looked him in the eyes. "It's okay, Sammy. Nothing will happen to you. I promise. I'll follow right behind you in my car, and you'll be able to see me the whole way. Mark will be in the police car with you, and we'll all be back home before you know it."

"But... we didn't do anything wrong," Sam sniffled.

"I know, darling. I know." She gave my little brother a firm hug and wiped away his tears with her apron. "Now can you be a brave young man and go with your brother? Remember, I'll be right behind you, and I won't let anything happen."

"Okay," Sammy said quietly. He turned and walked back to Officer Hevia, who led us into the back of his patrol car.

On the short drive to the police station, I tried to cheer Sam up. "This is kind of like an adventure, Sam. You can tell all your friends tomorrow that you got to ride in the back of a police car. Maybe we'll even get fingerprinted."

"You think so?" he asked with a half-smile. Sam leaned into the perforated opening in the Plexiglas divider. "Excuse me, are you going to fingerprint us?"

Officer Hevia's partner answered, "Nah, I don't think so. We just have to fill out some paperwork for you, and then we release you to your mother."

"Oh." Sam looked vaguely disappointed. "How come you didn't handcuff us?"

"It was tempting for awhile there," Officer Hevia laughed. "I thought we might have to Mace you to get you to cooperate."

"What's Mace?" Sam asked. The two policemen explained tear gas, billy clubs and other instruments of law-enforcement persuasion for the rest of the ride. I wasn't sure whether they were trying to entertain us or intimidate us, but we mostly enjoyed the conversation.

When we arrived at the Walton Township Police Station, Sam and I couldn't believe our eyes.

"Hey, Mark," said Sam as we entered the musty municipal building, "I don't think I'll need to wait until school tomorrow to tell my friends what happened. Half of them are right here."

He wasn't kidding. There were dozens, perhaps hundreds, of scared kids and their angry parents milling about the stationhouse, as frantic officers tried to maintain order.

"Holy cow," gasped Officer Hevia. "What the heck is going on around here?"

What was going on was unknown to all but a handful of bureaucrats in the local government, such as School Superintendent Frank Rito, but the rest of us would soon find out.

Normally in a town the size of Walton, the police make about one arrest a day during the busy periods, so they were totally overwhelmed by the chaotic scene taking place. A sergeant with a clipboard came by and asked our arresting officers for our names. "Okay, Hoffman. Got it. Greg, you're going to have to wait with these kids for awhile while we process some of the others that came in ahead of you. We'll get you on a desk in about twenty minutes."

"What's this all about?" asked Officer Hevia's partner.

The sergeant rolled his eyes and replied, "It's a long story, Joe, and you have no time to hear it. Greg can process these two by himself. You need to get back in your car and pick up another one of these little perps over on Spruce Street."

"Jeez-o-Pete, why don't they just give us a list of who not to arrest?" the cop named Joe asked. "It looks like half the kids in Walton are already here."

"Yeah, well never mind that," said the sergeant. "Just get over to Spruce on the double."

As Officer Joe headed out the front entrance of the station house, our mother entered, looking worried as she scanned the room for us.

"Over here, Mom," I waved at her.

As she approached us, she continued to look about the room, and her expression became even more troubled. "What on earth…?" she asked no one in particular. Officer Hevia, Sam and I all shrugged in reply.

Moments later Neil Jones walked through the front door—or rather, Neil was pushed unwillingly through the front door by a huge plainclothes cop wearing dark sunglasses, a cheap black suit and a sneer. Neil's hands appeared to be cuffed behind his back.

"Knock it off!" Neil yelled. "I'm suing you for false arrest and excessive use of force!"

"I'll be happy to show you some excessive force anytime you want," said the plainclothes cop in a deep, intimidating voice. "Now have a seat." He grabbed Neil by the shoulders and pushed him to the floor next to a file cabinet. Neil grimaced in pain as he landed on his cuffed wrists.

For some reason, that cop's voice seemed very familiar.

Our mother charged into action. "I saw that!" she yelled. "That's a thirteen-year-old boy for goodness sake, not some common criminal. How dare you treat him like that!"

The cop's sneer broadened to a wicked grin as he approached us, and even our brave mom took a step back. "Well, well, well, if it isn't Walton's favorite family of dope dealers and criminals, the Hoffmans. I should have known these delinquents would be here."

I did know that deep voice, and that evil face. He was Karen's father!

Our mother looked really confused and scared now. She looked to Officer Hevia for an explanation, but he wasn't about to provide one. In fact, Officer Hevia looked somewhat intimidated himself by the plainclothes lieutenant.

"Mom, that's the cop who arrested Dad," I said.

"Oh," she said as she glared at Lieutenant Thomas. Man, I thought I'd seen her angry before, but nothing like this. Her green eyes shot pure hatred at the man who had taken away her husband and the father of her children. Her usually pink complexion changed to crimson, while her knuckles turned white from clenching the straps of her purse.

"It's okay, Mom," said Sam, trying to comfort her. "Everything is going to be okay, remember?"

She looked down at Sam and nodded, as she loosened the death-grip on her purse. Then she turned to Lieutenant Thomas and motioned toward Neil, "I demand that you un-handcuff that boy immediately. He's no threat to anyone."

Lieutenant Thomas laughed humorlessly. "You're in no position to demand anything, lady. Just consider yourself lucky that I didn't get to arrest your two little hoodlums myself. But there's always next time, and with their type, there is always a next time. The apple doesn't fall very far from the tree, does it?" He pointed to Sam and me, and then he walked across the room to speak to another police officer.

We all watched Lieutenant Thomas for several seconds, until our mother snapped out of it and turned to Officer Hevia. "Well, what happens now? What do I have to sign?"

"The thing is, ma'am, we're a bit overwhelmed at the moment, as you can see," said Officer Hevia sheepishly. "It's going to be awhile before I can process them."

"How long?" our mother asked.

"Sorry, ma'am, but I don't know the answer to that. I'll do the best I can."

Noise and mayhem filled the room, as the small police force of Walton tried to cope with an unprecedented situation. Children cried while parents yelled. Then parents cried while children yelled. At one point a young female police officer cried while parents and children yelled at her.

For the most part, our group sat there quietly in the middle of the chaos as the minutes ticked away. Every few minutes, Officer Hevia would check with the officer with the clipboard to see if a desk had opened up, but would always return shaking his head. After nearly an hour, Sam, our mother and I were all sitting on the cold tile floor, since all the chairs were taken.

While we were waiting, I also had some time to think and try to sort the pieces of the puzzle.

"Sam, have you noticed anything about all the kids in this room?" I asked.

"Yeah, almost all of them are balling their eyes out."

I shook my head. "I meant besides that." Glancing toward Neil, who Lieutenant Thomas had left unguarded sitting on the floor, I motioned for him to come closer to us. Because Neil's hands were still cuffed behind him, he couldn't boost himself up, so he awkwardly scooted across the floor toward us.

"So what did they bust you for?" I asked Neil as he approached.

"A whole bunch of garbage," Neil scoffed. "Operating a business without a license, operating a business in a residential area, failure to collect New York State sales tax, failure to collect social security and Medicare taxes from my employees."

Our mother arched an eyebrow. "What employees?"

Neil smiled. "Gee, Mrs. Hoffman, you didn't think Mark and Sam were the only good businessmen at John Dewey, did you?" Sitting up straight and throwing his chest out slightly, Neil added, "I just opened my fifth business last week, and some of my tackle just got picked up for the summer LL Bean catalog." Everyone wished Neil heartfelt congratulations, including Officer Hevia.

"How about you guys?" Neil asked. "They get you for the same thing?"

"More or less," I answered.

"Goodness," my mother exclaimed. "Are all of these children here for running black-market businesses?"

I nodded. "That's what I've been thinking, Mom. There's Harrison and David Wolfe over there. They run a trading card and comic book shop. And that pretty little girl over there is Bethany DeLoof, who started a radio station...." As I pointed from kid to kid, I was able to identify at least one underground enterprise operated by each of them. I hadn't thought about it for awhile, but our children's economy had really been booming lately. Would today be the day it all ended? I wondered.

Our mother shook her head in bewilderment. "But it doesn't make any sense. Why would they pick on all these kids for running little businesses? Kids have always had lemonade stands and newspaper routes for as long as anyone can remember."

"Maybe they're jealous," Sam suggested. We all looked at him, but said nothing.

After another hour had passed, Lieutenant Thomas returned and lifted Neil by the collar, which was impressive, since Neil was a husky thirteen-year-old. "On your feet, Jones. Your old man is in the next room signing you out."

Our mother rose to her feet next. "But he came in after us." She paused and covered her mouth, as if she had just said something terrible. Turning to Neil, she explained, "Oh, I'm so sorry, Neil. I would never want you to stay in this place a second longer than you have to. It's just that—"

Neil shrugged. "Don't worry about it, Mrs. H. Fair is fair. Go ahead."

Lieutenant Thomas held up a finger. "Nobody goes anywhere until I say so. Jones is next." Turning to Officer Hevia and waving toward Sam and me, he added, "These two don't get processed until everyone else is done. Got it?"

"But I—" Officer Hevia started to protest.

"Got it?" Lieutenant Thomas repeated in a menacing whisper.

"Yes, sir."

Chapter Fifteen

The Hostile Takeover

Just as Lieutenant Thomas ordered, the police processed every other kid in the room before Sam and me, regardless of when they arrived. Officer Hevia's partner returned with his perp from Spruce Street, who happened to be my friend Vic Sanjay. We talked to him for about thirty minutes while the police waited for Vic's parents to come for him. Just as we suspected, Vic was busted for running an illegal business. When Vic's parents arrived, they signed a few forms, and minutes later they were leaving with him.

Szuck the Truck, I mean Celeste Szuck, our business partner in Desserts Express, arrived in the station house under police escort a few minutes before Vic's release. Apparently the Truck had put up quite a fight when the police came for her, and like Neil she wore handcuffs behind her back. She looked quite pale and sweaty, even more than usual. I wondered if it was possible for an obese twelve-year-old girl to have a heart attack.

"Please take the handcuffs off me," she begged the female officer escorting her. "They're cutting into my wrists. I can't feel my fingers!"

I wasn't surprised at that. Celeste's wrists were thicker than the average adult's calves.

With a sigh, the female officer reached for her key chain and Celeste's handcuffs. "If I take these off and we have a repeat of the scene at your house, I'm locking you up in the county jail."

"I'll be good," said the Truck as she rubbed the black-and-blue chafe marks on her freed wrists. "I promise. Thanks."

Not wanting to be rude, I waved discreetly to Celeste. After making a quick phone call and apparently not reaching anyone, Celeste pointed to us and spoke to her arresting officer, apparently asking permission to talk to us. The cop nodded, and Celeste waddled over.

Celeste told us that she put up a big fight when the police came to get her, because she somehow convinced herself that it was just another cruel prank arranged by the meaner kids at our school. How she imagined that some kids would have the power to get real police—or any adults—to participate in such a scheme was beyond me.

"We're all in this together, Celeste," I explained. "I think I've seen just about every kid in our school here today."

"Oh yeah?" said Celeste in a tone that was even more paranoid than usual. "What about Karen Thomas? I'll bet little miss perfect hasn't been through here."

As a matter of fact, now that she mentioned it, I hadn't seen Karen, although I had seen entirely too much of her old man.

"But Karen is in just as deep as the rest of us," Sam pointed out. "She's been running all those private parties right under her dad's nose."

Karen's parties had become the pre-teen, suburban version of the scene at an exclusive New York City nightclub. She and her friend Wendy Siegel leveraged the popularity of their middle-school clique into a lucrative enterprise. Although Karen usually dressed up her parties with some big theme to justify the high cover charge, kids were paying top dollar for the privilege of hanging out with the cool crowd for a few hours on a Saturday afternoon. And, just like a trendy nightclub, admission was tightly controlled so that there was always a wait list, which made the parties all the more desirable for kids with low self-esteem.

"Phooey!" Celeste scoffed. "Do you think that matters? She's connected. Her father is one of these cops."

"We know," I sighed, as I explained how Lieutenant Thomas decreed that Sam and I would be the last ones to go.

"Well, there you go," said Celeste triumphantly. "Karen Thomas has her father wrapped around her little finger, just like she has all the idiots in our school. She's probably behind this whole thing. She'll drive the rest of out of business, just because she can."

I shook my head. "That's crazy. I don't know why Karen isn't down here with the rest of us, but I'm sure she didn't have anything to do with this."

Celeste arched half of the single bushy eyebrow that spanned the length of her forehead and smiled suspiciously. "How do you know, Mark? Is Karen Thomas your girlfriend?"

"Heck no!" Like I had time for a girlfriend, especially one whose father put my own father in prison and apparently wanted the rest of my family there as well.

"You sure seem awfully protective of her."

Looking away, I mumbled, "Yeah, well, I'm not protective. I'm just trying to be fair." I wanted to tell Celeste that it was Karen who recommended her to me as our dessert supplier, but somehow it didn't seem like the right time.

About an hour later, Celeste's mother arrived and—after a lot of yelling and confusion—signed whatever forms she needed to sign and took Celeste home. Just as Celeste was finishing up, Officer Hevia finally escorted Sam, my mother and me to a desk. As promised, we were the last kids left. The three of us sat down in chairs in front of the desk, while Officer Hevia took a seat at an ancient-looking computer terminal.

"Okay, Mark and Sam, you are each being charged with one count of operating a retail food business without a license, conspiracy to operate a food business without a license, endangering the public health, willful violation of an order of the Department of Health, hiring under-age employees, unlawful hiring practices, and juvenile delinquency. Do you understand?"

"Not really," I said.

"Sounds like a bunch of baloney to me," Sam added.

"Me too," our mother concurred.

"Mrs. Hoffman," Officer Hevia continued, "you are charged with two counts of child neglect."

Our mother looked stunned. "How's that?"

"Well, you know," Officer Hevia mumbled. "You let Mark and Sam get away with all this stuff, and possibly even encouraged them."

Our mom stood up and slammed her hands on the desk, so that everyone, including the police officers nearby, jumped. "Encouraged them? You mean I encouraged them to be productive? Is that now a crime?"

"Of course not, Mrs. Thomas. But there are certain regulations that must be followed. Please take your seat."

"Oh, I know all about those regulations," she said with contempt. "Those stupid regulations are what drove my dessert shop out of business."

"The law is the law. If you don't like it, you can try to change it, but you can't disobey it without suffering the consequences."

Officer Hevia read aloud our address, birth dates and social security numbers from the screen to verify that they were correct. He spent another five minutes typing who-knows-what into the computer before finally pushing himself away from the monitor while the printer noisily spat out some documents.

"While that's printing, I'm going to need to get a set of fingerprints from each of you," he said. "Mrs. Hoffman, if you could give me your right hand, just the first three fingers…"

"Cool," said Sam as he watched up close the procedure he had seen so many times on television.

Our mother turned to him and replied brusquely, "It most certainly is not cool, Sam."

"But on the way over here, you said you weren't going to fingerprint us," I pointed out.

Officer Hevia shrugged. "Boss's orders." We didn't need to ask the name of the boss. Lieutenant Thomas was giving us the full treatment.

"Now then," Officer Hevia said after he finished fingerprinting us, "I do have some good news."

"What's that?" our mom asked suspiciously.

"There won't be any need for you to post bail. The family court judge has decided that, given the age of most of the defendants and the non-violent nature of their crimes, they are neither a flight risk nor a danger to the community."

"That's what you think," Sam blurted.

"Sam!" our mother snapped.

"The three of you are scheduled to appear in family court, room three, at 9:00 a.m. next Wednesday," Officer Hevia continued. "If you do not appear, another warrant will be issued for your arrest."

The three of us looked at each other and then at Officer Hevia, who stared back blankly. Finally, our mother asked, "So are we free to go?"

"You're free to go."

It was dark outside when we left the station, and our mom's old Subaru station wagon was the last car in the parking lot. I scraped the frost from the windshield, while Sam waited in the backseat and our mom tried to start the car. The cold engine made a slow, straining noise on the first three cranks. Please let the car start, I thought. After the day we had, the prospect of going back inside the police station and asking for a jumpstart was probably more than any of us could bear. On the fourth attempt, the engine mercifully turned over, and I jumped into the front passenger seat.

Nobody spoke much on the ride home. We were all trying to grasp just what in the world happened that day. It looked like they had arrested just about every kid in Walton. Why? How? I could see them getting wind of one or two underground businesses, but not all of them. We were too disorganized—or rather, decentralized, as our business school tutors would say. There was no way the police and the Board of Health could have pulled together so much information about all of us, unless somebody we knew and trusted was ratting us out.

The obvious suspect was Karen Thomas. She and her friend Wendy Siegel were about the only kids in town who didn't pass through the station house today, and her father was a high-ranking cop. Maybe Celeste was right about her. But it just didn't make sense. Or maybe it did make sense, but I couldn't admit it. Karen was pulling in as much money as any of us, maybe more. If she put the rest of us out of business, there would be a lot less disposable income to spend at her parties.

Most of all, I really liked and trusted Karen. She was a bit of a goody-two-shoes (except for the illegal business she ran, of course), and she was too respectful toward authority figures like teachers, police and parents (in her case, police and parent being literally one in the same). But everybody from teachers to students really liked her, and always had, and she seemed to get along with everybody. She was definitely the most popular girl in school, and with good reason. Having all of your classmates arrested just wasn't something that a popular girl would do. That sort of thing has a way of alienating people.

As we pulled into the driveway, the headlights shined across the front of the dessert shop. "What the heck?" our mom whispered loudly before slamming the gear-shifter into park. She pulled her keys from the ignition and jumped out of the wagon to get a better look.

What now? I wondered. Sam and I saw what our mother had noticed as soon as we climbed outside. The snow on the lawn between the driveway and the entrance to the store was smashed down, and frozen clumps of shredded sod stuck out here and there. The evergreen shrub to the right of the doorway was bent over, its trunk cracked.

As we approached the entrance, we noticed a letter on some sort of official stationery glued to the window. "Premises closed and contents removed by Order of the Board of Health."

"Oh dear," our mother whimpered.

"It looks like they took everything, even your display cases," I said as I cupped my hands around my eyes and pressed them to the frosty glass. Sam ran around to the back entrance and quickly returned to tell us that the kitchen had also been cleaned out.

We're finished, I thought. We had no kitchen, no inventory, and we were facing criminal charges. The three of us trudged back to our house, kicked the snow off our boots, and went inside.

Frank was waiting for us in the kitchen. Sam and I glared at him with sheer loathing, while our mother studied him with an odd, sad look on her face.

"Come on, Sam," I said, motioning towards the stairs. "Let's find out if anyone else has any news."

"If you're heading for your computers," said Frank, "don't bother. The police confiscated those too."

"What?" Sam and I yelled.

"Evidence," Frank replied with a shrug and a condescending grimace.

No computers. That was the perfect ending to a rotten day. Not knowing what else to do, we watched television in a stupor until dinner, which we ate half of before going to bed early. None of us got much sleep that night, except probably Frank.

The next morning at the bus stop, we compared notes with the other kids, and everyone had more or less the same story. Everyone faced similar charges of permit violations, tax violations and employment violations. Any computers, goods or documents that could be possibly linked to an underground business were confiscated.

On the bus, the only missing kid (aside from Neil, who was now officially homeschooled) was Karen Thomas. She wasn't at school that day either. Vic and several of the other kids I talked to agreed that Celeste's theory had some merit. I was beginning to have some doubts myself.

At lunchtime, I called home to check on my mother. She was surprisingly upbeat.

"I just talked to our attorney," she blurted. "This whole situation just gets stranger and stranger. And Frank called from the municipal building. The mayor's office and the Health Department have been getting angry calls all day, and not just from the parents of the kids they arrested."

"What do you mean?" I asked.

"Hold on. There's someone on the other line." After a few seconds of silence, I heard her gasp for breath. "That was our attorney again. It's just getting bizarre. I have to talk to him. Go back to class, sweetie. We'll talk when you get home."

Like I really wanted to go back to class after that conversation. Luckily, I saw Vic heading in, so I caught up with him.

"Strangest thing," I said to Vic as we headed to our lockers. "I just talked to my mother—"

"I just got off the phone with my father," Vic interrupted. "But I couldn't make heads or tails of what he was saying. He started yammering at me in Indonesian, he was so excited, but his English didn't make much more sense."

As far as Vic could tell, the gist of his father's frantic message was that the county prosecutors were already hinting at some sort of deal. They were hoping for a plea bargain. That made some sense, we both agreed, as all of our illegal enterprises accounted for perhaps one hundred or more separate cases, which is more than they probably handled in a typical year. If they didn't want to clog the courts, they would have to find some way to avoid going to trial.

On the other hand, they would never let us off scot-free. We were going to have to pay some sort of price. The question was, how big? Maybe they would throw the book at just a few of us to scare the rest by example. I didn't like the odds of Sam and me being the ones to avoid prosecution. The justice system had already shown its willingness on more than one occasion to play hardball where our family was concerned.

When Sam and I arrived home from school that afternoon, we saw a black Lexus parked in our driveway.

"Must be the lawyer," Sam observed.

Sure enough, we barged into our kitchen to see a fat, balding middle-aged man with a stained trench coat and tight-fitting suit seated at the table. He was eating a slice of one of our last remaining pies and had crumbs in his scraggly brown beard. I was surprised that the cops hadn't confiscated all the desserts from our home refrigerator as evidence.

"Ray Smirnoff," the lawyer said with his mouth half-full, extending a pudgy hand towards Sam and me.

After shaking hands, introducing ourselves, and splitting the last slice of pie, Sam and I joined the attorney and our mother at the table. Luckily, Frank was nowhere around.

"So, Mr. Smirnoff—" I began.

"Call me Ray," he said.

"Okay, Ray, what's happening? I hear you might have some good news for us."

Ray glanced at our mother, who nodded for him to proceed. "Well, yes, Mark. That is, it may be good news, but like everything else, there are strings attached. I don't know if you and Sam will think those strings are so good."

"What do they want?" Sam asked.

Exhaling loudly, Ray said, "The health department and the county prosecutors are willing to drop all the charges against the three of you, um, if you boys transfer ownership of Desserts Express to your mother, the kitchen and shop are brought up to code, all employees of Desserts Express are brought onto the tax rolls, and all underage employees are terminated."

You could have heard a pin drop. For about five seconds, that is. Then the ear-splitting sound of a twelve-year-old and an eight-year-old trying to shout over each other filled the small room.

"Are they out of their minds?" Sam yelled.

"Are you out of your mind?" I yelled.

"That's the stupidest thing I ever heard!"

"Did you tell them to drop dead?"

"Where did they come up with such a stupid idea?"

"Boys, put a sock in it this instant, and maybe Ray can explain!" our mother finally shouted over both of us. We quieted down to a soft rumble and stared at our attorney.

Ray loosened his tie and coughed. "It's like this, boys. You may not realize it—heck maybe you do, you must be bright to have built such a huge business so fast—but Desserts Express is one of the few bright spots in this region's economy."

"Say what?" I exclaimed.

"Well, I should say Desserts Express and all the other little enterprises you and your friends apparently created when no one was looking. All the old established businesses have been closing down, and people have been leaving our fair town in search of opportunities elsewhere."

"Yeah, yeah, this town is a rat hole, and all the rats are fleeing," I agreed. "Everybody knows that."

"Mark!" our mother chided. "That's no way for a boy to talk about his hometown." Sam giggled, and she shot him a withering look.

"Be that as it may," Ray continued, "it's fair to say that your hometown is economically depressed and has been for some time. That puts a lot of pressure on our local government leaders."

"Sure," said Sam. "Nobody wants to be mayor of an empty rat hole."

Ray nodded and continued quickly before our mother could scold Sam for his hometown blasphemy. "You're quite correct, Sam. Unfortunately, they don't have a lot of options for reinvigorating the economy. They can't spend money on big new projects to get things moving. All the revenues in the municipal budget are more than accounted for by ongoing expenses, and they've raised taxes past the breaking point. Raising them again would just drive more families and businesses out. And the town can't even borrow anymore, because it's already too far in debt as it is."

I thought about this for a moment. "Why don't they just cut costs?" I asked.

"Yeah," Sam agreed. "Starting with Frank."

"Sam!" our mother snapped. She was used to me being disrespectful, but this was a new side of my little brother, who until very recently had the reputation of a sweet, innocent angel.

"They've considered that," said Ray, "but that's impossible for the mayor and town council politically. Even if all the municipal employees weren't protected by civil service rules, there are simply too many folks in this town who are on the government payroll. If they start laying people off, they can kiss their own jobs goodbye next November."

"Oh," said Sam.

"So too bad for Walton Township," I said. "But what's that have to do with us?"

"Think about it, Mark," Ray said. He paused to let Sam or me come up with the answer ourselves, but when we didn't, he continued. "Just when it looked like this place was going to become a ghost town, you kids come along and somehow get things moving again. People are working, albeit under the table. The economy is growing in new, unexpected directions. While everyone else is firing people and closing businesses, you kids are somehow opening businesses and hiring people!"

I nodded, starting to get the drift. "Okay, but then why mess with a good thing? If we're the only ones breathing life into this place, the last thing they should do is bust us."

Ray raised a finger and said, "But you forgot one thing. You kids aren't playing by their rules. They need your jobs and your new businesses, but they need you to do it their way. You weren't paying taxes, and you weren't playing nice with their regulators."

Now red in the face, Sam leaped out of his chair. "Duh!"

"I'm warning you, mister," our mother hissed as she pointed at Sam. "Mind your manners and sit down this instant, or you'll get such a spanking you won't be able to sit!"

Sam didn't sit down. "Of course we didn't follow their stupid rules!" he continued. "If we did, we would have gone broke too!"

Ray nodded. "You may be right, young man. But being right, unfortunately, will not keep your mother out of jail or you two out of the government foster care system. They've got you kids cornered, and they're not going to let you go until you give them what they want."

Chapter Sixteen

Valentine's Day

Sam sat back down uncertainly, and the four of us glanced at each other in silence. So this was their game. We either surrender our businesses that we built from scratch, or they put us all in one form of prison or another.

My brother and I were both watching our mother. Except for scolding us for our bad manners, she had been awfully quiet through the whole discussion. She was absent-mindedly blowing on her teacup to cool it off, even though she had filled it over twenty minutes ago.

Glancing up at us from her tea and catching our eyes, she shifted in her seat uncomfortably. "Why are you two looking at me like that? I'm not any happier about any of this than you are. This wasn't my idea."

I looked at Sam and noticed that his eyes were beginning to tear. "Don't cry, Sammy," I said, as our mother came over to our side of the table and put an arm around each of us.

"But I don't want to go to a foster home!" he bawled, and then the floodgates opened. To be honest, I sort of felt like crying myself, although of course I didn't.

Our mom lifted Sam in her arms and dabbed his eyes with a paper napkin. "Listen to me, Sammy. Nobody here is going to a foster home, I promise you."

Sam tried to nod with his face buried in our mom's hair. "Yes we are," said his muffled voice. "They're going to put Mark and me in foster homes, and they're going to put you in jail, and we'll never see each other again!"

"You're not listening to me, Sammy," she said. "I promise you that you and Mark aren't going to a foster home, and I'm not going to jail. I love you two more than anything in the world, and I would never, ever let that happen to you."

I wanted to say, "We you love you too, Mom." That was true, of course, but it was also true that I was really angry about what they were about to do to our business. So instead, I asked, "You mean you're going to go along with their stupid plan? You're going to take Desserts Express away from Sam and me and fire us?"

The hurt look on her face made me regret my words immediately. "I'm really, really sorry, boys, but we don't have any choice. The government is forcing our hand. They already took your father. I'm not going to let them take the rest of us. Do you understand?"

"Yes," I said with a nod.

But I still didn't like it. Not one bit.

We talked to Ray Smirnoff for a few more minutes, and he told us that he would call us tomorrow with additional details about the deal. They wanted us to all go down to the county prosecutor's office and sign some papers promising not to be involved in any more businesses until we were eighteen. Ray said he would try to negotiate a better deal so that we could just sign over the business to our mom without having to make any promises about the future.

None of us had much of an appetite at dinner, except for Frank, who was all smiles and had seconds of everything. Our mom could tell that Sam and I were looking for any excuse to wipe that grin off Frank's face, so she excused us from the table early.

Sam and I decided to ride our bikes over to Neil's house. Vic was there too. Everybody looked like their best friend had just died, except that all of our best friends were right there. We headed down to his basement rec room and took turns kickboxing each other on Neil's Playstation while we discussed the latest news. Everybody had received the same offer from the prosecutors.

"So are you guys going legit and selling out to your parents?" I asked.

Neil nodded as his kickboxer attempted to flatten mine with a flying sidekick. "We don't have much choice. The cops have all our money, our computers, our fishing tackle and our raw materials."

"They even took our worm farm," Vic added.

"You're kidding!" I exclaimed. The worm farm for Vic and Neil's bait supply business was an old wooden trough about twenty feet long, filled with dirt and worms. It probably weighed over a thousand pounds. "How in the world did they get it out of Neil's garage?"

Neil shook his head and scowled as my kickboxer connected with a vicious left hook. "They came over here with one of those huge flatbed trucks and a big motorized hook and chain that they use to tow cars. They winched the whole thing up onto the truck. But that trough is so old and damp, a few of the rotted boards along the bottom crumbled off. I got hysterical, because I thought the whole thing was gonna fall apart. But it looked like it mostly held together, at least when they left here. Who knows what happened to it when they got down to the impound lot."

Vic shrugged. "All the worms are probably dead by now anyway, if they were dumb enough to leave it outside in the snow." Neil nodded in agreement and scowled again.

"The person I really feel bad for is Alana Poponna," I said.

"Who?" Neil asked. "Oh yeah, that little girl that runs the bank. Why do you feel worse for her? She's in the same boat as the rest of us."

I shook my head. "No, she's not. Didn't you hear? Because she was printing money and operating a bank, the FBI actually got involved in her case."

"No way!" Vic yelled.

"Yeah," I said. "And unlike the rest of us, her business is illegal no matter what, so she doesn't even have the option of turning it over to her parents. She's out of business for good."

"But it's not illegal to run a bank," Sam argued.

"It is when the bank prints its own money," I said.

"Unless it's the Federal Reserve Bank," Vic observed. "It's only okay when the government does it. If a normal person does it, all of a sudden it's a felony for some reason. Even if Alana wasn't printing her own currency, just to run a bank she'd have to have federal insurance and a bunch of government licenses. There's no way she could afford to be in that business unless she was already a millionaire in the first place."

"This sucks big time!" Neil yelled, just as his kickboxer was knocked unconscious.

The rest of us nodded. Being the winner of the video game competition, I had the option to play the next challenger. However, I wasn't in the mood for another match, so I forfeited my game controller to Sam, while Vic took Neil's place.

Lying back on the old threadbare carpeting that covered Neil's basement, I stared at the pink insulation and heating ducts in the unfinished ceiling. It was inconceivable to me that they were going to take away everything we created, and there was nothing we could do about it. Well, at least our mother would be back in business, I told myself. Hopefully, she would do better this time around in steering clear of the insane health department regulations.

"Know what doesn't make any sense?" Neil asked as he bounced a basketball against the wall.

"Besides everything?" I asked.

"If they cut us out, and they go back to taxing and regulating everything to death, what makes them think the businesses we built won't just end up in the same sorry mess as everything else around here?"

"Beats me," I said. "But I know I won't be buying anything from any of the shops they're stealing from us."

"That goes double for me," said Vic.

"And triple for me," added Sam.

At school the next day, there was even less education than usual taking place. Everyone was preoccupied with the business forfeitures and our possible response. I mentioned our idea for a boycott, and all of the kids I talked to agreed that it was the only sensible thing to do. It might not get us back our businesses, but it would help us get our revenge, which was the next best thing as far as I was concerned.

I sat at the usual table for lunch with Vic. The meatloaf sandwich my mom packed was delicious, but I didn't have much of an appetite. I nibbled absent-mindedly while glancing around the cafeteria. My eyes practically popped out of my head when I saw Karen Thomas walking straight toward me. She hadn't been on the bus or in class since before the police raids.

Karen looked at me uncertainly and gave me a half-smile, which to be honest was still twice as nice as most people's full smile. "Hi, Mark," she said. "Mind if I sit down?"

I shrugged and answered coolly, "All the seats at this table are taken."

"Oh." She looked hopefully at Vic and the other boys at our table, as if expecting one of them to be chivalrous and offer her a seat, but none of them was budging.

"That was some nifty police work your dad pulled off," said Drew Baxter, who was sitting across from me. "Thanks a lot."

Karen's smile faded and her mouth hung open. "What do you mean, thanks a lot? You don't think I had anything to do with that?"

With a mouthful of sandwich, Vic said, "You were conspicuously absent when the rest of us got hauled down to the police station."

"No, you don't understand," she pleaded.

"What's to understand?" Vic asked. "You cleared out all your competition—not that any of us were really competing with you."

Instead of answering Vic, Karen looked at me. "Is that what you believe too, Mark? That I put my father up to that?"

I took another bite of sandwich and said nothing. All of us watched her complexion change from peaches and cream to blushing red before our eyes. As she turned and ran out of the cafeteria, I thought I noticed a tear rolling down her cheek.

Vic went back to eating as if nothing had happened. I looked down at my sandwich and then over to the door that Karen Thomas had just run through.

"You think she's telling the truth?" I asked Vic.

"I doubt it," Vic answered, "but stranger things have happened."

With a sigh, I pushed myself up from the table and hurried for the door, trying not to catch the eye of any of the kids who were now staring at me.

As I entered the hallway, Karen was leaving the girls' bathroom. There were no tears on her cheeks, but her eyes were now nearly as red as her complexion. She glanced at me and turned quickly to walk in the opposite direction.

"Hey, Karen. Wait up." She stopped and turned.

"Yes?"

"Um, I'm, uh, sorry for doubting you," I mumbled.

"Whatever," she said.

A bit more sincerely, I added, "You've never lied to me before, so I had no business thinking you would start now. If you say you had nothing to do with it, I believe you."

She raised her eyebrows and almost smiled. "Really? I'm glad to hear you say that, Mark. You really hurt my feelings before."

"I'm sorry," I repeated. "But you have to admit, it does look really suspicious. You and Wendy were the only ones who weren't arrested, and your dad pretty much ran the whole thing."

Karen shook her head. "I know. In a way, I guess I can't blame you. Wait, yes I can. I can't really blame the rest of them, but you of all people should know better."

I smiled, and she smiled too, which was somehow a big relief.

"So what was it you wanted to say before?" I asked.

"Huh?"

"You know, back at the lunch table, when I was acting like a jerk."

"Oh," Karen said. "I wanted to give you—well, it doesn't matter."

Now I was curious. "You wanted to give me something? What?"

"Forget it. It's too late."

When I put my mind to it, I could be a real pest, something I must have picked up from my brother Sam. "Please, please, please, please, please, pleeeease," I whined.

Karen rolled her eyes and then glanced around the hall nervously. We were alone, except for a hall monitor at the other end. She opened the binder under her arm and sheepishly handed me a small stack of ripped red paper.

"What's this?"

"Until five minutes ago, it was a valentine card," she said. "Happy Valentine's Day."

Oh.

Hmmm.

I must have blanked for a few seconds. Clumsily unwrapping the envelope shreds from the card shreds, I tried to piece my first valentine back together. Well, it was my first unforced valentine, at any rate. I don't count all those crappy little valentines that the teachers had ordered us to give to every single kid in class—boy and girl alike—throughout elementary school. Thankfully, that stupid tradition did not carry over to Dewey Middle School.

"Um, thanks, Karen, I guess."

"You're welcome, Mark, I guess."

Looking up from my mangled card, I said, "You know, I didn't get you a card. I didn't know…"

Karen grinned. "Gee, what a surprise."

"Okay, I do have one surprise for you."

"Oh, yeah? What's that?"

That's when I leaned in and kissed her. It was quick and dry, but it was a kiss.

Then I braced myself for—I don't know what—a slap, a scream, a laugh, or another kiss. Instead, all Karen did was smile her beautiful dimpled smile, and her face blushed all over again. This time, however, the blush made her look even prettier than usual.

"Happy Valentine's Day," I said quietly.

"Thanks."

I was trying to decide whether I was supposed to hold her hand on the way to class, but before I could make up my mind, the bell rang and dozens of kids came streaming out of the cafeteria. Instead, we walked together and talked, but without touching, back to Miss Farkas's classroom.

All of a sudden, I wasn't having such a bad week anymore.

Chapter Seventeen

The Sentence

"You kissed her?" Neil asked gleefully that evening when he, Vic and I met at his house. "Awesome."

I nodded.

"So what does that mean?" Vic asked. "Are you two boyfriend and girlfriend or something?"

"I don't know," I said truthfully. "I guess not. It's just a valentine—a ripped up valentine at that."

"And a kiss," Neil reminded me. "Don't forget that."

After a few more minutes of congratulations and reliving my moment of glory, Neil got back down to business. "So she didn't have anything to do with the arrests, huh? Then why weren't she and Wendy busted with the rest of us?"

"Well, when her dad found out what was going down, he did butt in on her behalf. Lieutenant Thomas can be very intimidating, as you know, and when he decided that Karen and Wendy weren't going to be arrested, nobody was going to challenge him on it. But that was all his doing. Karen didn't ask him to butt in."

"So she says," Vic said.

I was starting to get annoyed with these guys. "Yeah, she does say that, and I believe her. And it's not like she's getting off scot-free. Her business is shut down just like the rest of ours."

"Really?" Neil asked.

"Really. Her dad doesn't have that much pull, and from what Karen says, he wasn't too happy about her being involved in any of this in the first place. He really let her have it."

The next morning, instead of taking the bus to school, Sam and I went with our mother to the law office of Ray Smirnoff, our attorney. Holding a bagel overflowing with cream cheese in one hand, Ray waved us into a small conference room with the other and gestured toward some empty seats.

"Mk yrslf at home," Ray grunted through a mouthful of breakfast. "I'll be rt bk."

The three of us sat down and waited for Ray. My brother and I fidgeted, while our mother tried to maintain her poise but revealed her anxiety by chewing on her fingernails.

A few minutes later, Ray returned with four manila folders stuffed with papers. He handed each of us a folder and kept one for himself. I opened mine and saw an intimidating stack of photocopied legal documents. The papers could have said anything; they were all in legal mumbo-jumbo. All I could tell was that our names and address appeared throughout them, along with the name and rank of the arresting officer, and various details about Desserts Express.

"These are the final papers for your plea bargain, which the district attorney's office faxed to me early this morning," Ray said. "I've been hashing out the details with them over the last few days, but for the most part it's the same deal that I described to you at your home the other night. I'd like to review these with you and make sure each of you understands the terms of these agreements, and I'll try to answer any questions that you have. Then, once you are comfortable with the language in these papers—"

"But I'm not comfortable," I interrupted. "I can tell you that without reading a thing."

Ray tilted his glasses down on the bridge of his nose and looked at me. "Nobody expects you to be happy with this plea bargain, Mark. You just have to be able to live with it. If you can't live with it, then that's another matter, but my advice as your attorney is that you take this deal. The county has a solid case against you, and if you lose in court, the outcome will be much less tolerable than this."

For the next forty-five minutes, Ray took us paragraph by paragraph through each document in the folders. After sitting through his explanation, I still couldn't tell you much more about the content of the papers than before we started. My mind was on Desserts Express and the injustice of the entire turn of events.

If only they had left us alone, I thought to myself. We weren't hurting anybody, and we weren't holding a gun to anybody's head. From our employees to our vendors to our customers, there wasn't anybody who ever dealt with Desserts Express who was unhappy with us. The only people who didn't like it were the government busybodies, who just wanted to grab a piece of the action for themselves, while forcing us out.

Our mother, Sam and I got in our beat-up Subaru wagon and followed Ray in his black Lexus to the district attorney's office, located in the large gray municipal building next to the county courthouse. Once inside, Ray led us to yet another conference room, where we waited outside the door for another group to finish. After a few minutes, Harrison and David Wolfe—until a few days ago, the owners of a thriving business in comic books and trading cards—emerged from the room along with their parents and attorney. They had just signed a similar deal to ours and were now apparently free, but from the looks on their faces, you would have thought they were heading off to jail.

"Hey Mark, hey Sam," the Wolfe brothers greeted us as they passed down the hallway.

"Hey Harrison, hey David," Sam and I answered as we entered the conference room.

A sour-faced, balding man in a blue suit sat near the center of the of the conference table. Ray led us to seats directly across from him.

"Good morning, counselor," Ray said cheerfully.

"Mr. Smirnoff," replied the other man, nodding curtly.

"These are my clients, Ellen Hoffman, Mark Hoffman and Sam Hoffman. This is Jonathan Stern, assistant district attorney."

"How do you do?" Mr. Stern asked each of us as he rose slightly from his seat just long enough to shake each of our hands.

"How do you do?" our mother replied.

Mr. Stern handed us original copies of the same documents we had just reviewed at Ray's office. He asked us if we had any questions, and we each said no. Ray took one last quick look at the papers to ensure that nothing had changed and then told us to sign wherever we saw an X and a blank line above our names. I picked up a felt-tip pen that Mr. Stern had placed on the table and—with a knot in my stomach—signed away my share of the business I helped create. I also signed away my rights to build any other business until I turned eighteen.

Sam signed his papers, and then our mom countersigned next to our signatures before turning to her own stack. Her papers gave her complete ownership of Desserts Express and committed her to run it above-board and without her sons' help going forward.

So that was it. Sam and I had just sworn to be idle bums and avoid any productivity until we reached adulthood, and in exchange the government promised not to throw our mother in jail or put us in a foster home. It wouldn't be so bad, I thought. I could get used to doing nothing useful again. It would be good training for life as an adult in Walton.

It was noon by the time we left the district attorney's office, so our mom drove us home and made us a quick lunch before taking us to school for afternoon classes. Ms. Farkas grimaced when I strolled into classroom just after recess, and then she really frowned when she saw that I had an actual note from my mother excusing my absence from the first half of the day.

For the first time in months, I made sort of an effort to pay attention in class. My life as an entrepreneur was over, and with our cash flow dried up, I sure couldn't afford the private tutorials from the business school students anymore. Maybe I could force myself to go back to being just a regular kid. I'd turn over a new leaf.

My new leaf lasted about an hour before I was bored out of my mind as usual. Miss Farkas spent the last hour of the day reviewing fractions and percentages, which I had down cold since early in the fourth grade. Not to mention that I had used percentages in running a successful business every day for the last five months. I could have taught the class, and I probably would have made it a lot more interesting than Miss Farkas.

As I gazed around the room and then out the window at the cold, empty playground, my eyes eventually met Karen's, who was sitting across from me (months ago she had convinced Miss Farkas to let her move to the front of the classroom) and was probably as bored as I was. Miss Goody-Goody had definitely seen her attitude at school take a turn for the worse lately, especially since the private tutorials. Of course, her reputation was a lot better than mine from the start, and Karen wasn't prone to be a troublemaker like me, so Miss Farkas still gave Karen the benefit of the doubt.

Karen wrote something and quietly tore that page from her notebook. Folding the paper in half, she discreetly slipped the note to me when Miss Farkas turned her back to write a problem on the board. Oh great, I thought. Mushy stuff in public. With one hand cupped over the top to shield it from prying eyes, I unfolded the note and read it.

"So, how did it go this morning??" the note asked. Little hearts and smiley faces decorated the edges.

I tore a new page from my own notebook and folded it in half. On the front, I wrote, "They sentenced me to six years…" Inside the fold, I added, "…in the Walton public school system!"

It occurred to me that I should reciprocate with some sort of hearts or smiley faces or other mushy stuff, but I thought better of it. That turned out to be good thinking on my part. I reached across the aisle to place the note on Karen's desk, when suddenly Miss Farkas spun around and glared at me.

"Mr. Hoffman, why are you trying to deprive Miss Thomas of her education?"

"Huh?" I said, stalling for a better answer.

Miss Farkas took a menacing step forward. "I said, why are you bothering the students who are here to learn? Is there something you want from Miss Thomas?"

In reply, somebody behind us made a loud, sloppy kissing noise, which prompted a lot of laughter from the other students. I immediately suspected Vic, and I whipped my head around to look at him, but he just shrugged innocently.

"Quiet!" Miss Farkas yelled, as she walked between Karen and me. I had already covered the note Karen passed to me, but Karen was too slow with the one I sent her. She and Miss Farkas reached for it at the same time. Karen was not about to challenge a teacher, so she let it go.

Miss Farkas cleared her throat and unfolded the note. She read the note to herself with a frown before reading it again out loud. "They sentenced me to six years… in the Walton public school system."

The class erupted in another burst of laughter. "I said quiet!" Miss Farkas yelled. "So, Mr. Hoffman, you find my class to be the equivalent of a prison sentence?"

I answered with a grin, "Well, yeah, except that we can't smoke cigarettes or lift weights here."

Over the giggles and howls of my classmates, Miss Farkas replied, "Not to worry, Mr. Hoffman. I have no doubt that a juvenile delinquent like you will have the opportunity to experience actual prison life soon enough. In the meantime, you can write, 'They sentenced me to six years in the Walton public school system' one thousand times for tomorrow."

Of course, I didn't bother writing that, which landed me in detention for a week. But I didn't care. With Desserts Express gone and no prospects ahead, I didn't care about much of anything.

A week later, my mother got a call from the police department telling her where to go to pick up our confiscated kitchen equipment and computers. She had to hire a moving van and crew to retrieve all the heavy stuff, and then it took her about another week to get everything back in its place and working properly. I would have given her a hand with the grunt work, but Sam and I were prohibited by our deal with the county from so much as lifting a spatula.

By the end of February, Desserts Express was back in business with my mom as sole proprietor and old Mrs. Whitney as the only employee. In reality, it was more a reincarnation of Ellen's Pastry Place, my mom's old shop, than the business Sam and I had built. She tried to use the customer list that we had put together to email each day's specials and solicit business, but none of our customers were interested. Most of them were sworn to boycotting the businesses the adults had stolen. The rest were just broke, now that our underground economy had dried up.

Vic and Neil reported similar news from their homes. Neither of their fathers had any luck running their sons' bait and tackle shop or the other enterprises they had going before the big raids. Not only had the customers disappeared, but running things the government's way meant taxes, licenses and regulations ate up what little revenue trickled in.

It was the same story all over Walton. Ted Wolfe wasn't selling any of his sons' comic book and trading card inventory. Drew Baxter's mom found no takers for his Internet-consulting business—which, stripped of its strippers and other titillating content, offered little appeal to Drew's puberty-stricken clients. Alana Poponna's bank was closed down altogether, but at least the FBI finally decided to drop its case against her due to her age.

All of us kids were hoping for an early spring, but even the weather disappointed us when March ushered in a record-breaking cold spell. There wasn't even much snowfall to go with it, which would have at least gotten us out of school for a few days. Just a solid week of sub-zero temperatures, cabin fever and an outbreak of temper tantrums. I beat up Sam about twice a day, just for something do, but honestly the little pest had it coming. One night before bed, I got a sickening taste in my mouth while brushing my teeth and sprayed spit across the bathroom mirror in a panic of disgust. Sam's stupid honking laugh gave away his hiding place behind the bathtub curtain.

A thorough pounding revealed that he had dropped his own toothbrush in an open toilet he forgot to flush, so he simply swapped mine for his. Our mother, of course, came to his rescue when she heard Sam's pitiful cries and grounded me for a week, which didn't matter because it was too cold to go outside anyway and there was nothing to do besides. But still, it really bugged me that he gives me a pee-soaked toothbrush, and I'm the one who gets in trouble!

Sam and I were just about at the breaking point of boredom and irritability when a new development caught our attention. Around mid-March, our mother suddenly had orders to fill at Desserts Express. It was really strange, because as far as I could tell, we kids were still holding the line on our boycott. She must have come across some new customers somehow, but whom?

At the same time, Neil reported that his father's fishing tackle business was slowly picking up. Now I was suspicious.

"Maybe the economy is just finally turning around on its own," Neil suggested one Saturday afternoon as we watched a "Spider-Man" DVD in his basement. "It had to happen sooner or later. It couldn't keep getting worse forever."

"I'm not buying that," I said. "There's something fishy going on. I just haven't figured out what."

"Vic says his dad's business is starting to pick up too."

"There you go," I said. "It doesn't add up."

Neil got up off the floor to change the DVD. "It doesn't make any more sense to me than it does to you, Mark. But if business is picking up all over Walton, that means the economy is growing. It's simple as that."

"Okay, then tell me this. Who are the customers? Did your dad mention who's been buying all this fishing tackle all of a sudden?"

"Well, no," Neil conceded. "What about your mom?"

"I tried asking her," I said. "But she won't give me a straight answer. She says the less I know about the business, the better, because of the plea bargain. Like the cops and the health inspectors can eavesdrop in our living room."

"Your mom's a smart lady," said Neil. "I wouldn't put anything past those creeps after what they did to us."

I couldn't argue with that. Still, something about this sudden reversal of fortune just ate at me. My Spidey Sense was tingling.

Since my mother wouldn't discuss it with me, and she sure as heck wouldn't let me anywhere near her store where I could take a look around, there was only one thing for me to do. I would have to break into Desserts Express at night.

Dinner was a drag that evening. My curiosity was taking over, and I just wanted everyone to go to bed so I could sneak out to the bakery shop. Frank's annoying jabber only made the clock tick more slowly. Ever since the raid and the takeover, Frank had become more pompous and irritating than ever.

"Yes sir, things are really looking up again in Walton," Frank crowed while serving himself a second helping of lasagna. "Sure we're still tightening our belts at the board of ed—"

"Why don't you tighten your belts around your necks?" I muttered as I reached for the salad.

"Mark!" my mother cried.

Frank smirked. "Don't waste your breath, Ellen. Your little angel is still pouting over his big wake-up call. Mark learned the hard way that the rules apply to him too. If it were up to me, of course, I wouldn't have let him off so easy. A few months in juvenile detention would have done him a world of good. At the very least, they should have thrown in some mandatory community service, teach him a little something about sacrifice and putting the greater good ahead of himself for a change."

I swallowed the salad in my mouth and replied, "I force down food while listening to your socialist babble, so some other family doesn't have to put up with you. That's my community service." Sam spit out his ice tea onto his plate at that one.

"Mark! Sam!" my mother gasped. "You too, Frank! Can't you three ever just be civil for twenty lousy minutes so we can eat our meal in peace? Is that too much to ask?"

"Mark, apologize to your mother," Frank said.

"Frank, your mother should apologize for not aborting you," Sam piped up.

"Whoa! Good one, Sammy. Gimme five!" The kid was definitely picking up some moves from his big brother.

Our mother held her forehead in her hands and sighed. Frank looked at Sam and me with disgust and decided to press on.

"Anyway, Ellen, as I was saying, we're still tightening our belts. The town's fiscal crisis isn't over by a long shot, but I definitely believe we've turned the corner. And I was telling Mayor Holstein just yesterday, it's a credit to her vision and leadership that she's been able to keep all essential government services up and running throughout this recession. It's hard times like this when the citizens rely on their government most."

Raising her head up and nodding sluggishly, our mom said, "Yes, well I suppose Mayor Holstein knows what she's doing. She's been at it a long time."

"You're darn right," said Frank. "Twenty-five years next week. And that's why this silver anniversary party next Thursday is so important. Every citizen in Walton owes her a debt of gratitude."

Frank suddenly slammed his mouth shut and grimaced at my mother. I looked over just in time to see her shoot Frank a quick look of anger.

"Party? What party?" Sam asked.

"Oh, nothing," our mother answered.

I guffawed. "A silver anniversary party? For Mayor Holstein? You gotta be kidding me! That's hilarious."

"Just keep it up, mister," Frank said with attempted menace in his voice.

"And who's paying for this big hoopla?" I asked. "As if I didn't know."

"Walton Township, of course," Frank answered. "As it should be."

"Oh, that's rich," I said. "Mayor Heifer taxes and spends this stupid place—"

"That's Mayor Holstein, smart mouth," Frank interrupted.

"Whatever the cow's name is," I continued unfazed, "she taxes and spends Walton into a ghost town over the last twenty-five years, and now the few taxpayers that are still hanging on have to pay some more to thank her for it."

Frank wiped his mouth with his napkin—missing a large gob of tomato sauce on his chin—and stood up from the table. "Every time you speak, you only display your ignorance, Mark. You think you're smart, but you're a stupid, fresh-mouthed little boy who doesn't know the first thing about the real world, and who certainly doesn't know his place. The taxpayers you are so worried about *love* Mayor Holstein. Who do you think has been re-electing her for the last twenty-five years?"

I grinned and replied, "She keeps getting re-elected by you and the hundreds of other clowns on the city payroll. The only day anyone ever sees them do actual work is on election day when they get out the vote for another four years of mooching off the regular people. Only most of the regular people smartened up and moved out of Walton years ago, which is why this crummy town is practically bankrupt."

"You disgust me," Frank hissed as he slithered out of the kitchen.

I was really steamed now, but I tried to push the stupidity of it all out of my mind. Shoving one last heaping forkful of lasagna in my mouth, I got up from the table and headed for my room, where I distracted myself playing Alien Insurrection on my computer until I was sure my mom and Frank were asleep.

Shortly after midnight, I fetched my camping flashlight from my closet. Creeping down the hall to Sam's room, I saw that he was still awake.

"Come on," I whispered. Together we tiptoed down the stairs and out the back door into the cold winter night.

Chapter Eighteen

The Secret Customer

When we got to the rear entrance of our mom's shop, I discovered that my old key no longer fit in the door.

"Darn, they changed the locks," I whispered.

"Hold on," Sam said. "I think mom left her purse in the living room by the coat rack. I'll go see if I can find her keys."

"Okay, but be quiet. If we get busted again, we're dead meat."

A few minutes later, Sam returned with our mother's key chain, and we quickly found the key that let us into the kitchen. After closing the door behind us, I turned on my flashlight. We didn't dare turn on the overhead light. For all we knew, the police were still patrolling our street on the lookout for any illegal productivity.

I swept the flashlight beam around the room until I found what I was looking for. On a small metal desk in the corner of the kitchen, our mother kept all of her current business paperwork in a stack of wire baskets. While Sam watched, I flipped through the recent receipts.

"Holy cow!" I yelled.

"Shhh!" Sam urged with a finger to his lips.

"Holy cow," I whispered. "Look at the name on all these incoming payments."

Sam peered at the starkly lit paperwork. "Holy cow!" he yelled, before covering his mouth.

There were seven bills issued within the last three weeks from the new Desserts Express ("under new management"), and every one of them was stamped "Paid in Full." Every one of them was billed to "The City of Walton." The details of the orders varied, as did the delivery addresses. Some went to the Department of Education, some to the mayor's office, and some to the Board of Health. One was sent to the police department.

"How do you like that?" I whispered to Sam. "Now we know who wasn't supporting the boycott."

"Yeah, I guess we should have seen that one coming," Sam replied. "You think that's how the other businesses are suddenly raking in so much money?"

I nodded. "No question about it. It makes perfect sense, in a warped, communist sort of way. The city is subsidizing the businesses they confiscated to make sure they don't fail."

After returning the receipts to their basket, I moved to the basket holding the active orders. There were four orders from various city agencies for cookie platters and another for a cake for a retirement party at the Department of Education. For a moment, I let myself imagine that my teacher Miss Farkas might finally be headed for the old witches home, but then I realized that she would never leave with three months remaining in the school year.

At the top of the pile, there was one large order consisting of several pages stapled together. The order listed three cookie platters, five Boston cream pies, five lemon meringue pies, forty individual tarts and a four-foot-by-six-foot yellow sheet cake with strawberry filling and white frosting. The instructions for the cake decorations were quite detailed: They wanted a candy replica of the official seal of the town of Walton and a frosting rendering of City Hall. The writing on the cake was to say: "Congratulations Mayor Holstein on 25 YEARS of service."

"Wow," was all I could think to say.

"No wonder Mom wanted Frank to shut up about the party," said Sam. "They gave her the entire dessert order."

I flipped to the last page of the order to see the final tab and let out a low whistle. "Eight grand."

"I think I'm going to be sick," Sam said.

"You and me both. Let's get out of here."

I replaced the active orders in the wire basket. After helping ourselves to some brownies that would have otherwise been wasted on the Walton Department of Consumer Affairs, we carefully opened the rear door of the shop, stepped outside, and locked the door behind us. We tiptoed quickly across the lawn to our house, and while Sam returned our mother's keychain to her purse in the living room, I headed upstairs to bed.

The next day, Sam and I met with Vic and Neil to fill them in on the previous night's discovery.

"We can't let them get away with this!" Neil bellowed as he slammed his fist against his basement wall. Fortunately, the wall Neil chose to take out his frustration was solid cinderblock, and so he only hurt his hand, instead of the plasterboard that made up the opposite wall. If he had punched a hole in that, Neil's dad would have hurt a lot more than his hand.

"Okay, but what are we going to do about it?" Vic asked with a note of defeat in his voice.

"Well, I don't know about you guys, but for starters, Sam and I are going to make sure that delivery to Mayor Holstein's party has a little something extra in it."

"Yeah," said Sam with a mischievous grin, "like maybe a big loogie for each year she's been mayor."

Vic chuckled as he popped open a can of grape soda. "Fine. And we'll all get a big laugh out of the Hoffman brothers' hijinks. Now tell me the part where your childish humor stops them from propping up their stolen businesses with stolen tax dollars, because I must have missed it."

Sam looked down at his shoes and furrowed his brow. "Shut up, Vic!"

"Don't tell Vic to shut up," I said as I punched Sam in the arm.

"Yeah," said Vic as he also hit Sam in the arm.

"And don't hit my brother in the arm!" I yelled as I punched Vic in the arm. "Only I'm allowed to do that." I hit Sam in the arm again to emphasize my point. Sam and Vic each punched me in the arm, and we spent the next minute rubbing our bruises while Neil laughed, from a safe distance so as not to get a punch in the arm himself.

When we were finished beating up on each other, we realized that Vic had a point. Sabotaging the mayor's anniversary party might feel good, but it wouldn't be enough to stop the creeps.

"As long as city hall is willing to prop up these businesses, then our boycott is meaningless," Neil observed.

"But they'll have to run out of money sooner or later," Sam pointed out. "About the only taxpayers left in this stupid town either work for the government or one of the businesses the government is propping up."

"That's true, Sam, but who knows how long it will take for the house of cards to collapse?" I replied. "It took the Soviet Union seventy-five years. I don't want to wait that long."

"What's the Soviet Union?" Sam asked.

"You'll learn about it in history class next year," Vic answered. "And the year after that. And the year after that. And the year after that."

"Forget I mentioned it," Sam said.

Neil tossed a basketball against the wall to help him think. "If the boycott won't do it, then we're just going to have to hit harder."

"What do you mean?" I asked.

"We've got to make it really awful and unpleasant for them whenever the town does business with one of our old companies." Neil stood up and started hurling the basketball harder, until it got away from him and landed behind the TV, miraculously not breaking anything. "Spitting in the pies for the mayor's party is a good start, but we can do better, I mean worse."

Vic nodded. "I think Pudgy here is onto something. If we can make them really pay a price—and not just in dollars, which mean nothing to these thieves—then they might think twice before doing it again."

You know, this just might work, I thought. "If we want to really get their attention, then we have to make this anniversary party our number one target."

The next day was Monday. On the bus to school and throughout the day, we quietly spread the word to all the former entrepreneurs. Everybody agreed to snoop around and try to find out whether their parents were providing any goods or services for the mayor's big party, or were handling any other government business. If so, then they were to do their best to throw a wrench into the works.

A few were reluctant to agree. "Don't you feel just a little bit guilty about sabotaging our own parents?" Wendy Siegel asked.

"Look," I said. "These businesses were stolen from us. As far as I'm concerned, we're still the rightful owners, so they're our businesses to destroy. But if it will help ease your conscience, only mess with sales that go to the local government. Any other legitimate business—if there is any other legitimate business—they can keep."

Sam and I made late-night visits to our mom's shop every night that week. Monday night we carefully opened all the boxes of sugar, washed their contents down the drain, and refilled them with salt before resealing them. On Tuesday evening, we replaced the baker's chocolate with Ex-Lax. By Wednesday evening, the giant cake and most of the dessert trays were already prepared and sitting in the refrigerated display cabinets. While Sam held the flashlight, I inserted assorted surprises into the desserts and then reapplied the frosting.

Some of the other kids in Walton were also busy preparing for the big event. Drew Baxter's dad had taken over Drew's web hosting business after it was closed down by the township, just like our mom had taken over Desserts Express. As with all of the other boycotted businesses, e-Baxter had few clients until recently. That changed when the local government started giving it jobs to keep it afloat. The most recent order was for a special website commemorating Mayor Holstein's twenty-five years in office, which would be launched at the big gala celebration on Thursday. Drew spent every night that week hacking a spoof version of the website that he planned to swap for the real one at the last minute.

Vic's parents had inherited the several businesses he started, including his underground weekly newspaper, *The Walton Whisper*. Unlike their New York-born son, Mr. and Mrs. Sanjay had poor English skills, making for an unintentionally amusing publication. They were naturally preparing a special commemorative issue for the mayor's anniversary, courtesy of the local taxpayers. The disk containing the final layout had been sent to the printer late Wednesday afternoon, and printed copies were scheduled for delivery to the party at City Hall first thing Thursday morning. Little did Vic's parents know, however, that Vic had switched disks on them.

By Thursday morning, the whole town was buzzing with excitement over the big party. Pressing my luck, I asked Frank if Sam and I could accompany him and our mom to the festivities at city hall. He laughed at that one before reminding us that our school bus would arrive in a few minutes. We grabbed our lunches and walked slowly toward the door. The moment we stepped outside, my brother and I trotted over to the garage and quietly retrieved our bicycles. There would be no school for us that day. As far as I knew, it was Sam's first time playing hooky. It was roughly the hundredth time for me.

Rain drizzled on us as we rode our bikes toward City Hall, and occasionally a passing car would splash us while driving through a puddle. By the time we arrived in downtown Walton, we were wet and shivering. Sam and I hid our bicycles behind some shrubs next to the municipal building and walked around back.

We found the delivery ramp, where caterers, decorators and TV news crews were busy hauling equipment inside. On the ride over, I had rehearsed in my mind an assortment of lies for talking our way past security, but it turned out to be unnecessary. There were no guards watching the rear entrance, and the men making deliveries had no interest in us. Sam and I hoisted ourselves up onto the loading dock and walked inside.

"Where do we go now?" Sam asked as we looked up and down a dimly lit hallway in the rear of the building.

"They're holding the celebration in the rotunda on the second floor. We have to make our way there. I think that's a stairwell up ahead."

The stairwell took us to a fire exit in the rear of the rotunda. It was perfect. As we quietly entered the room, we saw many of the same disinterested workers from the loading dock bringing their wares through the double doors of the main entrance. A couple of cops were standing outside the entrance, but they were facing away from us, looking for people trying to get in.

When I was certain that none of the workers were watching us, I motioned for Sam to follow me onto the stage. We walked as quietly as we could across the dais while trying not to look suspicious. Sam nodded his head toward the red velvet curtain lining the wall behind the podium and raised his eyebrows at me. Hmm, that just might not be a bad hiding place, I thought. I found an opening in the center of the curtain, and we both slipped behind it.

"Stand up straight as you can with your back to the wall," I whispered, "and try not to let your feet stick out."

"Okay," Sam whispered back.

There was nothing to do now but wait and give Sam an occasional elbow whenever he fidgeted.

Chapter Nineteen

Flying Pies

"We'll be getting started in just a few minutes, folks," we heard the mayor's chief of staff announce over the microphone. "The governor's motorcade just pulled into the parking lot. Thank you for your patience. Please help yourselves to coffee or tea."

That announcement confirmed my suspicion that the party had been delayed from its 10:00 a.m. scheduled start. It felt like an eternity since Sam and I had hidden ourselves behind the curtain, but I didn't dare lift my arm to check my watch. We had been listening to people walk around the dais, and every time the footsteps came near us, my stomach churned in anticipation of somebody throwing open the curtain and exposing us.

After another twenty minutes or so, they finally got started.

"Ladies and gentlemen, honored guests, thank you all for coming this morning," the aide said, struggling to talk over ear-piercing microphone feedback. "Sorry about that. Is it better now? Anyway, thank you again for being here. We are gathered today to honor an extraordinary public servant who has been at the helm of our township for a remarkable quarter of a century now. Mayor Holstein has led Walton through good times and bad. Through it all, she has touched all our lives in countless ways…"

The chump blathered on like that for several minutes. He was straining my patience and probably killing my high-strung little brother. Although we tuned out most of his speech, we both perked up when we finally heard him lead into his closing.

"...But I am going to keep my remarks brief this morning, because I know I'm not the person you came to hear. We are honored this morning to have a special guest, who is going to say a few words and then introduce Mayor Holstein. Ladies and gentlemen, I am honored to present the governor of the great state of New York, Jeffrey Scott."

Oh no, I thought we had just heard the introduction, but it was only the introduction to the introduction. Governor Scott was an even bigger windbag than the mayoral aide. I sighed and pressed my head back to the wall.

"Thank you, thank you," the governor said. "Please sit down. You know, Janet Holstein and I got into this business of public service about the same time, and it's remarkable where the years have taken us. Little did I know twenty-five years ago..."

Just great, I thought. Here come the never-ending war stories. The governor proceeded to thrill the audience and bore Sam and me with one lame anecdote after another about the many times their paths had crossed over the years. He was even more long-winded and insufferable than the mayoral aide who preceded him.

"Oh, man," Sam moaned.

"Shut up!" I whispered, and then I was angry with myself for even saying that much out loud.

After half an hour of gubernatorial gobbledygook, the governor finally said, "But this is a celebration, after all, so enough with the political speeches. Let's bring out the lady of the hour and get this party started!" There was much applause. Apparently the audience wasn't so thrilled with the governor's war stories after all. "Ladies and gentlemen, it is my privilege to present your friend and mine, the mayor of Walton for the last twenty-five years, Janet Holstein!"

Applause was the only sound for the next minute or so. This roomful of toadies and ignoramuses was really beginning to get on my nerves. Finally, the mayor cleared her throat, and the crowd settled down.

"My dear, dear friends," Mayor Holstein cooed. "You have no idea how touched I am. If I start crying, please forgive me."

"If I start vomiting, please forgive me," Sam whispered.

"You're gonna start bleeding if you don't shut up," I warned him.

Another ten minutes of boring history of a depressed New York City suburb passed before Mayor Holstein got to the part we had been waiting for.

"Now, as some of you probably know, I have a bit of a sweet tooth," the mayor confessed. The crowd chuckled nervously, probably not sure how much they should laugh at her pear-shaped figure that made her fondness for sweets no secret. "I couldn't help noticing some delicious-looking treats in the rear of the rotunda, including a spectacular cake. Let's see if it tastes as good as it looks, shall we?"

Oohs and ahhs filled the room. I couldn't see anything, but if I had to guess, some lackeys wheeled the cake across the rotunda and brought it up on the stage.

"Ladies and gentlemen," the mayor's aide was now speaking into the microphone, "before we cut this lovely cake, let's sing 'happy anniversary' to Mayor Holstein."

Oh man, I thought.

Sure enough, the entire audience broke into song:

"Happy anniversary to you!
Happy anniversary to you!
Happy anniversary, Mayor Holstein!
Happy anniversary to you!"

"That was terrific," the aide announced. "While we're cutting the cake and the servers are bringing around the other lovely desserts for those who want them, I'd like to call your attention to a couple of other tidbits. By now, at the center of each table there should be copies of this week's special souvenir edition of *The Walton Whisper*, commemorating Mayor Holstein's twenty-fifth anniversary."

I could hear voices mumbling and papers rustling as people reached for their souvenir paper, followed by a few horrified gasps.

"Is there a problem?" the aide asked.

"Is there a problem!" someone shouted. "I'll say!"

"It's outrageous!" another person yelled.

The puzzled aide said, "Let me see that."

Although Sam and I wouldn't see a copy until later in the day, Vic's substitute lead story for the paper began as follows:

FRAUD IN TOWN PURCHASING!

Scandal Stains Mayoral Anniversary

A widespread scheme of improper government purchases has been used to prop up politically favored failing local businesses, an exclusive investigation by The Walton Whisper reveals. The businesses are the same ones that were stolen from local children earlier this year under orders from city hall and with the cooperation of the Walton Police, the district attorney's office and other branches of town government....

"What the—" the aide stammered.

The room echoed with general pandemonium. "Is this true?" some woman yelled.

"Please, people, if everyone could just calm down," the aide pleaded. "I'm not sure what's going on here, but there's obviously been some terrible mistake. These aren't the newspapers that we ordered, I mean, that is, not that we order the story, but… If you could just discard the papers, we'll continue cutting the cake and serving the dessert."

Nobody discarded their papers, of course. In fact, the reporters in attendance, including some from the New York City radio and television stations, were eagerly grabbing copies, we later learned. They had undoubtedly dreaded the assignment to dreary Walton Township for a lame political celebration, but suddenly it had the potential for real news.

While the audience continued to grouse about the scandalous newspaper, and the serving of vandalized dessert strangely failed to appease them, the aide decided to try another diversion.

"If everyone could turn their attention to the large video monitor to my right, I'd like to show you our final, um, surprise, I mean, our other tribute to Mayor Holstein's anniversary," the aide said nervously. "If I can just get this computer to work… ah, there we go. Now I just log on to waltontownship.gov and click on Holstein Anniversary. And—uh-oh."

The website the aide had called up was titled, "Celebrating 25 Years of Corruption!" Drew had used Photoshop to superimpose a particularly unpleasant picture of Mayor Holstein's head onto the body of an obese cartoon queen sitting on a throne surrounded by piles of treasure.

The audience gasped.

"Is this your idea of a joke?" someone yelled.

"I assure you," the aide croaked, "I don't know how that got up there."

An irate Mayor Holstein spoke up. "In that case, could you be a dear and turn that thing off?"

"Huh? Oh yeah, of course." He switched off the computer.

People were shouting from every table.

"This party stinks!"

"It's an insult to Mayor Holstein!"

"It's an insult to Walton!"

"Everyone please calm down!" cried the aide. "Please! Quiet!"

The crowd only grew louder. "Why don't you be quiet, you twit!" an angry old man in the front row yelled. "This is horrible! Even these desserts are horrible!"

"Which desserts?" the aide asked.

"This dessert!" the man yelled, as he hurled a large slice of lemon meringue pie at the aide. Or so Sam and I were later told, since we were still hiding behind the curtain at that point.

The man didn't have very good aim, however. The pie sailed past the aide and hit the governor in the chest.

"You hit the governor, you jerk!" another audience member yelled, just before throwing a slice of Boston cream pie at the original thrower. He had slightly better aim, hitting his intended target squarely on the side of the head, but the pie filling splattered onto everyone else sitting at that table.

That group wasn't going to just sit there and take such abuse, of course, and since the inedible dessert had already been served to their table, they quickly returned fire. Their marksmanship varied from person to person, and several nearby tables were brought into the fray. In a matter of seconds, it escalated into a full-blown food fight.

"People! People! This is outrageous!" the mayor's aide shrieked into the microphone. "There are VIPs and media present! Hey, you hit me! Eww, that tastes disgusting!"

The room was now so loud and out of control that Sam and I laughed freely.

"What do you think, Mark?" Sam asked. "Should we get in on the fun?"

"Might as well," I answered. "Not much point in hiding anymore."

At that moment, the curtain concealing us flung open. Frank stood inches in front of us, clenching the end of the curtain in his fist, his nostrils flared.

"I should have known!" he hissed. "Do you two have anything to say?"

"Yeah," I replied. "Duck."

"What?" he yelled. A split second later, a piece of yellow cake nailed Frank in the back of the head.

I shook my head in mock sadness and said, "I told you to duck."

"*You* better duck, you little punk!" Frank roared as spit sprayed from his mouth.

I did duck, and so did Sam. We ran across the stage and jumped into the center of the food fight. Three or four police officers were making a futile effort to restrain the crowd, but they were badly outnumbered by frenzied pie-throwers. Sam and I each grabbed handfuls of cake from the catering cart and hurled them with abandon. To my brother's delight, he hit Mr. Wilkens from the Department of Health—the agent who closed down Desserts Express—on his first throw.

Frank pushed his way through the frenzy and clumsily grabbed at Sam and me, but we were too quick for him. I got him right between the eyes from close range with a lemon tart, which apparently stung, because he doubled over clutching his face. While I laughed at the hapless public school superintendent, Sam started waving frantically and pointing toward the exit.

"Mark, quick! The big fish are getting away!" I turned and saw Mayor Holstein and Governor Scott slinking up the aisle.

"Governor, mayor, you forgot something!" I yelled. Okay, it wasn't very creative, but it worked. The governor and mayor stopped and turned toward me momentarily, which was all the time I needed to hit each of them with cake one last time.

The mayor wiped frosting from her face and glared at me through eyes that looked unusually red and beady, but that might have been the strawberry filling.

"Officers, arrest those two delinquents!" she bleated.

The cops were distracted at that moment with trying to restore order elsewhere in the room, but they wouldn't be for long. When Mayor Holstein gave an order, everyone on the city payroll usually jumped.

"What do you say we leave this party now, Sam?" I asked.

"Sounds good to me," Sam said. "I hear the dessert is terrible anyway."

We scrambled back through the rear fire exit where we came in, ran down the stairwell to the basement, and then out the delivery ramp to recover our bicycles hidden behind the shrubs. It was raining much harder now then when we arrived, but my brother and I both wore huge wet grins as we pedaled home, deliberately rolling through every puddle along the way.

Chapter Twenty

Let's Make a Deal

The mayor's anniversary party in sleepy Walton, New York, which was supposed to be filler for the end of the evening news programs, instead led the broadcasts at six and eleven. The next morning, it was on the front page of every paper from Albany to New York City. They covered everything from the pie fight to the hacked website to the accusations of corruption in the souvenir edition of the *Walton Whisper*. All weekend, we had reporters stalking around town, searching for people young and old to interview.

Frank appeared to have finally snapped. All weekend, he just slouched on the couch in front of the television with a dazed look on his face, surfing channels for more coverage.

By Monday morning, the state attorney general announced that he would be launching a formal investigation into the corruption allegations.

"Wow, I have to hand it to you guys," Neil said approvingly, as we shot basketball hoops in his driveway on the first semi-warm day of spring. "That went better than I ever imagined. I posted all the news footage to YouTube, and I still laugh every time I watch it."

"Yeah," Vic agreed. He added pessimistically, "But it doesn't solve all our problems. We may have gotten some revenge, but it won't get our businesses back. It's not like the attorney general will suddenly return everything to us after the investigation."

I nodded reluctantly. I liked Vic a lot, but sometimes he really had a way of raining on our parade.

Vic, Neil and I played basketball for the rest of the afternoon. It was great to run around outside without being bundled up. The three of us liked to play full contact, and we each took some hard falls to the ground that gave us some impressive scrapes and bruises. We were about to head inside for some video games when Neil's father stepped outside with his phone in his hand.

"Mark, your mother called," Mr. Jones said. "She wants you and Sam to come home right away."

"Why?" I asked. "She usually doesn't serve dinner for another hour."

Mr. Jones shrugged. "Do I look like your mother?" he replied with a smile.

I laughed. "Okay, okay. I'll see you guys later." I got on my bike and rode towards home, stopping along the way to yell for Sam, who was shooting bb guns at soda cans in the backyard of one of his little friends.

When we got home, our mother was waiting in her station wagon in the driveway. She rolled down her window when she saw us approach.

"Come on, park your bikes and get in!"

Sam and I looked at each other and then at our mother. "What's going on?" I asked suspiciously.

"Just hurry up!" she snapped. "I'll explain on the way."

My brother and I pushed our bikes into the garage and ran back to the car. Our mother slammed the car into reverse, and the tires screeched against the asphalt as we pulled out onto Walton

Street. She didn't look before pulling out, and an oncoming cement truck blared its horn as it barely swerved to miss us.

"Okay, now will you tell us?" Sam pleaded as our mother floored the gas pedal, which we had never seen her do before. Usually she drove about ten miles under the speed limit.

"I don't want to get your hopes up, but there is a very small chance that you two will be getting Desserts Express back," she said. "But we need to get out of here before the state investigators show up at our house."

"Huh?" I gasped. Now I was really confused.

Our mother honked her car horn furiously as she accelerated through a yellow traffic light that was turning red.

"I've been on the phone all afternoon," our mother explained in rapid bursts. "You boys really stirred up a hornet's nest at that party last week. First the state attorney general's office called about that investigation they announced this morning. They want to send some investigators over to talk to us."

"Good," said Sam. "We've got plenty to say."

"Yeah, well somehow they got wind of it down at city hall," our mother continued, "and the powers that be are none too pleased."

"Even better," I said. "We're pleased that they're none too pleased."

A railroad crossing arm came down in the road just in front of us, and along with the clang of the warning bell, we could hear a train whistle in the distance. Our mother looked like she was considering whether to drive around the crossing arm but then thought better of it. She grudgingly shifted the car into park, and with a sigh she turned around to look at us.

"Listen to me, boys. I think they may be ready to cut a better deal. They asked us to come down to the district attorney's office this afternoon for a talk, but they gave me strict instructions not to speak to any of the investigators beforehand."

Sam and I were stunned. Could this really be true?

"Do you really think they'd give us back Desserts Express?" Sam asked.

"All I know," our mother answered, "is that we have a lot of ambitious small-time crooked politicians in this town who still think they can be big-time crooked politicians, but this investigation could put an end to that for good. The governor was mentioned in the news stories, because he showed up at the wrong place at the wrong time. He's so angry and humiliated, he probably gave the state attorney general orders to bury Holstein and her crew. So it's probably safe to assume they're desperate right now. Are they desperate enough to give you kids your businesses back? I don't know."

We'll find out soon enough, I thought.

Our old Subaru pulled into the parking lot outside the municipal building. A black Lexus was parked a few spaces down from us, which meant that our attorney, Ray Smirnoff, was already inside.

Ray stood and smiled broadly at us as we entered the dingy conference room where Sam and I had surrendered our business to these thieves weeks ago.

"Hello, boys," Ray chirped. "Hello, Mrs. Hoffman. Please have a seat here next to me. We're still waiting for a few people."

I looked across the room and saw the same bald-headed assistant district attorney we had dealt with last time. "Who else is coming?" I asked.

"The mayor's chief of staff," Ray replied.

Our mother and I took our seats, but Sam walked to the end of the long conference table and grabbed the edge. He looked like he was trying to lift it, which was silly, since his sixty-pound body was no match for a several-hundred-pound slab of mahogany.

"Samuel Edward Hoffman, what on earth are you doing?" our mother gasped. She loved to call us by our full names when she was mad at us.

"I thought we were here to turn the tables!" Sam answered with a guffaw. He slapped the tabletop and doubled over in laughter. The assistant D.A. turned crimson and shuffled his papers.

"That's enough, young man," our mother hissed. "Get over here and take your seat this instant."

A minute later, Mayor Holstein's chief of staff entered the conference room. It was the same mayoral assistant who had hosted Friday's anniversary party. After everybody introduced themselves and exchanged some awkward small talk, we got down to business.

"As you, um, gentlemen are aware," the chief of staff began, "Mayor Holstein was quite embarrassed by the unfortunate events that took place at last week's anniversary celebration."

"I would imagine so," I said.

The chief of staff ignored me. "Furthermore, those unfortunate events included a number of outrageous, politically motivated accusations against this administration. Mayor Holstein is appalled that anyone would stoop to such baseless slander."

"If you're talking about the newspaper and the website, every word is true," I argued.

"Yeah!" Sam shouted. "You creeps stole our businesses!"

The assistant D.A. shook his head and scowled. "Counselor, your clients are out of order," he warned Ray.

Ray looked amused. "This isn't a courtroom. Lighten up, Jonathan."

"Boys, quiet down and just listen, will you?" our mother pleaded.

"Thank you," the chief of staff said. "As I was saying, these malicious political attacks are as embarrassing as they are untrue. To make matters worse, these accusations have aroused the attention of the state attorney general's office."

"Well, I'm sure the attorney general will get to the bottom of it," said Ray coyly. "The truth will come out."

The assistant D.A. winced. "Er, yes. Of course it will. In the meantime, unfortunately such a politically sensitive investigation could do irreparable damage to Mayor Holstein's sterling reputation. It would almost certainly stifle Walton Township's current economic recovery, which the mayor has worked so diligently to bring about."

"Yup," I agreed. "A reputation for stealing small businesses once they become successful could really hurt new investment. I can see that."

Now the assistant D.A. was on his feet and shouting at Ray. "This is outrageous! I'm not going to sit here and take this from some smart-mouthed punk!"

Ray wasn't going to take that sitting down either. "That's my client you're defaming!"

"How dare you call my son a punk!" our mother added.

Everybody shouted and waved their arms for the next minute or so, until finally the mayor's chief of staff stuck two fingers in his mouth and let out a piercing whistle.

"Okay, people, let's take a deep breath and sit down. If we all speak at a normal volume and one at a time, we can get this done and go home."

We all grumbled as we took our seats. Ray Smirnoff tried to steer the conversation back on track. "Look, we all know why we're here. The administration would deeply appreciate it if my clients reconsidered the way they remember certain events. If they wrack their brains sufficiently, they might realize that they don't have anything of interest to say to the attorney general's investigators after all. Is that the gist of where this is going?"

"Precisely, Mr. Smirnoff." The chief of staff allowed himself a small smile.

"Okay. And why exactly would my clients wish to make this effort on the administration's behalf?"

There was an uncomfortable silence. The chief of staff glanced nervously at the assistant D.A., who shuffled some papers in a manila folder. He clearly wasn't looking forward to whatever he was about to say.

"Um, it is the opinion of the district attorney's office that Masters Hoffman and Hoffman, due to their young ages, may deserve a reconsideration of the earlier cases against them. That is to say, um, we are prepared to rescind the contracts they signed assigning their former business to Mrs. Hoffman."

Sam looked really confused. "Can somebody repeat that in English?"

"It means they want to give us back Desserts Express, dummy." I answered.

"It's true then?" Sammy exclaimed with a huge smile. "We'll be back in business?"

The assistant D.A. frowned and replied, "Unfortunately, yes." He was obviously going along with the whole thing against his will.

"That is, if you agree to the considerations toward this administration that your attorney Mr. Smirnoff just explained," the chief of staff quickly added.

Our mother nodded. "So, we keep our mouths shut to the attorney general, and you give Mark and Sam their business."

Now the chief of staff was frowning along with the assistant D.A. They obviously didn't want any of us speaking so bluntly about the bribe they were offering. "Your understanding is essentially correct, Mrs. Hoffman. Do we have an, er, deal?"

"Deal!" our mother cried.

"Deal!" Sam echoed.

"No deal," I said calmly.

"What?!" everyone else in the room shouted.

"I said no deal."

Climbing out of his seat, Sam bounded around our mother and grabbed me by the coat sleeve. "Mark, are you nuts? They want to give us Desserts Express back! Don't blow it!"

I shook my head. "Before there's any deal, I want a few other things thrown in."

"Of all the nerve!" the assistant D.A. yelled.

"What do you want?" asked the chief of staff.

Before I could answer, the assistant D.A. said, "Don't even bother. We are not negotiating with juvenile delinquents. This whole cockamamie idea was a mistake."

"Suit yourself," I said, as I stood up to leave. "Have fun at the big house. Say hi to my dad."

"Now let's not be hasty," said the chief of staff, whose forehead was now sweaty, despite the chill in the office. "Let's hear Mark out. He seems like a reasonable young man."

I smiled as I turned toward the table, but I didn't sit down. "We'll see if you still think I'm reasonable after you hear me out. At any rate, the following terms are non-negotiable."

The assistant D.A. glowered and looked like he would have given anything to strangle me right then and there, but he said nothing.

"One," I began, "I want all of your government lackeys to stay out of our way. We don't need any licenses or permits to do an honest day's work."

"Unfortunately," the assistant D.A. said sarcastically, "that would be a violation of state and municipal law." He smirked as if he just settled the matter.

With a shrug, I replied, "Then change the law. Get the mayor to lean on whoever it takes to get these bureaucrats off our backs. That goes for all of the other kids' businesses you'll be returning, but in particular, I don't want to see a health inspector anywhere near Desserts Express, not even on the same street. Agreed?"

"Agreed," said the mayoral aide. The assistant D.A.'s jaw dropped.

"Good," I said. "Two. I want all of these stupid employment laws nullified, especially the minimum-age law and the minimum-wage law. If we want to hire a ten-year-old to sweat over a hot oven at ten cents an hour, that's between him and us."

"Outrageous!" yelled the assistant D.A. "The children need our protection!"

"Your 'protection' is what's keeping them poor and miserable," I said.

"Agreed," said the mayoral aide. "What else?"

I glanced over at my mom and brother, and they nodded their approval.

"Three," I continued, "we don't want to see any tax collectors from New York State or Walton Township, or even the IRS for that matter. No income tax, no sales tax, no property tax. Walton is a tax-free zone as far as our kid-owned businesses are concerned."

The assistant D.A. shook his head. "Now you've done it, kid. You should have quit while you were ahead."

"I'm afraid I have to agree, Mark," said the mayoral aide. "There isn't much point to reviving your businesses, from the town's perspective, if they don't generate any tax revenues."

Leaning across the table, I said, "You're wrong about that, mister, but I don't have time to explain basic economics to you."

"And what would an uneducated child like you know about economics?" the assistant D.A. asked. "We all know you'll be lucky to make it out of middle school, seeing as you so rarely attend."

Sam was indignant. "My brother doesn't have time to waste at that stupid school. He takes *business school* classes with tutors from Columbia University!"

Our mother raised her eyebrows. That was probably the first she had heard of our custom-made MBA program, and it caught her off-guard. "I'll explain later, Mom. Anyway," I continued, turning toward the mayoral aide again, "it's not important whether you see the importance to this dying town of dozens of successful start-up businesses, even if they don't pay taxes. The important thing, as far as you're concerned, is that it will keep us from talking to the attorney general. Right?"

The mayoral aide paused to remove his glasses and rub his forehead. "Yes, Mark, I suppose that's correct. But I must warn you that you are pushing your luck. I hope that was the last of your demands."

"Not quite," I said.

Silence filled the room as everyone looked at me.

"Well?" the assistant D.A. finally bleated in exasperation. "Let's hear it. What else can we do to please the Walton Street tycoons? Fly in showgirls from Las Vegas? Build you a yacht club? Maybe provide you with armed guards?"

"No," I replied. "No, but you're getting warmer. With the kind of money we'll soon be making, there is no way we can rely on this hick police force to protect us. So us kids will need to carry our own guns."

"Guns?" asked Ray, as if he didn't hear me correctly.

"Guns?" repeated the mayoral aide.

"Guns!?" gasped the assistant district attorney.

"Big guns," I said. "Big scary guns. I'm totally serious. You don't have to pay for them. You don't even have to like them. But you have to keep your Keystone Cops from hassling us or trying to confiscate them."

To my surprise, the assistant D.A. no longer looked angry. He shook his head and appeared almost sympathetic, in a patronizing way, as he began to speak. "Look son, let me explain this to you as simply as I can. If my boss, the district attorney, ever found out that I agreed to something as insane as allowing children to carry guns openly—"

"They'd be concealed, for the most part," I interrupted.

"—I'd lose my job," he continued, ignoring me. "As it is, I'll be lucky if they don't fire me for the conditions we already agreed to. So what do you say we all just quit while we're ahead, forget your last demand, you kids can go home and re-open your stupid cookie factory, while I go home and drink myself into a stupor."

The mayoral aide nodded. "He's right, Mark. We've given you an awful lot here. Don't be greedy and stupid, or you'll blow the whole thing."

Maybe the gun bit was too much, I thought. Oh well, it was worth a shot, so to speak.

I would have given in at that point and gone along with the rest of the deal just to get Desserts Express back, but just as I was about to open my mouth, I looked up and caught the assistant D.A. and the mayoral assistant smirking at each other. They knew they had us. Man, did that make me sore.

Sam saw it too, and their smugness made him even angrier. He tapped me on the shoulder, and I turned to him. I had never seen an eight-year-old look so serious.

"Come on, Mark," he said quietly. "Let's get out of here."

I nodded and patted him on the shoulder. Not bothering to discuss it with our mother or attorney, the two of us walked toward the door.

"Hey!" the mayoral aide yelled. "Where do you two think you're going?"

"Home," I answered. "I think there might be someone there from the attorney general's office who wants to talk to us."

"Can't keep an important man like that waiting," Sam added.

The mayoral aide knocked his chair over as he raced over to head us off. "Stop! If you two kids walk through that door, you're through! We will not re-open these negotiations. Do you hear me? No Desserts Express!"

"Okay," I said. "Now can you step out of the way, please?"

The mayoral aide looked down at us and sighed. "Hold on." He then looked over at the assistant D.A.

"Oh no," said the assistant D.A. "Forget it."

"We don't really have a choice, Jonathan," the aide said through gritted teeth.

The assistant D.A.'s voice cracked as he spoke. "Let little kids walk around Walton carrying guns? Are you out of your mind?"

"It's a hunting and fishing town," Ray observed. "They'll fit right in."

"Heck yes," said the mayoral aide, trying to muster enthusiasm. "Remember when we were all kids? We used to roam around the countryside with .22's over our shoulders, plinking tin cans and squirrels. Nobody ever got hurt. That wasn't so long ago, was it?"

The assistant D.A. sat down and thumped his pen on the table. "So we're really going to arm these little monsters," he muttered.

"No, we don't take welfare," Sam protested. "We'll arm ourselves."

After a minute of silence, the mayoral aide finally whispered, "Deal."

"What's that?" I asked.

"Deal," he repeated more loudly. "Right, Jonathan?"

The assistant D.A. stood up again. "Not so fast. Now it's my turn to thrown in some conditions. You kids listen to me, and listen good. We're not going through this all over again with every brat in town. If we make this deal, it's the same deal for everyone. You kids are going to leave this office, go home, and before you touch a mixing bowl, you're going to call all your juvenile-delinquent friends, and tell them this is our final offer. They're all to get their butts down here and sign off by 9:00 p.m. this evening. I don't care if they're in bed dying. If I don't get every kid in town's signature on a deal—this same deal—by the time I leave this office tonight, all of you will regret the day you were born. Got it?"

"But I'm not the boss of all the other kids!" I protested.

"Then you better learn to be very persuasive," the assistant D.A. growled. "You have four hours to get them all in here."

"Deal?" the mayoral aide asked hesitantly.

"Deal," Sam said.

I paused just a moment before answering. "Deal."

We were back in business.

Chapter Twenty-One

Growing Pains

The hardest part about selling the other kids on the deal Sam and I negotiated was getting them to believe it. Everyone agreed that we handled it perfectly, and nobody was in a mood to mess things up by trying for more. By 6:30, a line of kids extended out of the municipal building into the parking lot as they raced to recover their stolen businesses.

The investigators from the attorney general's office made their rounds that evening and all day Saturday, but they were met by closed mouths and closed doors. They returned to Albany on Sunday, suspecting that the whole bizarre story of government corruption and child capitalism in Walton was a big hoax.

All the kids were in such a giddy mood from our surprise victory, they went on a massive shopping spree to celebrate. As soon as the investigators left our house on Saturday, we went to work almost non-stop until Monday morning, with just a few breaks for naps. With just a week until Easter and hundreds of baskets to fill with treats for our returning customers, we didn't have a minute to spare.

Around 7:30 Monday morning, Sam and I stuffed the last handfuls of plastic colored grass into the Easter baskets that lined our storage room. We purchased the grass in bulk on Sunday from a wholesaler in Poughkeepsie, which saved us hundreds of dollars over buying it from the local retail stores, none of which even had such a large quantity available at that late date.

Through a gaping yawn, I said to Sam, "Why don't you go get cleaned up for school? I'll stay here and take care of labeling the orders from this weekend that have to go out this afternoon."

"No, I think I'll stay here and keep working," Sam replied.

"Forget it," I said. "It's hard enough on Mom that I'm always cutting class. You don't need to follow my bad example."

Sam shook his head. "Mom will get over it. Besides, I'm learning way more here than I ever would at that stupid school. The only kids in my class who can do long division are the ones like us, who run businesses. The rest of them won't even start until next year in the fourth grade. I could miss the rest of the year without falling behind."

"Heck, you'd probably be even further ahead of them," I agreed. "Well, at least let's both take a break then. We'll go back to the house and get some breakfast and maybe a few hours sleep. We deserve it."

Our mom was waiting for us at the backdoor of our house. "Good heavens, it's about time you two took a rest. I was just about to come over and drag you home."

"You can't do that," I said with a grin that turned into another large yawn. "You work for us now."

"You two may run Desserts Express, but I run this family," she clucked. "Don't either of you forget it, or I'll be forced to spank my bosses, and don't think I won't do it. Now sit down and have some eggs, and wipe those smiles off your faces!"

"Yes, ma'am," we happily answered in unison.

While Sam and I dug into our eggs, bacon and home fries, our mother continued to fret about our sleep-deprived appearances. "If you makes yourselves sick, you'll end up bed-ridden or in the hospital. Then how will you run your business?"

"Awww, Mom," I groaned.

"Don't 'aw, Mom' me, mister," she snapped. "And I'm not just nagging you as your mother, but as a concerned employee."

"Huh?" Sam asked through a mouthful of toast.

"Look, boys," she said as she pulled up a chair across the table from us, "a lot of people will depend on you now. What you two accomplished in building this business and fighting those crooks downtown to get it back is just remarkable. You've done everything your way, and you've been right each step along the way, while people who were older and supposedly wiser were dead wrong."

"Gee, thanks, Mom," Sam said with a beaming smile.

"So I'm not about to start telling you how to run your business now," she continued. "Not that you'd listen to me anyway."

"Of course not," I said as I reached for the jelly jar.

Our mother smiled. "Of course not. But I just want you to remember one thing. All of us employees are counting on you now. We can't afford for the two of you to work yourselves to exhaustion." She rose from her chair and turned to the sink to wash the frying pan.

Sam and I looked at each other but said nothing. Our mother was right, and we knew it. Many of our employees—some as young as Sam—were now the sole wage earners for their families, since their parents had lost their jobs. In a way, that put even more pressure on us to return to the shop and get back to work. On the other hand, we could feel the fatigue setting in, and that was going to start affecting our performance sooner or later.

After finishing breakfast in silence, Sam and I both walked upstairs to our rooms and collapsed on our beds.

Sam was still out cold when I woke up just after 2:00 p.m. I decided to let him sleep while I headed down to the shop to supervise the afternoon delivery rush.

"How's everything going?" I asked cheerily as I strode into the kitchen.

"Watch it," yelled Mrs. Whitney, as she raced past me with two large sheets of cookies just out of the oven. "Hot stuff coming through." For an old lady, she had more energy than some of our employees who were sixty years younger.

Across the room, another employee—a fifth-grader who had decided a day at work would be more useful than a day at school—was grumpily sweeping up a twenty-pound bag of flour that had broken open on the floor. Eight other flour sacks stood lopsided on the counter behind him.

"Thanks for cleaning up that mess, Audrey," I said with a grin. "I think I'll lug a few of those sacks back to the storage room before we have another avalanche. Want to give me a hand when you're finished sweeping?"

Audrey shrugged. "If there was any space in the storage room, I would have done it myself by now."

"What are you talking about? Sam and I were just in there a few hours ago." I opened the storage room door, and crates of candies stacked to the ceiling now joined the Easter baskets we had stuffed with plastic grass earlier in the morning.

"What the heck is all this?" I asked anyone who might be listening.

"Sam ordered those yesterday, I guess, and they arrived about an hour ago while you were sleeping," Audrey answered. "You have 500 chocolate bunnies, 500 chocolate eggs, a couple thousand marshmallow chicks, and a bunch of other stuff I can't remember. I left the invoice over there on the bulletin board."

I looked toward where the bulletin board was supposed to be, but it was hidden behind crates of eggs and milk that had also been delivered within the last hour.

"Holy moly," I groaned. "Why doesn't somebody put that stuff in the refrigerator before it spoils?" I opened our large commercial refrigerator and stared at the shelves that were packed to capacity. "Oh."

Just three days after the return of our business, and I already felt like we were in over our heads. A few weeks out of the game had made us rusty. We would get back into the swing of it before long, I told myself. The problem was that Easter week was absolutely one of the worst possible times to be working out kinks.

Not knowing what else to do, I picked up a crate of eggs and carried them back to our house to keep in our home refrigerator for the time being. Then I called Celeste to see if she could take any of our excess inventory at her place. Naturally, she was already at capacity. I walked back over to the shop and asked a few employees to help me carry the milk and eggs to the front of the store, where the public used to make their purchases when it was Ellen's Pastry Place. That way, we could at least keep our perishables away from the oven heat.

Sam came down from his bedroom around 4:00 p.m., and I updated him on the situation. By that time, the afternoon deliveries to our customers were starting to go out, freeing up some much-needed space in the kitchen. But the place was still a cluttered, overcrowded mess.

We really need to get this place under control," Sam agreed. "Nobody has room to work."

"Well, maybe things will slow down after Easter, and it won't be so crowded," I suggested.

Sam raised an eyebrow. "That's your plan for handling our business growth? Just hope it's only temporary?"

I shook my head and felt embarrassed that my little brother had to point out the obvious. In my defense, he got more sleep than me. But the pipsqueak was right. We needed to keep growing, and we needed room to do it.

We busted our butts to make it through that first day of back-in-business madness, until the day's last order went out at 9:30 p.m. When it was over, Sam and I rode our bikes over to Celeste's house to talk things over.

Our meeting produced two good ideas. The first was that we would try what one of our business-school tutors called "just-in-time" production. This was a fancy way of saying that we wouldn't accept any deliveries of raw ingredients from our suppliers until we received orders from our customers. We would then rush all the orders to our customers as quickly as possible, keeping our inventory to a minimum. It sounds obvious enough, but when you're dealing with huge quantities coming and going, keeping everything in sync can be a problem. Our tutor told us he could put together a computer system to coordinate the whole thing between our suppliers and us. For a fee, of course. Fine, we said, you're hired. Just make the crates of eggs, milk and candy go away so we can move around in our kitchen.

The second thing we decided was we needed a bigger kitchen and production facility. Even with all the just-in-time jazz, we were simply growing our business too fast. We didn't have enough ovens at our shop and Celeste's house to keep up with demand.

As it turned out, we wouldn't have to wait long to find a new place. On Wednesday afternoon, Karen Thomas sent out a spam email to everyone in her address book announcing she was diversifying out of her party-hosting business and into real estate, of all things. I gave her a call and asked if she did commercial properties.

"Of course, silly," she giggled. "Commercial real estate is all I'm doing. I'd love to sell residential real estate, because there are plenty of folks looking to move out of Walton, but there aren't any buyers looking to move in. But with all of our little businesses growing so quickly, I had a hunch that you and everyone else would be looking for more space before long."

"Smart girl," I said.

Karen giggled again and asked, "So when do you want to look at some properties?"

"As soon as possible," I replied. "We're bursting at the seams over here."

"Okay," she said. "I'll send a car to pick up you, Sam and Celeste tomorrow at noon, and we'll go shopping for dessert factories. See you then. Bye-bye."

Did Karen really say she would send a car for us?

Sure enough, I peeked out the window of our shop at noon on Wednesday and saw a silver limousine idling in our driveway. I walked over, and the driver opened a door for me.

"Wow, nice ride you have here," I said to Karen as I stepped in and the driver closed the door behind me. The car was even bigger inside than it looked from the outside. That didn't stop me from sitting just inches from Karen on the long, plush blue velvet seat.

"Thanks," Karen said with a big smile, her snow-white teeth sparkling along with her sea-blue eyes under the limo's dim track lighting. "Where are the others?"

"The what?" I asked absented-mindedly. There was something different about Karen, I thought. I looked her over as discreetly as I could, which probably wasn't very discreet at all.

Karen had the same long blond hair with the soft curls, and the same peaches-and-cream complexion. She never wore make-up—only a few girls our age did—except for lip-gloss.

She wore a black mini-skirt that just barely covered her butt, just like the rest of the girls in our grade, and her legs did look nice, all the way down to her black mid-calf boots.

Her top was a pink knit short-sleeve blouse with a collar. It was nice enough, but nothing fancy. I wouldn't have given it a second thought, except that I suddenly noticed what was different about Karen.

Breasts!

Sometime over the long cold winter, when everyone was bundled up, Karen Thomas had developed breasts. Nice ones, if I do say so myself. Okay, they weren't breaking any records in the size category, but there they were, two unmistakable round bulges beneath that beautiful pink knit top.

"Mark?" Karen asked.

"Huh?" I replied stupidly.

"I said, where are Sam and Celeste?"

"Who?" I broke myself from the hypnotic spell of Karen's budding womanhood. "Oh, they can't make it. Sam is holding down the fort in our shop. There's no way we could both get away with our workload. And Celeste is just as bogged down over at her place."

"So it's just the two of us?"

"Yep," I said with a grin. "Just the two of us in the back of a big limousine."

"In that case—" Karen said with an even bigger grin. To complete her thought, she wrapped her hands softly around my cheeks, pulled our faces toward each other, and gave me a kiss. Only this wasn't a quick, nervous kiss like the one we had on Valentine's Day. This was a long, warm, and only slightly nervous kiss.

"Hey, good idea," I said. I went back for another kiss, and this time both our mouths opened and our tongues met.

We spent the next ten minutes—or was it thirty minutes?—making out in the back of the limo. We only took a breather long enough for Karen to answer when the driver, a gravel-voiced old-timer, asked, "Am I driving youse two love-birds anywhere, or are we just going to park in this driveway?"

"Take us to the old Tastee Treets plant on Route 17," Karen gasped, "just past that abandoned rail yard." She reached over and pressed a button that raised the Plexiglas partition between the driver and us.

We continued to neck on the ride to the first property. I kept one hand behind Karen's head, caressing her hair, and another on her arm. I really wanted to work one hand over toward Karen's breasts, but I was too nervous. Plus, it's not smart to try to take advantage of a girl who carries a Glock, as Karen gleefully did ever since we won the right to bear arms in our deal with the township. That would not only protect her from puberty-afflicted boys her own age, like me, but possibly from her maniac father. She never said anything, but it wouldn't surprise me if Lieutenant Thomas beat Karen or her mother.

The limousine turned off the road and onto the driveway of an old run-down factory. Karen and I unlocked lips so we could look out the tinted windows. Most of the factory's windows were broken or boarded up. Old tires and a stained mattress were scattered across the property.

"Why are we stopping?" I asked. "Do we have to look at the map or something?"

"No, silly," Karen answered. "This is the first place."

I shook my head as I stared out the window. "In that case, we might as well keep on going to the second place."

"Come on," she urged as she tugged my arm. "At least look at it before you make up your mind. It's not so bad on the inside."

The driver stepped out of the car and opened the door on Karen's side. He held out his hand and helped her step out of the car. I glared at him until he put his hand down so I could get out of the car unassisted like a guy.

Karen had a key to the front door and let us in. We stepped inside, and Karen groped the wall until she found the light switch. As the fluorescent lights flickered on for the first time in ages, we were able to see what had once been a large reception area, but which was now dusty and barren except for a desk and some Styrofoam coffee cups scattered about the floor. The famous interlocking double-T logo of the defunct Tastee Treets company was etched into the glass doors that separated us from the factory floor.

"See, this is pretty nice, or it will be once it's cleaned up," Karen offered hopefully. "You could have a crew of fourth-graders scrub this place spotless for a few packs of bubble gum."

"That's what you think," I snorted. "Some of those fourth graders demand top dollar these days, and the good ones get it.

But okay, yeah, I guess I can see some potential here. Let's keep going."

As Karen led me through the glass double doors onto the factory floor, I had to admit to myself that—underneath the layers of dust and grime—the old place showed promise. It was a convenient coincidence that the former owners had been in more or less the same business as Desserts Express. I assumed a lot of the machinery would have been sold or destroyed by now, but much of it looked to be intact. The factory had everything that we had in our current shop, but on a much more massive scale, plus some equipment I had never seen before.

On the wall next to us were some large metal doors that undoubtedly led to a refrigerated storage room. A row of mixing bowls the size of hot tubs occupied the floor space directly across from the refrigerators, and the mechanical beaters that hung from the ceiling above looked like canoe paddles. A series of elevated conveyor belts began just in front of the mixing bowls and stretched in dozens of directions across the factory floor from ovens to cutting machines to gizmos that might possibly have wrapped the products. I couldn't even guess at the purpose of some of the equipment.

"Wow," I said, letting out a low whistle as I took it all in.

"I knew it," Karen exclaimed. "I knew it from the moment I found this place that it was the perfect place for Desserts Express."

It did look perfect for us, but I didn't want to tip my hand for the price negotiations. "Well, I don't know if I'd call it perfect. A lot of this junk is pretty old and will have to be replaced. It's going to mean even more work for us short-term, and we can't afford to take our employees away from making desserts so they can renovate a factory."

"So outsource it," she said with a wave of her hand. "I even heard the DeLoof boys, Adam and Jeremy, have started a handyman business. Where there's demand—"

"—there's supply," I finished for her. "Yeah, I know. Okay, so let's cut the small talk. How much do the owners want for this dump?"

"If you hurry and make a deal before anyone else starts bidding on it, I can get this factory for you for only $12,000 a month on a two-year lease. The equipment will be extra."

"Uh-huh," I said. "Nice try. I won't even be insulted, because I'm sure your clients put you up to that ridiculous price. Now here's a real offer: $4,000 a month, equipment included."

Karen smiled and playfully punched me in the arm. "Mark Hoffman! You think that just because you're a good kisser, you can push me around?"

I smiled back. "Really? You think I'm a good kisser?"

"Well, yeah," Karen said, blushing. "I mean, it's not like I have anything to compare it to, but you seemed pretty good to me."

"Thanks. You weren't half bad yourself, Karen."

"Gee, thanks," she said. "I think. But seriously, anything less than $10,000 a month isn't a serious offer."

"Yeah, right," I answered sarcastically. "Like people are really lining up to rent this dump in the middle of nowhere." We dickered back and forth as we walked back to the limousine.

We told the driver to take the scenic route home, so we could have more time to finish negotiating, not to mention more time to make out.

Chapter Twenty-Two

Easter

By early Friday afternoon, we had most of our Easter baskets prepared and delivered to our customers, so Sam, Celeste and I could ride our bicycles out to the old Tastee Treets factory together. My partners were skeptical that I could keep my feelings for Karen from clouding my business judgment.

One of the biggest surprises of the day, aside from leasing a new factory, was Celeste Szuck agreeing to such a long bike ride. It was at least four miles from Celeste's house to the factory. When I hung up the phone on Celeste and told Sam what the plan was, he didn't think Szuck the Truck would make it to the end of her block without stopping for a snack or a heart attack. I agreed with him.

When Sam and I pedaled up Celeste's driveway a few minutes later, we couldn't believe our eyes. Apparently Karen Thomas wasn't the only girl in Walton to blossom over the winter. Only Celeste's transformation wasn't just bigger breasts. It was smaller everything else.

Sam put it bluntly when he greeted Celeste, "Jeez, you look like you lost a hundred pounds!"

I smacked Sam in the head. "It's okay," Celeste laughed. "Thanks for noticing."

It would have been hard not to notice. Celeste was straddling a girl's mountain bike, wearing pink bicycle pants that hugged her now-slender hips and thighs. Even more impressive, she wore a purple halter, exposing a midriff that was flat and hard as a pool table.

While my brother and I sat there on our bikes with our jaws hanging open, Celeste pulled her long brown (no longer greasy) hair back into a bun and yelled, "Come on, you sissies! I'll race you there!"

She was off like a rocket. Sam and I stepped down hard on our pedals and pumped furiously to catch her, but she had too much of a lead. Truthfully, I probably could have caught up (I think), but Sam's legs were too short for that kind of speed. We dropped back and contented ourselves just to keep Celeste in our view on the road ahead.

"What the heck!" Sam yelled to me, as we huffed and puffed our way up a steep incline, while Celeste smiled and waved mockingly from far above. "Did you notice what great shape she was in when we had our meeting on Tuesday?"

"Nope!" I yelled back, gasping for air. "But we were pretty tired and had a lot on our minds!"

"You think we were tired then?" Sam panted. "I'm exhausted! Can't we stop and take a break?"

"Come on, Sam!" I urged. "You can't let a girl whip you in a bike race!"

"Good point!"

When we arrived at the factory, Celeste was glistening with sweat, which wasn't that surprising since the old Celeste perspired from just walking across a room, but this sweat looked good on her. Her skin, which I now noticed had lost almost all of its usual acne (although the large birthmark was still on her cheek), had a healthy, pink glow from the workout. And she wasn't breathing hard at all.

"It's about time you two slowpokes got here," she smiled mischievously. "What took you so long? You look tired."

"Who's ... tired?" I croaked as I dismounted and doubled over, clutching my bike for support. "Are... you... tired... Sam?"

"Nope," he gasped.

My partners' doubts deepened as they looked over the outside of the factory for the first time. Once Sam and Celeste saw the inside, however, they agreed the place was perfect for us, and we stopped by Karen's house on the way home to seal the deal. Sam and I weren't in the mood for any confrontations with Lt. Thomas, so we sent Celeste to ring the doorbell while we waited at the bottom of the driveway.

After a minute the door opened halfway, and we saw Celeste speaking with someone inside, probably Karen. The door closed, and Celeste walked back down the driveway by herself.

"Come on, and be quiet," Celeste whispered as she grabbed her bike and walked it up the driveway. "Karen's dad is in the living room watching TV. She's going to meet us out back in the horse barn."

As we walked around the Thomases' house, I eyed the large pond in the backyard. This is where it all started, I thought to myself. How did we go from a simple day of fishing to a sprawling black-market economy run by kids? I noticed that almost all of the ice covering the pond had melted. Soon it would be time for Karen to host another for-profit fishing party. A doe and her small spotted fawn walked casually along the far side of the pond, leaving the woods for the evening. I wondered if we could talk Karen into hunting the property this fall. Probably not, if only because of her stupid dad.

"Watch where you're stepping," I told Sam as we approached the barn.

"Eww, gross," Sam whined as we tip-toed through the turds. "There's horse poop everywhere."

We leaned our bikes against the side of the barn and rolled the large door open. Starlight, Karen's horse, pricked her ears and looked up briefly before deciding that her pile of hay was more interesting.

A minute later, Karen joined us in the barn. I noticed she was wearing her riding boots and helmet. She must have been planning to take Starlight for a trot after we finished our business.

"Hi, guys," she greeted us with a broad smile, while sliding the barn door closed. "You look terrific, Celeste."

"Thanks, Karen," Celeste smiled back. "You don't look bad yourself in that get-up."

"Thanks. It's been so rainy lately, and I've been so busy with my businesses, that I haven't had a chance to go riding in days." Karen turned to the horse and fed her a carrot she'd been holding. "Right, girl? You've missed me, haven't you? I've missed you, too."

"Um, Karen," I said, clearing my throat, "aren't you forgetting something?"

She shook her head. "How could I miss you, Mark? We just saw each other yesterday, silly."

"No, that's not what I mean. Did you leave the lease in your house?"

Karen shook her head again and grinned. "Step into my office." She was pointing to an empty horse stall next to Starlight's. Celeste, Sam and I looked at each other and shrugged, but we followed Karen into the stall. We all did a double take when we looked inside.

It turned out the stall wasn't empty at all. A small computer station and chair were pushed up against the wall closest to Starlight, just out of sight of anyone who hadn't opened the stall door. The desk had a notebook computer, a printer, a cell phone and a small stack of papers. Karen plucked the lease for our new factory from the top of the stack.

"You keep your office out here now?" Celeste asked incredulously.

"Well, my dad still doesn't approve of me running my businesses, regardless of our deal with the city," Karen explained. "He was snooping through my room when I wasn't home, and on Monday he threw away all my papers and erased my data from my computer. Luckily I had everything backed up on CD-ROMs. So now I just keep everything out here. Daddy won't come out here because he hates Starlight, or I guess Starlight hates him. It's the strangest thing. She has such a sweet disposition, but she always snorts and bites at Daddy whenever he approaches."

"Now that's what I call good horse sense," I said, as I reached over the stall wall to stroke Starlight's white mane.

Karen handed me the lease and a pen. "Take your time reading it over, but it's the terms we discussed last night."

"Highway robbery," I muttered as I skimmed the document. "You should be ashamed of yourself for taking advantage of us like this."

"Oh, puh-leeze," Karen huffed. "You guys are getting a steal. And you'd never find another real estate broker who charges commissions as low as mine."

Celeste took the lease and pen from me so she could sign and said, "Other real estate brokers have a lot more experience and business expenses, like licenses."

"And an office that isn't shared with a horse," Sam added.

"True," Karen conceded with a laugh.

Celeste signed and handed the lease and pen back to Karen, who said she would drop it off with the property owner on Monday. She added that we would be able to start fixing up the place anytime we wanted.

"When do you think we'll have the place up and running, Mark?" Sam asked.

I raised my palms up and shrugged. "I don't know, Sam. We've got a lot of work to do there cleaning up that dump, and we still have to keep things running from the old shop in the meantime. If we bust our butts and there aren't any surprises, I'd guess maybe June."

"At least we'll be in for the summer," Celeste said. "My home kitchen gets so hot, I wouldn't be able to stand being in there all day in July." Celeste paused for a moment and added. "You know, I just had a great idea. We should have a big ribbon-cutting party when we move in."

"A party?" Sam scoffed. "You girls and your stupid parties. Sounds like a big waste of money to me." The kid was getting cheap in his old age.

"Come on, Sam, it'll be great," Celeste pleaded. "We'll give all our employees the day off and invite them. Everyone will need a break after all the work we're going to put them through."

I nodded. "That's not a bad idea really. We might even be able to get some good publicity for Desserts Express out of it, if we do it up right."

"And I just happen to have an excellent party-planning company that you can hire," Karen said with a wink.

"I suppose we'll let you submit a bid," I conceded with mock reluctance.

Sam rolled his eyes and said, "Okay, fine. We'll have a big party. But let's focus on getting the place cleaned up first, if that's all right with all of you."

As we were walking out of the barn, I turned and took another look at Starlight. "She sure is beautiful," I said.

"Will you and Karen cut it with the mushy stuff?" Sam moaned.

"I was talking about the horse, not Karen, you retard," I said while Karen blushed, obviously embarrassed.

"Oh," Sam said quietly. "I knew that."

"Do you want to go for a ride on her?" Karen asked. "All of you, I mean?"

"Sure!" I answered enthusiastically.

Celeste thought about it momentarily before declining. "No, but thank you. It's been a really long week. I think I'll just go home and get some rest. Maybe some other time."

"Yeah, me too," Sam added. "We'll let you love birds take your romantic horse ride by yourselves." He made smooching noises and darted for his bicycle just before the back of my hand could reach the side of his head.

Celeste and Sam took off, and I waited outside while Karen saddled Starlight. A few minutes later, she rode out on top of her white horse. Each was beautiful alone; the two of them together were stunning.

"Come on!" she yelled. "Hop on while there's still some daylight left!"

"How am I supposed to do that?"

Karen sighed. "Put your left foot in the stirrup, grab the back of my saddle with two hands, and swing your right leg up and over. Do you need me to come down and help?"

"Of course not," I scoffed. I proceeded to put my foot in the stirrup, grab the back of her saddle, lift my right leg, and fall backward with a thud onto the ground.

"Oww!" I yelled.

"Mark! Are you okay?" Karen cried.

"Yeah, luckily the big pile of horse poop I landed in broke my fall."

Karen giggled. "You get used to the manure. It's part of the equestrian experience. Give it another try."

I stood up and tried again, and this time I was successful. I wrapped my arms around Karen just as she snapped the reins. Starlight took off in a trot, and I tightened my hug to avoid falling off again. Plus, it was just fun holding Karen.

"Hang on!" she yelled as she cracked the reins again and nudged her heels into the horse's sides, prompting Starlight into a full gallop.

We slowed down to a walk as we approached a path through the woods. That was fine with me, because my butt was already sore from the fall and from bouncing along the back of the horse without a saddle. I relaxed a little and enjoyed the scenery. A few sprigs of green were starting to sprout from the tree branches. Some small mounds of melting snow were still scattered along the path. After a few minutes of listening to nothing but the soft thud of Starlight's hooves on the leaf-covered trail, we started talking.

"Man, Celeste looked incredible today," I said.

"Excuse me," Karen huffed. "We may both be new at this dating thing, but I'm certain it's not a good idea to tell your girl how nice another girl looks."

"Oops," I said. "Don't worry, Karen, she's still not in your league, and you know it. You're the prettiest girl in all of Walton."

"Aw, that's much better." She reached down and patted my thigh.

"But still," I persisted, pressing my luck, "what a change. It just happened overnight."

"You boys are so unobservant," Karen tisked. "It was anything but overnight. Ever since Celeste joined Desserts Express and the business took off, it gave her the self-confidence she never had to feel good about herself. She's been watching what she eats and exercising for months."

"She has?"

"Mmm-hmm. I can't believe you didn't notice."

"You know I don't notice any other girls but you, baby," I said.

Karen groaned. "Oh, please. You sound like Austin Powers."

"Hey, I have an idea. We're wasting all this private time riding this horse. Why don't we give Starlight a break?"

"Good idea." Karen pulled back on the reins, and the horse came to a stop. I was about to jump down and look for a good make-out spot, but Karen suddenly stood up in her saddle, turned around, and sat down facing me. She smiled and said, "Okay, you can put those arms back around me again." Amazingly, Starlight stood perfectly still while we sat on her back kissing for the next ten minutes. The horse snorted once or twice, but I'm pretty sure she wasn't snorting at us.

By the time we finished, it was dark out, and we had to follow the trail home by moonlight. Fortunately, Starlight's eyesight was excellent, or she just knew the trail by heart. We made it to the barn without incident. I said goodbye to Karen and gave her one more kiss before she went to work taking the saddle off and I headed home.

On Saturday, Sam and I did some work around the shop for a few hours before deciding to call it an early day. We spent the afternoon coloring Easter eggs our mom had boiled. Our family had a strange Easter tradition that had been passed down from our mother's family and that Sam and I loved. Instead of just eating our Easter eggs on Sunday morning, we had an egg-bucking contest. Each person would select his favorite egg and slam it pointed-side first into an egg held by another family member. The winner was the person whose egg stayed unbroken while breaking the most other eggs. Therefore, instead of the usual nice pretty Easter egg colors and decorations, Sam and I would dye them dark—almost black—and use crayons to write names on them that were more suitable for monster trucks, like The Egg-sterminator and The Egg-secutioner.

Sunday morning, we found the baskets that the "Easter Bunny" had hidden and sneaked a few pieces of chocolate before breakfast. After the week we had, I didn't think either of us would be in the mood to even look for Easter baskets, but we were still happy to have them. We headed into the kitchen, where our mother was pouring juice and Frank was waiting impatiently at the table.

"Happy Easter, boys!" our mother greeted us. "Have a seat."

"Happy Easter, Mom!" we replied in unison. I added, "Happy Easter, Frank."

Frank eyed me uncertainly before replying, "Um, happy Easter to you, Mark."

"Here," I said as I reached into the basket in the center of the table and pulled out a red, white and blue egg. "I made this one especially for you."

"Uh-huh," he said, looking at the egg but not taking it. "You sure are being nice to me today."

"Yeah, what can I say? I'm just a nice guy, and it's Easter." I took the black Egg-secutioner egg for myself. "Ready for a challenge?"

"You must think I'm pretty stupid, young man," Frank said.

"Frank!" our mother gasped. "Mark is trying very hard to be nice this morning."

"No he isn't," Frank barked. "He's trying to make me the butt of one of his stupid little jokes. And he thinks I'm so stupid that I'll walk into the same trap he set for me last year."

"What was that?" our mother asked.

"Don't you remember? Mark 'accidentally' decorated a raw egg for me last Easter, and when we bucked eggs, I ended up with a mess in my hand and lap."

Sam laughed so hard that he spit the orange juice he was drinking back into his glass.

"Frank, you're being paranoid," I assured him. "Come on, take the egg I made for you."

Shaking his finger at me, Frank bellowed, "We have an old saying where I come from, mister. Fool me once, shame on you. Fool me twice, shame on me. I'll take *your* egg, if you don't mind."

"But—" I stammered.

"No buts. Hand it over. And *you'll* use the egg you made for me."

"But—"

Frank held out his hand in silence. I looked at Sam, then back at Frank, and sullenly handed him The Egg-secutioner. Then I picked up the red, white and blue egg and held it pointed end away from me.

"Now then," Frank declared smugly, "we'll see who laughs last. On the count of three. One, two, three."

Splat.

As our eggs collided, the raw insides of The Egg-secutioner splattered in Frank's hand and lap. "My good suit!" he yelled, lurching up as yolk dripped from his pants.

I shook my head and raised the red, white and blue egg victoriously. Our mom struggled not to laugh while Frank washed himself with a sponge at the kitchen sink.

What a dope, I thought.

Chapter Twenty-Three

Missing Pieces

April and May flew by, as we worked furiously to clean up the old factory we were leasing, while keeping the current business running from home. We pulled a lot of sixteen-hour days, but by early June, we were ready for the big ribbon cutting.

We invited everyone to the celebration—our employees, all the other kids in town, and even the adults. Our mother even badgered us into inviting Frank. To our surprise, he accepted.

Frank's mood had been especially foul for the last few weeks. He couldn't believe that we were actually doing well enough to lease a factory, and he took every opportunity to make ominous warnings about how we were headed for a fall. Sam and I dismissed his threats as empty, since we had our deal with city hall. Looking back on it now, we should have kept our guard up.

"Hey, do we have to dress up for this stupid party tomorrow?" Neil wanted to know, as he, Vic and I splashed around the above-ground three-foot-high swimming pool in Neil's backyard.

I replied with a shrug, "What do I care what you wear?"

"Man, that's what I told my mom," Neil whined. "But she said she talked to your mom and that you were wearing a tuxedo! I knew that was crazy." Turning towards his house, Neil bellowed at the open windows. "Maaaaa! Mark says he's not wearing a tux!"

"Well, I didn't exactly say that," I corrected him. "I just said I don't care what you wear."

Vic arched an eyebrow. "Does that mean you really are wearing a tux?"

"Yeah," I answered. "Sam and I both are. And Celeste is wearing a fancy dress. This is a big publicity event for Desserts Express, and we want to look good for the cameras."

Neil chuckled. "Szuck the Truck is wearing a dress. I'll bet they charged her extra for the material."

"Neil, when was the last time you saw Celeste?" I asked.

"I dunno. Probably not since my folks took me out of school. Why? How much does she weigh now?"

I smiled. "A lot less than you, chubby. She really got herself into shape."

Vic was skeptical. "Szuck the Truck? Get out of here."

"Whatever," I said. "You guys will see for yourselves tomorrow, and you're going to be sorry you ever called her the Truck."

Neil was now standing on the rickety aluminum wall of the pool. "I'll believe that when I see it," he snorted before doing a belly flop that splashed half the water out of the pool onto the lawn. "Ow!" he groaned, clutching his stomach.

Late the next morning, Sam and I struggled to get into our tuxedos, while our mother flitted from one of our bedrooms to the next, tying our bowties, adjusting our cummerbunds, wetting down our hair, and generally making all of us nervous wrecks.

"You boys better step on it!" she yelled from Sam's room. "The party starts in less than twenty minutes."

"We're paying for the party!" I yelled back. "Nobody is going to start without us!"

I looked myself over in the mirror and reviewed my mental checklist. I had some notes on index cards in the breast pocket of my jacket, so that I could make a statement at the ribbon cutting without getting tongue-tied. Then I reached in my front pants pocket and felt the check to Karen's party-planning company for the balance of our bill. We had run up quite a tab on this party. Whether the party was good for our business or not, I thought, it sure turned out to be a big windfall for Karen's.

There wasn't anything left to do, I told myself, but I still had a strange feeling I was forgetting something important.

"Come on," our mom called as she rapped on my door. "Sam and I are heading down to the car now!"

I was agitated. "I'm not ready yet! Give me five minutes!"

A minute later she was knocking on my door again.

"Your brother has ants in his pants, Mark! If I don't get him to the party now, he's going to have a conniption. Frank says he'll wait and drive you there, so I can take Sam now."

"Fine!" I yelled.

Riding with Frank wasn't exactly going to put me in a festive mood, I thought, as I listened to my mom's station wagon start up and pull out of our driveway. Then again, this was our big day, and Frank would be in an even worse mood. Needling him as we rode would cheer me up.

Now I just had to get myself together and get out the door. I tried to remember what I was missing. Glancing around my bedroom, I spotted the leather strap of my shoulder holster hanging off my headboard. Of course, I wasn't wearing my gun! No wonder I felt naked. The day after we made our deal with the city, I bought a used Sig Sauer nine millimeter from Neil, who had expanded into the small arms business with his father. I hardly went anywhere without it since.

I removed my tuxedo jacket and tossed it on the bed so I could slip on my holster. When I lifted it off the headboard post, however, the holster felt too light. As I looked down, my stomach churned. The gun was missing.

How the heck could that happen, I wondered. I looked under my pillow and on the floor around the bed, but the gun was nowhere in sight. This was bad. I'm a well-known slob when it comes to leaving my clothes and food wrappers all over the house, but I would never absent-mindedly set my gun somewhere. I began frantically searching my dresser and closet, while the knot in my stomach tightened.

"Missing something?"

Startled, I jumped about a foot before turning towards the door. Frank stood in the doorway with an even nastier sneer than usual on his face. Holding my gun.

And pointing it at me.

"Very funny, Frank," I said, holding open my left hand as I took a step toward him. "Give me back my gun."

"I don't think so." Frank raised the pistol so it was now aimed directly at my head from less than four feet away. "Not just yet anyway. And you would be wise not to take another step toward me, young man. In fact, why don't you slowly take a seat on the end of your bed? Now!"

For the first time ever, I did exactly as Frank told me.

"Okay," I gasped, trying not to show my fear and failing badly. Frank had finally lost his mind, I thought, and he hadn't started with a lot of mind in the first place. "Let's neither of us do anything we'll regret. You want to tell me what this is all about?"

Frank corrected me, "Please tell me what this is all about, sir."

"Please tell me what this is all about, sir," I said in as unsarcastic a tone as I could manage.

"That's better," Frank said with a crocodile smile. "I'll teach you some manners and respect yet. It's a pity you won't live to use them."

That last part didn't sound good at all.

"What the heck are you talking about?" I exclaimed. Frank furrowed his brow, and I quickly added, "Sir?"

"Ah, Mark," he sighed, as he took two menacing steps into the room. "Mark, Mark, Mark, Mark. This is a day I've been waiting for a long time. It's the day this whole black market run by anarchist juvenile delinquents gets shut down for good. And even better, it's the day you shut up for good."

I couldn't believe what I was hearing. "You'll never get away with this, Frank. Put the gun down, and we'll both forget this ever happened."

"Oh, I'll get away with it. Don't you worry about that. You'll be just another tragic teen suicide victim, who took his life with his own gun." Frank shook his head in mock sadness.

"But I'm not even a teen!" I protested.

Frank chuckled. "So we're off by a month. Everyone knows the great Mark Hoffman was advanced for his age. And when the town of Walton learns about the tragic suicide, everyone will realize once and for all just how foolish it is to let any civilians own guns, especially the children. And when they read the suicide note you will have, ahem, written—confessing to a myriad of unethical business practices, from cheating your employees and customers to urinating in the desserts you sold—the good people of Walton will realize once and for all that unregulated, untaxed business is sheer madness. And they'll demand that their leaders in government put a stop to it."

I was at a loss for words as I tried to absorb everything Frank was telling me. My mind wouldn't focus on anything but the gun aimed at me. Not only was it at point-blank range, but it was between me and the only doorway in the room.

One thought finally occurred to me. "Nobody will believe it was a suicide, you know. The coroner will be able to tell the wound wasn't self-inflicted."

"The who?" Frank asked with an ironic grin.

"The cor... oh, right." I understood why Frank was grinning. My pathetic hopes hinged on a government hack vindicating me. Even if the coroner weren't a friend and political crony of Frank's (which he was), he wouldn't exactly be eager to stop the big-government comeback that Frank was orchestrating.

Now I was really desperate. So desperate that I was ready to beg Frank for mercy.

"Please, Frank!" I groveled. "Don't do this! You've been like a father to me."

Frank snorted. "Please, you've insulted my intelligence enough."

"But what about my mother? How can you kill her son? I know you hate Sam and me, but you must care for her."

Frank nodded. "She'll need a lot of comforting and support over the next few months. I suspect this terrible tragedy will bring us even closer together. She'll realize that I was right, and you kids were wrong the whole time, and she'll beg my forgiveness." Frank's smirk turned positively evil. "She'll probably even finally marry me."

I was seething with rage while Frank yammered on about my mother and his disgusting plans for the two of them. As I seethed, I shoved my hands in my pants pockets and shook in anger. Inside my pockets, I crossed my fingers on my right hand, while my left hand fumbled for the 9-1-1 buttons on my cell phone.

"Calling the police?" Frank asked mockingly. "But aren't you the smug brat who demanded that law enforcement steer clear of this property and the dubious activities that take place here? Ah, well. Any port in a storm, I suppose. Here, let me help you." Frank cupped his hand over his mouth and turned his head slightly toward the door. In a soft voice, he said, "Help, police. Help, police."

At first, I thought Frank was just mocking me. Seconds later, I was astonished to hear what sounded suspiciously like a walkie-talkie crackling to life from the hallway beyond my door. The sound grew louder, and I thought I distinctly heard the voice on the walkie-talkie say something about a garbled 9-1-1 call. I'm getting delirious under the pressure, I told myself.

I was even more astonished when the walkie-talkie entered my bedroom on the hip of a uniformed police officer.

It was Karen's father, Lieutenant Thomas.

Lieutenant Thomas glanced at Frank and then at me. He picked up the walkie-talkie from his hip and pressed the button on the side. "Car 3 responding to the 9-1-1 on Walton Street. Situation is under control. No need for backup. Repeat, no need for backup. Over."

"Over," the voice on the other end replied.

I shook my head, resigning myself to my fate. "I should have figured you'd be in on this too," I said. Frank really covered all his bases this time.

"That's Walton's Finest for you," Frank said gleefully. "Responding to the crime before it happens. What do your make of this situation, Lieutenant?"

Lieutenant Thomas peered over his dark sunglasses. "Clearest case of teen suicide I ever saw."

"Now that's what I call good police work," Frank cackled.

"Shut up and finish it already," Lieutenant Thomas growled.

Frank looked offended. "You're right," he said glumly. "Goodbye, Mark."

I closed my eyes just as a deafening shot rang out. I felt the blood rushing to my head, and I momentarily thought I would lose consciousness.

My ears were ringing from the gunshot, but I quickly realized the bullet didn't hit me. I opened my eyes just in time to see Frank collapse to the floor in a pool of blood.

I was shocked. Lieutenant Thomas killed Frank? Why? However, when I looked up from Frank's body, I saw that not only was the lieutenant just as shocked as I was, but his gun was still in his holster. He reached for the weapon but stopped instantly when another voice said, "Don't move."

I knew that voice. My father stood in the doorway, his smoking gun barrel now lodged in Lieutenant Thomas's back.

Chapter Twenty-Four

Family Reunion

"Huh?" was all I could think of to say. What else was there to say? Just when I thought my day couldn't get any weirder, it did, but in a wonderful new direction.

"Hi, Mark," my dad said solemnly. He was older, grayer and thinner than the last time I saw him, but he looked like a million bucks to me. The old man gave me a wink, but didn't allow himself to smile just yet. "This isn't exactly how I pictured my homecoming."

"But why… how?" I stammered.

"Somehow, my mandatory sentence got commuted," my dad replied. "Apparently my sons have influence in high places. We need to talk later." Placing his free hand on Lieutenant Thomas's shoulder, he said, "Spread your legs and put your hands on the wall."

Lieutenant Thomas didn't budge, except to twist his neck so he could see my father. "Put the gun down now," the lieutenant commanded. "You're going right back to prison. I don't care who commuted your sentence; felons can't possess weapons in New York."

"Don't make me shoot you too," my father requested sincerely but firmly. "There's been enough bloodshed already. I'm not going to tell you again. Spread your legs, and put your hands on the wall."

Drawing his holstered gun, Lieutenant Thomas suddenly crouched and spun. My father fired first. The force of the gunshot at close range slammed the cop's body onto the floor. Blood splattered over everything and everyone in my room.

"Mark! Get me the first aid kit from the bathroom now!" my father the doctor screamed. "And then call an ambulance!"

My father worked frantically to stabilize Lieutenant Thomas and Frank until the paramedics came. When they arrived minutes later, Lieutenant Thomas had a weak pulse and was in shock, and they rushed him to the hospital.

They pronounced Frank dead at the scene.

Dozens of police officers from Walton and surrounding towns soon surrounded our house. I called Sam at the ribbon-cutting party and told him to call off the festivities and hurry home with our mother. By the time they made it back, the county sheriff was questioning my father and me while we sat handcuffed in the back seat of a patrol car. Our mother called Ray Smirnoff, our attorney, who met us at the sheriff's office. A few hours later, we were both released but told not to leave town until the investigation was completed.

Our whole family, together for the first time in over a year, stayed up all night laughing, crying and talking. Our mother did most of the crying, as she clung to our father tightly on the living room couch.

"What a day!" our mother exclaimed for about the hundredth time. "I can't believe you're home, darling! I can't believe Frank is dead! I can't believe Frank was really going to kill Mark!"

"I can!" Sam countered. "Mark and I always told you Frank was a total creep."

"Sam," our father admonished quietly, "you shouldn't speak ill of the dead. Not even Frank Rito."

"No, Sam is right," our mother insisted. She let go of our father long enough to pull Sam and me into a firm embrace and started crying again. "Frank was a total creep. I don't know how I could have been so blind. Boys, please forgive me! When I think of what I put you through, and that I let that monster into our home—"

"Forget it, Mom," I said. "You were just scared and lonely without Dad around. We all were. And Frank was slimy enough to take advantage of that. He lived his whole life as a parasite. But Dad's back now, and we never have to worry about Frank again."

Mom squeezed us some more, went back to hugging Dad, and before long all four of us were in one giant hug. Normally it would have been nauseating, because I'm not much for hugging and crying and all that girly stuff, but considering our dad just got out of prison and I almost got killed, I didn't mind too much.

Eventually our mom let go, and she put on a pot of coffee while the rest of us caught our breath. Now it was Sam's turn to get all emotional.

"But Daddy," Sam whimpered as he sat in our father's lap, "what about what that cop said? Felons aren't allowed to own guns. Are they going to send you back to prison for that?"

Our father paused for several seconds, looking uncertain how to answer Sam's question. "Well, son, they haven't charged me with anything yet. They still could, and it will probably be months before this whole mess gets cleared up one way or the other. But that attorney of yours, Ray, seems like a pretty sharp fellow, so I'm not too worried. I wish I would have had him instead of that bum of a lawyer who defended me when I went away."

"I'm not worried either," I said with a big smile. "We'll get you off one way or another. What I want to know, Dad, is where you got that gun in the first place."

Our father winked and grinned. "Boys, this was my house long before it was your house. You think you're the only ones with secret hiding places for your things? When the bus dropped me off and I saw Thomas's squad car parked in our driveway, I had a feeling nothing good was happening. So I sneaked in quietly, and before I went upstairs I got my gun from…" He stopped himself just in time.

"From where?!" Sam and I yelled.

"None of your business," our father answered. "Anyway, it was a good thing I had it."

Our mother handed him a mug of coffee. "I'll say. And it was a good thing for Lieutenant Thomas that you had your medical kit here too. Not that he deserved saving."

Sam snorted. "Really. I would have let him bleed to death."

Our father looked Sam in the eye. "No, you wouldn't have, Sam. You're better than that. I don't regret using deadly force to save Mark, but I would have regretted it if I didn't do everything I could to try to save their lives once we were out of danger."

"That's why your father is such a wonderful doctor," our mother gushed.

Our father corrected her, "You mean that's why their father *was* such a wonderful doctor."

"What?" Our mother was aghast.

He shrugged. "They revoked my medical license when I went to prison, Ellen. You know that. Just because I'm out now doesn't change that fact. And shooting two people today isn't exactly going to impress anyone on the medical board into giving my license back."

"So you're not going to be a doctor anymore, Daddy?" Sam asked.

Our father smiled at Sam. "I'm afraid I don't have a choice, son. Your old man is just another ex-con who can't find work. Maybe you boys can give me a job in that pastry business of yours until I get back on my feet."

"Oh, don't worry, we'll get you work, Dad," I assured him. "But as a doctor, not as a dopey pastry chef. No offense, Mom."

"None taken," she said cheerfully.

Shaking his head, our father protested. "Believe me, I'd love nothing more, Mark. But like I said, I don't have any choice. You can't practice medicine without a license."

"That was the bad old days," I said with a grin. "Things have changed in Walton. We do business. We don't do licenses."

Chapter Twenty-Five

Mark's Birthday

"Did you boys put everything in the truck yet?" our mother asked. It had been a month since our father came home from prison, and he, Sam and I were driving out to the eastern end of Long Island for a day of fluke and striped bass fishing to celebrate my thirteenth birthday.

"Everything but Sam," our father answered as he poured himself a second cup of coffee. "He's having a bit of trouble getting out of bed this morning."

Yawning and stretching as I stumbled into the kitchen, I said sarcastically, "I can't imagine why. It's already 3:30 a.m. He must just be lazy."

Our mother shook her head as she set a bowl of oatmeal on the table in front of me. "Lazy, my Aunt Martha! You both have been working way too hard again lately. I'm so happy you at least decided to take today off."

"We probably shouldn't even be doing that," I said. "With the baking plant running twenty-four seven now and our new fleet of delivery trucks arriving this week, we're up to our ears in work."

"Too bad," our mother replied. "Desserts Express can wait. You two need some rest."

"Then what am I doing up at 3:30?" I asked.

She shrugged with exasperation. "Heaven only knows why you boys think this is fun."

My father and I smiled at each other knowingly.

Sam finally made it downstairs, half-dressed and his eyes half-shut. Our father convinced our mother to just let Sam go back to sleep in the truck rather than force a hot breakfast on him. We had at least a three-hour drive ahead of us to get to Montauk, and we had to leave immediately if we wanted to get some fishing in before the morning's slack tide. After we promised to make sure Sam ate something before getting on the boat, and after we promised that we would all wear lots of sunscreen, and after we promised that we would bring home lots of fish, she kissed us goodbye and went back to sleep.

While our father drove and listened to country music on the radio, I slept restlessly in the front passenger seat of the new Ford Expedition—a Father's Day gift from Sam and me. In between naps, I thought about the fishing ahead of us, as well as everything that had happened over the last few weeks.

The shooting made the front page of the local paper and dominated the news broadcasts for about a week. The district attorney didn't know what, if anything, to charge our father with, since popular sentiment was clearly with the old man. They didn't even bother with any charges directly related to the shootings, since it was clearly a case of self-defense. In the end, the district attorney made a vain attempt to bring an indictment on illegal gun possession charges, but he couldn't get the grand jury to go along with it. Our father was officially free.

Lieutenant Thomas didn't make out as well. While he did make a full recovery from his gunshot injuries, he was indicted on attempted murder and corruption charges while he was still in intensive care. By the time his stitches were removed, ex-Lieutenant Thomas was a patient of the prison hospital. It was the same prison where our father had been incarcerated. He was eventually sentenced to twenty years in prison. With the way our crummy system works, I expect he'll be out in five, if the other prisoners don't kill him first. A lot of his fellow inmates were people he had put away, and they were eager for a reunion.

There was a funeral service for Frank Rito a few days after the shooting, but none of us attended. I heard from some friends (the few who still bothered to show up for class) that the school system bussed all of the students to the service on the last day before summer vacation "to help the children cope with the loss of their beloved superintendent." Probably it was just so the funeral wouldn't be totally empty.

The shooting and the indictment of Lieutenant Thomas put a damper on my and Karen's relationship. My father was out of prison, her father was in, and Karen had a difficult time handling that. We talked about it a lot, and while her head told her that her father was a total dirtbag, I guess her heart just couldn't accept it. So we broke up, but we agreed to stay friends. That was fine with me. I was only thirteen, and I had a thriving business. The last thing I needed was a steady girlfriend.

Speaking of business, it was taking off like a rocket. We were already running the plant at full capacity, and we would probably need to shop for a second one before long. Most of our new business was now coming over the Internet from far outside of Walton, as word of our amazing desserts spread. A wholesale food distributor even called us about a supermarket deal. Sam and I figured that we would be national by the end of the year.

Vic's, Neil's, Karen's and the other kids' businesses were doing great too. A reporter and photographer from *Entrepreneur Magazine* even came to town to do a cover story on us. The cover showed us all wearing business suits and piled on the monkey bars at the playground. The photo caption called us "The Walton Street Tycoons."

To our father's amazement, we were able to get his medical practice up and running again—without a license, of course. Nobody from the government bothered him. The local and state bureaucrats had finally learned their lesson not to mess with the Walton kids. Or their parents.

Everybody was busy being productive and getting filthy rich. Our parents were proud of Sam and me, and we were proud of ourselves.

"Okay, sleepyheads, we're here," our dad declared. "Let's get this gear on the boat before the captain leaves dock without us."

I opened my eyes and saw the sun coming up over the harbor. The captain of the boat we had chartered was hosing down the stern. As I opened my door, the cool salt air quickly revived me, and I helped my father carry a cooler onto the boat. In a few hours, the sandwiches and soda weighing down the cooler would be replaced with fresh fluke and striped bass.

I hopped down onto the stern deck, and Sam handed me our rods and reels. We caught each other's eyes and grinned.

Neither of us would think about work for the rest of the day. Business is business, but fishing with your father is important.